POLICING
WOMEN

In the series
Critical Perspectives on the Past
edited by
Susan Porter Benson, Stephen Brier, and Roy Rosenzweig

POLICING WOMEN

THE SEXUAL POLITICS OF
LAW ENFORCEMENT AND THE LAPD

Janis Appier

TEMPLE UNIVERSITY PRESS
Philadelphia

Temple University Press, Philadelphia 19122
Copyright © 1998 by Temple University
All rights reserved
Published 1998
Printed in the United States of America

⊗ The paper used in this publication meets the requirements of the American National Standard for Information Sciences—Permanence of Paper for Printed Library Materials, ANSI Z39.48-1984

Text design by Tom Scheuerman

Library of Congress Cataloging-in-Publication Data
Appier, Janis, 1952–
    Policing women: the sexual politics of law enforcement and the
LAPD / Janis Appier.
        p.   cm. — (Critical perspectives on the past)
    Includes bibliographical references (p.   ) and index.
    ISBN 1–56639–559–3 (cloth : alk. paper).—ISBN 1–56639–560–7 (pbk. :
alk. paper)
    1. Policewomen—United States—History—20th century. 2. Police
administration—United States—History—20th century. 3. Police
professionalization—United States—History—20th century.
    4. Police social work—United States—History—20th century.
I. Title.   II. Series.
HV8023.A66 1998
363.2'082—DC21   97–9965

For Peter

Contents

Acknowledgments

Throughout all the phases of research, writing, and revision of this book, I have received the help and support of many people. I am extremely grateful to Sarah Stage, a superb teacher and advisor, for her penetrating criticism, intellectual guidance, and constant words of encouragement. I owe her a great debt, for she has always been unfailingly generous in sharing with me her deep understanding of women's history.

I also owe a large debt to Susan Porter Benson for her enthusiasm and words of advice, and to Clarice Feinman for her interest and help at two stages of the project. In addition, I thank Estelle B. Freedman, Leila Rupp, and a group of thoughtful graduate students in women's history at The Ohio State University for reading and commenting on different portions of the manuscript. All these scholars have helped me to sharpen my thinking.

I am grateful to my editor, Janet Francendese, for her hours of work on this book. Her kindness and sense of humor are wonderful. Many thanks, too, to Debby Stuart, a tireless copy editor who made many excellent suggestions.

This book would have been greatly impoverished without the generosity, kindness, and support of George and Helene Staininger. They warmly welcomed me into their home day after day, allowed me unrestricted access to their much-cherished private collection of documents and pictures, talked with me freely about their memories, and wished me well at every step. I will always be thankful to them.

A number of people who either worked for the Los Angeles Police Department as policewomen themselves or had mothers or aunts who did, were amazingly generous with their time. I thank Raymond Wells, Mary Galton Stevenson, Patti Smith, Elizabeth Shadle, Fanchon Blake, Nancy McCard Rene, and Sidney Crabtree. Several people assisted me with my research of Los Angeles County Juvenile Court records: Michael Rousseau, Los Angeles County Juvenile Court Administrator; the Honorable Paul Boland, Judge of the Los Angeles County Juvenile Court; and the Honorable Jaime R. Corral, Judge of the Los Angeles County

Juvenile Court. I would also like to thank Robert Freeman, former Director, Los Angeles City Archives; Jay Jones, present Director, Los Angeles City Archives; Hynda Rudd, Records Management Officer, Los Angeles City Archives; and Ruth Gordon, President, Sojourner Truth Industrial Club.

Librarians at many institutions gave me assistance. I would particularly like to thank Muriel Suleiman and Randolph Elliott of the University of California, Davis; Jane Nowak and Bettye Ellison of the Los Angeles Public Library; and Matthew Gilmore of the District of Columbia Public Library.

Two people, David Dixon and my father, Roy Appier, did not live to see this book finished; each in his own way gave me invaluable help. Annabelle Dixon, D. B. Jones, Diana Hart, and Scout provided steadfast friendship. The Sherman family—Henry, Lillian, and Steven—gave me love and words of encouragement when I needed them most; the love of the Appier family—my mother, Mary Jane, and Tim and Lynda—has always sustained me. For Peter Sherman, words of thanks are hopelessly inadequate.

Parts of Chapters Two and Four of this book contain material from Janis Appier, "Preventive Justice: The Campaign for Women Police, 1910–1940," *Women and Criminal Justice* 4, no. 1 (1992): 3–36. Copyright 1992 Haworth Press, Inc., 10 Alice Street, Binghamton, New York, 13904-1580.

POLICING
WOMEN

"A Man's Job":
Gender and Police Work

In 1930, an editorial entitled "Women as Police Officers" appeared in a mid-western newspaper. According to its unidentified female author, the movement for women police, then twenty years old, was a terrible mistake because police work was a "distinctively masculine" occupation. Nature, the author explained, had "peculiarly fitted" men for police work just as it had fitted women for nursing. Moreover,

> *there is to most of us something highly distasteful in the idea of a woman walking a beat, carrying a billy [club] and going into all sorts of low places.... Though we may feel ourselves equally capable as the men in many ways, it is better that we do our work well than to try to do men's poorly. Women have great power as law enforcers. But that power should be used in the home.... We can still do more good ... as mothers and teachers than as policewomen.*[1]

The idea that police work is a "man's job" has long plagued policewomen. It proved particularly troublesome to the pioneering generation of women police who, as one policewoman phrased it, "stormed the fortress" of U.S. police departments between 1910 and 1930.[2] In this book I take a close look at pioneer policewomen and their struggle to redefine police work as a job a woman could do as well as, if not better than, a man. Using gender as a category of analysis, I explore pioneer policewomen's ideas, their working lives, and the problems they encountered when they invaded a male institution. I also analyze their profound impact on the development of twentieth-century police methods, functions, and subculture.

Historical scholarship on policewomen is generally sparse and limited in scope, largely because, until 1970, women composed only about 1 percent of all sworn personnel in the United States.[3] (Since 1970, their percentage has risen to 10.)[4] Moreover, until the 1970s, police departments severely restricted police-women's range of duties and opportunities for promotion. With few exceptions, female officers worked as jail matrons, as juvenile officers for girls and prepubescent boys, or as clerk-typists. Policewomen's low numbers, together with their low-status positions, made them nearly invisible to historians. But it is women's marginality in police work that most needs explanation. As historian Joan

Wallach Scott observes, "We can better understand the full meaning of occupational identities when we see not only who is included in them but how differences among practitioners are dealt with, which differences matter, how they are understood, and whether and how they change over time."[5]

To understand the history and legacy of pioneer policewomen it is not enough to ask when and how women became police officers. Although these questions are important, they produce answers that simply add women into the story of the police as minor characters. More fruitful are inquiries that ask how women's entry into police work affected the discourse and direction of police reform, how policewomen and their supporters contested male hegemony in police work, and how the police, as an arm of the criminal justice system, incorporated gender into its operations and organization. These lines of inquiry not only illuminate the marginalization of women police, they also uncover another aspect of police history that historians have overlooked: the processes whereby police work in the 1930s and 1940s became increasingly identified with the "masculine" activity of war and the "masculine" characteristic of aggression.

Since the mid-1970s, the masculine identity of the police has received close attention from sociologists and criminologists. In 1975, for example, Thomas Gray pointed out that police work has a "subculture whose members share an acute sense of masculine identity . . . [and place] a high value on the exercise of authority, secrecy, and group solidarity."[6] In 1982, Nanci Koser Wilson argued that police subculture has placed women at a severe disadvantage because it encourages the notion that traditional "masculine" characteristics—aggression, physical strength, and toughness—are essential to successful job performance. In Wilson's view, "the link between masculinity and criminal justice is so tightly bound that we may say it is true not merely that only men can be crime fighters, but even that to be a crime fighter means to be a man."[7]

Although men have always dominated police work, police work itself has not always been synonymous with a narrow construction of masculinity. In the nineteenth century, U.S. municipal police departments routinely cared for lost children and provided free lodging (and often food) to homeless people.[8] Nurturing and sheltering activities like these corresponded to female rather than to male gender stereotypes, but because all police officers were men, conflicts over gender and occupational roles did not arise. By definition, all police work was men's work. In the Progressive Era, however, men lost their monopoly over law enforcement. As this study reveals, concern over changing sexual mores, particularly the increasingly overt public sexuality of working-class female youth, impelled middle-class women activists during the 1910s to push for the employment of women police. They hoped that by arming women with police power they could reduce the vulnerability of women and girls to sexual exploitation and the perceived dangers of premarital sex.

To make the case for women police, female activists drew on middle-class gender stereotypes. They claimed, for example, that women's inherently compassionate nature would make them better than men at performing some police duties, such as preventing crime, handling female and juvenile cases, and protecting the moral and physical safety of women and girls in public. Their arguments for the appointment of women police quickly became the basis of a new, female-gendered model of police work, the crime prevention model. This model has attracted little historical analysis. As a rule, historians of the police have not taken into account how law enforcement policies incorporate gender ideologies and relations of power, so they have either overlooked the existence of the crime prevention model or interpreted it as an early, impractical component of other models, such as the crime control model.[9] The key role of pioneer policewomen and their supporters in twentieth-century police reform has therefore not received scrutiny. When placed in the context of Progressive Era female social activism, the crime prevention model is revealed as a gender-specific critique of existing police practices and philosophy.

The crime prevention model had three main tenets: police work developed to its highest form is social work, crime prevention is the most important function of the police, and women are "inherently" better than men at preventing crime. According to pioneer policewomen and their advocates, successful implementation of the model hinged on the employment of middle-class women social workers as police officers. Once sufficient numbers of policewomen were hired, the argument went, their womanly compassion and social casework methods would gradually transform police departments from cold-eyed law enforcement agencies staffed by poorly trained working-class men into humane social work agencies employing middle-class professionals of both sexes.

Thanks to the efforts of middle-class women activists, hundreds of women became police officers in the 1910s and 1920s. But despite women's presence in police departments, the anticipated gender- and class-based transformation of police work never took place. Instead, year after year, pioneer policewomen remained a tiny, beleaguered minority within police work, resented and even despised by most of their male colleagues. Yet although policewomen did not have the impact on policing they wanted, they did make a difference. As this book reveals, the mass entry of women into police work during the 1910s and 1920s fundamentally changed the nature and gendered representation of law enforcement in unintended ways. Whereas prior to the 1910s, the occupation of police work was presumed to be sex-specific (only men could be police officers), during the 1910s and 1920s it became an occupation with an array of gender-linked functions. According to pioneer policewomen and their advocates, men were best at performing certain police duties, while women were best at performing other police duties. In this book, I argue that women's gender division of police work in the 1910s led to the development of the overtly masculine crime control model of police work, still in use today, and the macho subculture of modern American police departments.

My examination of gender relations of power in police work and the role of pioneer policewomen has three levels of analysis. I analyze the origins of the nationwide movement for women police, linking the movement to native-born middle-class women's efforts in the late nineteenth and early twentieth centuries to make government more responsive to the perceived needs of women and children; the ways gender shaped police work during the first half of the twentieth century; and the working lives of pioneer policewomen with the Los Angeles Police Department (LAPD).[10] Drawing on arrest statistics, original case records of the Los Angeles County Juvenile Court, and the personal papers of leading Los Angeles policewomen, I explore the kinds of arrests policewomen made (and refused to make), the programs they instituted, their close relationship with the local female activist community, and the limitations placed on them by male politicians and police officials. Unlike most historical studies of the police, *Policing Women* examines ordinary interactions between individual policewomen and the people whose cases they handled.

The LAPD provides an ideal setting for the study of pioneer policewomen. In 1910, by a decree of the reform-minded Los Angeles City Council, the LAPD appointed Alice Stebbins Wells, an assistant pastor and social worker, to the Juvenile Bureau. The hiring of a woman police officer swiftly became front-page news in many cities across the United States and Canada, making Wells famous but causing much derisive comment and speculation. Within six months of joining the LAPD, Wells took full advantage of her reputation as the first policewoman in the country by launching a nationwide speaking tour funded by local women's organizations. Everywhere she went, she inspired thousands of middle-class women to rally to the cause of women police. In 1915, she became the founder and president of the International Association of Policewomen.

Four years after hiring Wells, the LAPD established the City Mother's Bureau, a separate bureau of women police specializing in crime prevention through social casework methods. In the mid-1920s, glowing accounts of its work reached Scotland Yard and sparked an interest. After extensive correspondence with LAPD officials, Scotland Yard pronounced the City Mother's Bureau "the first effective preventive department established by any police department" in the world.[11]

The growing historical scholarship on women and the state provides a major framework for this study. In recent years, this scholarship has examined areas of public policy that overtly affected women, such as the development of family law, as well as areas of public policy in which women and dynamics of gender were long thought to be absent, such as war and diplomacy. Partly as a result of this new scholarship, the field of women's history has expanded to include an evaluation of the gendered bases of social processes and institutions.[12] Although gender analysis sheds a great deal of light on the history of the police, no one should assume that it alone can explain all changes that have affected the police. Class, race, gender, ethnicity, and culture simultaneously shaped law enforcement policies and practices.

This book has two parts. The first part, composed of Chapters One and Two, traces the nineteenth-century origins of the movement for women police, examines the public discourse over Progressive Era police reform, and analyzes some of the class and occupational battles fought by pioneer policewomen. The second part, composed of Chapters Three, Four, and Five, focuses on policewomen in Los Angeles. Chapter Three discusses the life and work of City Mother Aletha Gilbert, Chapter Four examines the work of policewomen assigned to the Juvenile Bureau, and Chapter Five explores the decline of the movement for women police and the death of the crime prevention model during the 1930s and early 1940s, when the LAPD moved toward the male-gendered crime control model of police work.

PART ONE

GENDER, THE POLICE, AND CRIMINAL JUSTICE REFORM

One of the heaviest crosses the policeman has to bear . . .

is the interference of the so-called leagues of reformers—the

short-haired woman and the long-haired man who want

to tell the police just how to run their business, how to do

police work, and how to conduct the city.

National Police Magazine
July 1912

"All over the Country There Is a Spirit of Cleaning Up": The Female Reform Tradition and the Origins of the Movement for Women Police

In the spring of 1910, Alice Stebbins Wells, a thirty-seven-year-old assistant pastor and social worker in Los Angeles, told her family, friends, and colleagues that she wanted to join the city police force. This news astonished everyone because police work had always been a "man's job." Moreover, even aside from her sex, Wells hardly fit the popular image of a police officer. The stereotypical officer was a working-class Catholic of Irish descent, nearly illiterate, with few scruples, plenty of muscle, and a fondness for strong drink. In contrast, Wells came from a middle-class Protestant family in the Midwest, held degrees from Oberlin College and Hartford Theological Seminary, stood two inches over five feet tall, and belonged to the Woman's Christian Temperance Union (WCTU). As Wells herself later wryly acknowledged, she personified the antithesis of every characteristic popularly ascribed to the police.[1]

When asked why she wanted to enter police work, Wells replied that women could perform some police duties better than a man could, such as comforting, guiding, and questioning an erring or abused child. She also claimed that women would know better than a man how to prevent women and children from becoming involved in crime, either as victims or as offenders. Armed with these beliefs, Wells persuaded thirty-five local clergymen and clubwomen to sign a petition urging city officials to provide for the appointment of a policewoman. In later years, she liked to recall the stares she received when she first asked people for their support. After pointedly assessing her small frame, people invariably asked, "How could *you* make an arrest?" Her reply summarized the basic goal of pioneer policewomen's work: "I don't want to make arrests. I want to keep people from needing to be arrested, especially young people."[2]

Wells argued her case to the mayor, the chief of police, the city attorney, and the police commissioners. When she was satisfied that these men understood her concerns, she submitted the petition to the Los Angeles City Council.[3] The idea of a woman officer preventing arrests rather than making them appealed to the council, then under the sway of the reform-minded Good Government League.

On August 2, 1910, the council unanimously passed an ordinance "providing for the employment of one police officer who shall be a woman."[4] A few weeks later, on September 13, Wells officially joined the Los Angeles Police Department (LAPD). Her job was to handle all female and juvenile cases and to investigate the social conditions that allegedly led some women and children to become involved in crime.[5]

News of her appointment spread quickly, and Wells soon became internationally known as the first policewoman in the United States. She received hundreds of letters and telegrams from people curious about her work. As she told an audience in New York City in 1912,

> When I applied for my appointment in Los Angeles I thought chiefly of the immediate work to be done right there by a woman. But when I was appointed, then came this—this terrifying publicity—and I realized what it meant. I realized that I should have to stand behind a sort of "movement" for women in the police departments of other cities, just because I was the first in the field.[6]

Wells took the responsibilities of leadership seriously. In 1911, less than a year after her appointment to the LAPD, she visited thirty-one cities in thirty days, promoting the idea of women police in a lecture tour jointly organized by the Los Angeles District of the California Federation of Women's Clubs and the Woman's Christian Temperance Union of Northern California. The following year she took a six-month leave of absence to deliver her speech "The Need for Policewomen" in cities throughout the United States and eastern Canada. Her hard work paid off. By 1915, women's clubs and organizations in at least sixteen U.S. cities had successfully campaigned for the appointment of municipal policewomen. By 1917, the number of U.S. cities with women police had risen to 125.[7]

Wells liked to take full credit for beginning the movement for women police. In 1940, she wrote, "The Police Department especially considered itself to be a man's world, and the public so regarded it, until I stormed the fortress."[8] Wells did indeed provide forceful leadership, but her efforts alone do not account for the success of the movement for women police. Instead, her ideas found fertile ground because of the convergence of several sets of circumstances in the early 1910s: the high level of female activism in social welfare reform, the juvenile court movement, and the ongoing revolution in sexual culture.

This chapter explores the roots of the movement for women police by first tracing the evolution of middle-class women's social action crusades over the course of the nineteenth century. Next, it illustrates middle-class women's gradually deepening involvement in criminal justice reform by describing the efforts of Chicago clubwomen during the 1880s and 1890s to change the ways local police and courts treated women and children. Chicago clubwomen's most famous reform, the juvenile court, receives lengthy analysis because it not only sparked the involvement of thousands of middle-class women in criminal justice reform but also institutionalized a female-gendered, maternalist approach to the problem of juvenile delinquency. The chapter concludes with a look at the rising concerns of middle-class women in the early twentieth century over the moral and physical safety of urban women and children, especially teenage girls. Within a few years, their concerns became the basis of a demand for women police.

Women and Social Welfare Reform

The movement for women police began as one of several contemporaneous movements in which middle-class women used exalted definitions of womanhood and motherhood to claim new roles for themselves in the public sphere as policymakers, workers, and electors. In recent years, historians have examined the links between these movements, which they have labeled "maternalist," and the emergence of the welfare state in the early twentieth century. Kathryn Kish Sklar, Robyn Muncy, Linda Gordon, and other scholars have shown that female reformers were far more likely than their male counterparts to look to the state to correct social inequities and cure social ills. Recent studies also show that women reformers realized their greatest achievements in shaping welfare policies for women and children. Well-known examples of maternalist reforms during the early twentieth century include mothers' and widows' pensions and protective labor legislation.[9]

Like other women activists of the nineteenth and early twentieth centuries, the leaders of the movement for women police drew upon a female reform tradition that had deep roots in the middle-class ideology of domesticity. This ideology first began to take shape in the Northeast during the late eighteenth and early nineteenth centuries, when profound changes in political culture, economic life, and family structure seemed to threaten women's traditional domestic roles. In response to the threat, white middle-class Americans gradually developed a highly refined gender ideology. According to its tenets, men and women occupied sexually differentiated social spaces and possessed different but complementary characters. Men presided over the morally dangerous public world of trade, politics, and industry, while women presided over the virtuous private world of the home. Because women were expected to devote their lives to their families, they were supposed to be pure, pious, submissive, and domestic. In theory, these virtues, together with women's exclusion from the amoral public world, elevated women to a position of moral influence, even superiority, over men. In practice, as historian Peggy Pascoe has noted, American society often did not accept middle-class women's claim to moral superiority.[10]

The conflation of femininity and domesticity in the gender ideology of the white middle class made the phrase "A woman's place is in the home" a popular adage throughout the nineteenth century. Despite its popularity, the adage did not reflect the reality of most women's lives. Financial necessity—or, for enslaved women, the law and the whip—compelled millions of women to work outside their homes. Furthermore, the adage often contradicted the diverse cultural customs and gender ideologies of Latinos, Native Americans, and immigrants from all over the world.[11] Even many privileged white middle-class women did not limit their activities to their homes but instead plunged into organized benevolence and reform. Inspired by the teachings and values of evangelical Protestantism, these women joined church missionary and relief societies, established moral reform associations, and directed a variety of charitable organizations. Some of the women's voluntary organizations relied on the leadership of clergymen, but many had female leadership. As Kathryn Kish Sklar has noted, the United States before the Civil War had more mass-based, politically autonomous women's organizations than any other nation in the world.[12] Through their multifaceted commitment to social activism, humanitarianism, and moral reform, middle-class American women of the nineteenth century made it clear that women's "proper" place was not just in the home.[13]

The ideology of domesticity, together with women's common needs and experiences, fostered a strong sense of female solidarity among women of the same class and family networks.[14] Among some women activists, this sense of solidarity was so strong that it crossed race, class, ethnic, and religious lines. Beginning in the early nineteenth century, some women's organizations identified and tried to help specific groups of women whom they labeled "unfortunate." During the 1820s, for example, a few Quaker women became interested in the plight of female prisoners in the Arch Street Prison of Philadelphia. Shut away in tiny, fetid, overcrowded cells, denied both physical exercise and mental stimulation, frequently abused and raped by male prison guards, female prisoners lived lives far removed from those of most middle-class women. At first, the Quaker women simply visited female inmates, but later they offered sewing and writing classes, as well as moral instruction. The Quaker women's efforts to "uplift their fallen sisters" eventually inspired similar efforts by women activists in other cities and culminated in the establishment of separate women's prisons in the 1870s.[15]

Although gender ideology and feelings of sisterhood bound women activists together, race, class, ethnic, religious, and ideological differences divided them into separate, but not always opposing, camps. Nancy A. Hewitt has found that white women activists from the most privileged socioeconomic backgrounds usually supported only the mildest reforms, while those from the lowest margins of the middle class often called for the complete overhaul of society.[16] Additionally, some women activists supported the ideal of the patriarchal family, while others explicitly rejected it; some used conservative interpretations of prevailing gender beliefs to make personal attacks on other women activists; white women activists barred women of color from their organizations; and in the two decades immediately following the Civil War, some women activists (notably those from elite backgrounds) rejected the idea of female moral superiority.[17]

Despite their differences, most women activists after the Civil War had one major strategy in common: they turned to the state for help. This strategy was not altogether new; a few women activists had begun to seek state funding for their organizations as early as the 1830s.[18] But after the Civil War, the trend gained momentum. In several states during the 1870s, women activists seeking to improve conditions for female prisoners campaigned successfully for positions on newly formed public boards of charities and corrections. Once in power, they pushed for the establishment of separate prisons run by and for women.[19] Like other women activists of their era, these prison reformers used direct political action to gain legal status from the government, as well as a sense of self-identity.[20]

Between 1880 and 1930, many women activists devoted their entire careers in social work and social science to identifying the welfare needs of working-class women and children and pressing for the establishment of government programs and institutions to meet those needs. As Kathryn Kish Sklar has argued, women activists sought to ameliorate class inequities through gender-specific means; that is, they created a public discourse on the sufferings and problems of working-class women in order to champion measures that would bring about a more just distribution of the nation's resources.[21] Moreover, most leading women activists expressed a firm belief in female moral authority and the unalloyed virtues of motherhood. In their eyes, motherhood and motherliness epitomized femininity at its best: nurturing, compassionate, protective, and morally vigilant. Despite their unity on these points, however, they did not share the same political commitments or views of women's role. They disagreed vehemently, for example, on woman suffrage and birth control. But underlying their political diversity was a strong commitment to the task of bringing the private, feminine virtues of motherhood to bear on the public, masculine sphere of politics, law, and government. This maternalist commitment, historically grounded in the Victorian middle-class ideology of domesticity, spurred and shaped female reform of the criminal justice system.

The Chicago Woman's Club, 1876–1907

The early history of the Chicago Woman's Club illustrates how middle-class women came to undertake maternalist reform of the criminal justice system. In fact, Chicago clubwomen's establishment of the juvenile court epitomizes the maternalist nature of much female criminal justice reform during the late nineteenth and early twentieth centuries, because it reflects middle-class women's belief that they had a moral responsibility to act in a motherly role toward the children of the poor. The maternalist nature of the juvenile court deserves attention because it clarifies the scholarly debate over the establishment and early operations of the court. Much of this debate has centered on the role of class, particularly the class bias of the court's founders. Once the court is placed in the context of maternalist reform, however, a new picture of its historical development emerges, one that is shaded by gender difference and gender ideology as well as by class dynamics. The same can be said of the historical development of many criminal justice reforms undertaken by the Chicago Woman's Club and other women's organizations in the United States between 1880 and 1930.[22]

The Chicago Woman's Club was one of many similar organizations formed by affluent women in cities across the nation after the Civil War. It began in 1876 as a literary and cultural study club.[23] Within four years, the members of the club's Philanthropy Committee resolved to abandon their nearly exclusive focus on self-improvement and undertake practical work on behalf of women. As they remarked, they wanted to do something that would "make them into a Committee of Philanthropy in fact as well as in name."[24] For their first project they arranged a public lecture series on women's health and hygiene matters. Within a short time, this series led to the establishment of the Woman's Physiological Institute of Chicago. Although committee members took a great deal of pride in the Institute, they soon realized that they had little to do with its routine operations once it got started. The Institute therefore did not offer them the kind of ongoing, hands-on work they yearned to accomplish. The opportunity to undertake that kind of work appeared two years later, in 1882, when the Chicago Woman's Club joined a nationwide movement, spearheaded by the WCTU, to install matrons, or female guards, in police stations and jails.[25]

The Chicago Woman's Club first heard of the movement for police matrons on May 10, 1882. On that date, club members Mrs. Sabin Smith and Dr. Leila Bedell discussed the plight of female inmates in Chicago jails and then asked the club if it would support the WCTU campaign for matrons.[26] The WCTU had taken up the cause of women in jail during the late 1870s, arguing that only female guards could protect female prisoners from sexual assault and provide them with sisterly comfort and moral guidance. The WCTU borrowed these arguments from the movement for separate women's prisons, then going strong.[27]

Smith and Bedell's discussion struck a responsive chord among club members. In what the club's annual report for 1882–83 calls "the only departure from the literary work of the Club," members passed a resolution in May 1882 "endorsing an effort being made by Miss Frances E. Willard to place women in police stations for the care of women prisoners."[28] The Philanthropy Committee was not content merely to endorse Willard's campaign, however. It also quickly instituted a successful search for a woman to become night matron at the jail, raised funds to pay her salary, and helped to persuade the Cook County sheriff to appoint her. (Committee members believed that it was more important to have a matron on duty during the night than during the day.) The committee continued to pay the night matron's salary for several years, until the city assumed responsibility for it.[29]

Shortly after the club became involved in the campaign for matrons, it formed the Jail Committee.[30] Through this committee's reports, club members gradually grew familiar with the conditions of local police stations, courts, and jails. Over the next twenty years, clubwomen worked to improve the ways these institutions treated women and juveniles. (Like other maternalist reformers, the members of the Chicago Woman's Club concerned themselves with the welfare of women and children.) In 1890 the Philanthropy Committee reported that its members had persuaded local police officials to abandon the custom of transporting women to the House of Correction in the same vehicle with men. In clubwomen's opinion, female offenders who were forced to be in the company of male offenders for even a brief time were almost inevitably degraded by the experience. Clubwomen's espousal of this view was an ideological triumph for female prison reformers, for they were the first to portray the female prisoner as less depraved than the male.[31]

In 1892, the members of the Chicago Woman's Club began to talk of the need to establish a separate police station in central Chicago for the exclusive use of women and children. This idea circulated for years but never went past the discussion stage. Among the clubwomen's concerns was the large number of destitute women and children who sought temporary overnight shelter in police stations. In early 1892, members of the Philanthropy Committee, together with representatives from other local women's organizations, formed an advisory board to the superintendent of police. The board investigated every Chicago police station that sheltered homeless women and children and insisted that certain improvements to the accommodations be made. A description of the kinds of conditions the advisory board found appears in a book by Walter Wyckoff, an investigative journalist. In December 1891, Wyckoff arranged to spend a night in a Chicago police station. He reported that the station offered no beds or cots to homeless people, only a bare concrete floor where men were packed in so close together that they had to lie "on their right sides with their legs drawn up, and each man's legs pressed close in behind those of the man in front." This mass of bodies, Wyckoff complained, created "an unventilated atmosphere of the foulest pollution."[32]

A few months after the police advisory board got under way in 1892, Mrs. Perry H. Smith suggested that the Reform Department of the club start a school for boys who were awaiting trial inside the county jail. (No mention of girls in jail appears in the published account of the club's activities.) According to the records of the club, some boys awaited trial in jail for months at a time. The club approved

Smith's suggestion and hired one of its own members, Florence Haythorn, to teach the boys. For the next half-dozen or more years, Haythorn taught a class that met for two hours every weekday morning in the corridor of the jail. After she retired, other women took her place. During the early years, class size ranged from fifteen to sixty boys between the ages of ten and sixteen.[33]

In addition to teaching at the Jail School, Haythorn acted as a juvenile probation officer; she was probably the first paid juvenile probation officer in the world. In this capacity she investigated the charges against her students, made visits to their homes, and accompanied them to court to speak on their behalf. When the juvenile court held its first sessions in 1899, Haythorn brought her records to court and advised the judge about each case. Ironically, had she pursued probation work in the 1910s, 1920s, or 1930s, she would have found that her sex barred her from handling the cases of her students. The professionalization of probation work in the early twentieth century generally restricted female probation officers to cases involving girls, women, and boys under the age of twelve.[34]

According to the records of the club from 1892, "The interest [in the jail] taken by the Women's Club began soon to have its effect."[35] In response to clubwomen's pleas, jail authorities began to house boys separately from adults, and they also began clean up the cells and corridors.[36] Club members wanted separate quarters for the boys because they believed that close association with adult prisoners both harmed and hardened juvenile prisoners. They viewed criminality in much the same light as an infectious disease, and they wanted to do all they could to ensure that boys in jail were "kept away from the contaminating influence of those more steeped in crime than themselves."[37] This emphasis on preventing crime through manipulation of the immediate physical and social environment became a keynote of female criminal justice reform in the Progressive Era.

Mrs. Perry H. Smith also recommended in 1892 that the club support the creation of a juvenile court. This recommendation led to fundamental changes in the treatment of children and adolescents by the U.S. criminal justice system. Smith doubtlessly made her recommendation at the request of Lucy Flower, a former club president who had been pressing for the legal establishment of a juvenile court since the mid-1880s. According to Flower's daughter, Flower had assumed leadership of the embryonic juvenile court movement in 1888, when local sentiment against the prevailing treatment of children by the courts crystallized "into a demand for a law removing children under sixteen years of age from the jurisdiction of the adult criminal courts and placing them under the control of a parental court."[38]

Flower and other early supporters of the court voiced two major objections to the way the criminal justice system handled the cases of children: They thought it wrong that criminal laws did not distinguish between adult and juvenile defendants, and they objected to a criminal justice system that focused only on the offense and ignored the offender.[39] In their view, the moral responsibility of children differed greatly from that of adults. Specifically, the founders of the court believed that a child was no more legally responsible for his or her actions than an orphaned child was responsible for his or her state of dependency. Children were victims of circumstance. This line of reasoning helps to explain why reformers created a court that handled cases of child dependency as well as juvenile delinquency.

The founders of the court further argued that if the state paid no constructive attention to juvenile offenders, many of them might well grow up to become adult criminals, especially if they were incarcerated alongside adult offenders, as was the custom, or allowed to return unsupervised to their former homes and haunts. The founders of the court believed that people became criminals through environmental influences, rather than through heredity ("bad blood"). Thus, the founders wanted to make the criminal justice system do more than simply find children guilty or innocent of a crime, institutionalize them or let them go free; they wanted to create a system that would prevent child offenders from growing up to become adult criminals. In sum, they thought the state should take responsibility for the well-being of every child in his or her own home. The ideal solution appeared to lie in the construction of a separate court and probation system for children.[40]

It took Flower and her associates approximately eleven years (1888–99) to write a juvenile court bill that was acceptable to all interested parties and to muster sufficient support for its passage among influential men. Toward the end of this long process, Flower held two meetings to introduce the bill to prominent men in Chicago. To the first meeting she invited judges, and to the second she invited representative clergymen from every denomination. Flower's daughter recalled that at these meetings, her mother "particularly emphasized that 'the bill was doomed to failure at Springfield unless men as well as women backed it.'"[41] This remark points up the early lack of male support for the bill and Flower's shrewd understanding of political realities.

Years after the founding of the court, Louise DeKoven Bowen, a member of the Chicago Woman's Club, described her dismay with the political process through which the juvenile court bill became law in Illinois. Her account suggests that politicians initially had little interest in a separate court for children.

> I well remember how that law was passed, because it gave me a feeling of great uneasiness. . . . I happened to know at that time a noted Illinois politician. . . . I told him I wanted to get this bill passed at once. . . . He went to the telephone in my library, called up one of the bosses in the Senate and one in the House and said to each one, "There is a

bill, number so and so, which I want passed; see that it is done at once." One of the men whom he called evidently said, "What is there in it?" and the reply was, "There is nothing in it, but a woman I know wants it passed"—and it was passed. I thought with horror at the time, Supposing it had been a bad bill, it would have been passed exactly the same way.[42]

In all likelihood, the "noted Illinois politician" dismissed the importance of the bill because it involved child welfare, a "woman's" issue that had not yet moved into the mainstream of public policy.[43]

On July 1, 1899, the Illinois State Legislature enacted the juvenile court bill into law. However, as amended and passed the bill made no appropriation for the payment of probation officers' salaries or the construction of juvenile detention homes.[44] Flower and other club members did not allow this obstacle to dismay or hinder them. They immediately chose the first probation officers, Emma Quinlan and Alzina P. Stevens, and raised money to pay their salaries. Club members continued to raise money for probation officers' salaries until September 1902, when Flower organized the Juvenile Court Committee to oversee court operations. This committee, headed by Julia Lathrop and composed of women representatives from many local organizations, paid the salaries of Cook County probation officers until 1907. (By that time the court employed twenty-two officers.) In addition, committee members raised money for the construction of a juvenile detention home in Chicago, oversaw its operations, placed court wards in foster homes, and sat beside the judge during the early sessions of the court to advise him on the disposition of various cases. Every year, when the circuit court judges began the process of choosing a new juvenile court judge, committee members interviewed all the candidates and informed the circuit court judges of their choice. Every year, the circuit court judges appointed the candidate recommended by the committee.[45]

Cook County took over the probation system from the Juvenile Court Committee in 1907, and the committee immediately disbanded. At first, committee members were pleased to relinquish their duties because they thought they were placing the probation system in the proper hands—the hands of the government. But political scandals and turnovers in administration soon caused them to regret their loss of control. In their opinion, the bureaucrats who oversaw court operations were both venal and uncaring. As one observer remarked bitterly in 1914, the whole juvenile justice system in Chicago had become "one more prize in the spoils of politics of its city."[46]

Although the former members of the Juvenile Court Committee swiftly reorganized under the name "Juvenile Protective Association," the demise of the Juvenile Court Committee marked the end of an era for women activists in Chicago.

Never again would they have so decisive a voice in shaping policy or overseeing the day-to-day operations of the juvenile court. By 1907, the Chicago Woman's Club had been involved in criminal justice reform for twenty-five years. During this time, club members pursued a course of action that featured several themes of maternalist reform. First, they focused their attention on women and children. Specifically, they tried to change the ways local institutions treated women and children. Second, they appealed to the state to implement their ideas and engaged in direct political action to achieve their goals. Third, they created new public careers for middle-class women (such as themselves) in the jails and the juvenile court. For years they privately funded most of the public positions they created, thereby contributing to the creation of what Sara Evans has called "the maternal commonwealth."[47] Fourth, and most important, they constructed their reforms in their own idealized image of womanhood and motherhood. This image gave the court a particularly strong and historically specific maternalist character.

The maternalist character of the juvenile court can be traced to its most basic feature, the removal of child defendants from the adversarial arena in which adult defendants were publicly tried. Chicago clubwomen and their allies eliminated the overtly adversarial aspects of criminal trials from the juvenile court because they believed that the state should act like a protective, nurturing mother to children, rather than like a foe.[48] In place of the adversarial criminal court, they designed a public agency that they claimed acted in the best interest of the individual child, rather than in the best interest of an abstract entity called the "state" or in pursuit of another abstract entity called "justice." Intent on eradicating the idea that the state and the child had opposing interests, the founders of the court did away with most of the physical trappings of the criminal courtroom. They insisted that the hearings (never "trials") be held in ordinary rooms furnished simply with a table and chairs. They explained that they did not wish to overawe the child with the majesty and power of the law. Instead, they wished to make the child feel as if he or she were in the company of wise and sympathetic friends. A spirit of feminine cooperation, not masculine antagonism, was supposed to prevail at every juvenile court hearing.

As the substitution of "hearing" for "trial" indicates, the court's founders not only got rid of the criminal courtroom, they also jettisoned the traditional language of criminal proceedings. In the lexicon of the juvenile court, the terms "petitioner" and "minor" usually took the place of "plaintiff" and "defendant." Similarly, rather than name an abstract political entity as the petitioner or plaintiff (e.g., the People of the State of Illinois), the court named the individual person who brought the child to the court's attention (usually a family member or a police officer). These changes in legal terminology reveal the founders' determination to remove all suggestion of an adversarial relationship between the state and the child. Moreover, the new terms indicate a purposeful rejection of conceptions of justice that were not rooted in an individual's social circumstances. The court's founders believed that the needs of an individual child took precedence over abstract conceptions of justice predicated on adult behavior. Like other maternalist reformers, they fashioned policies that they ardently believed served children's best interests.[49]

For the court's founders, serving children's best interests meant keeping them living at home whenever possible under a court-supervised system of probation. Under this system, probation officers regularly visited the homes of delinquent children to monitor behavior, investigate conditions, and give advice to everyone concerned. These visits were often filled with class tensions, for as a rule, probation officers came from a significantly more privileged socioeconomic background than the children they visited, and they typically used their visits to try to implant middle-class moral and behavioral standards in working-class families.

Gender shaped the system of juvenile probation as well. Indeed, the founders' determination to keep delinquent children at home reflects a deep reverence for the home, the seat of middle-class women's power. The founders extended their reverence even to homes they considered inferior, such as the those of immigrants, people of color, and the working class as a whole. Their reverence did not, however, prevent them from thinking that they knew better than working-class parents what kind of homes children should have.[50]

The passage of the juvenile court bill in Illinois in 1899 marked the beginning of a new era of middle-class women's involvement in criminal justice occupations and reform in the United States. Throughout the country, women's clubs and organizations heard of the leading part played by Chicago clubwomen in founding a juvenile court, and they began making plans to emulate Chicago club women's success. As in Chicago, women activists everywhere applied political pressure to establish the court, often paid probation officers' salaries until public funding became available, and formed juvenile court committees.[51] They undertook all this work with a sure sense that by rescuing children from brutalizing contact with adult defendants and adult criminal courts, they were helping to prevent children from becoming adult offenders.

Why did the juvenile court so quickly attract mass support from women activists? The timing was critically important. During the 1890s, middle-class women's clubs and organizations across the nation began to turn their attention away from cultural study and toward civic work.[52] The first decade of the twentieth century thus found thousands of organized women eager to undertake reform of public institutions. Moreover, the juvenile court provided women activists with a perfect vehicle for their maternalist reform energy because of its focus on children, a traditional area of women's concern.

Women activists were also drawn to the juvenile court because of the court's implicit promise to treat children more gently than traditional courts had treated them. The idea that children needed gentleness gained popularity in the United States during the decades following the Civil War, thanks in part to the recommendations of child-rearing manuals written by middle-class women. These manuals repeatedly advised parents to treat children with kindness, humor, and gentle discipline, rather than with harsh words and physical punishment.[53] Parents who took this advice to heart probably cherished the Victorian vision of the home as a peaceful haven from a competitive and often ruthless world. The founders of the juvenile court sought to extend this class-specific, female-gendered vision of home into the public sphere.

The juvenile court found particularly enthusiastic supporters among female settlement workers, social scientists, and social workers. For these groups, the court's appeal lay in part in its implicit recognition of child offenders as victims of bad social conditions. In this respect, the juvenile court represented a departure from the nineteenth-century hereditarian view of crime, which held that criminals composed a separate, almost subhuman, biological class.[54] During the early years of the twentieth century, female social scientists contributed a great deal to the success of the juvenile court movement by providing quantitative data pointing to the causative links between poverty and crime. For example, in 1912, Sophonisba Breckinridge and Edith Abbott, both of the University of Chicago, published *The Delinquent Child and the Home,* an influential study in the new field of criminology. Their study reported that nine-tenths of the female juveniles who appeared before the Chicago Juvenile Court between 1899 and 1909 came from poverty-stricken families.[55]

Finally, women activists across the nation worked hard to establish the juvenile court in their states because, like the clubwomen in Chicago, they thought it would solve a problem that had long troubled them: the arrest and incarceration of children in adult jails. The magnitude of Chicago clubwomen's accomplishment in creating the juvenile court has obscured the fact that they were not the only middle-class urban women during the late nineteenth century who tried to change the ways the police and courts treated children. The experience of women activists in Los Angeles was probably typical. According to the recollections of two residents of the Los Angeles College Settlement House, city police during the 1890s arrested an increasing number of children for relatively minor offenses, such as stealing a piece of fruit from a grocery store or playing in the streets. One of the residents of the College Settlement House, Bessie Stoddart, recalled that prior to the founding of the Los Angeles County Juvenile Court in 1903, she and other resident women "often went out on the street and pleaded with the police to keep them from taking the little fellows off to jail." By "little fellows," Stoddart explained, she meant boys age seven and older. "The women of the College Settlement House used to bring food and little playthings to those children who were housed in the jail. . . . As time went on things grew worse and the women of the club became desperate."[56]

When the women of Los Angeles Settlement House learned of the new juvenile court of Chicago, they invited Martha Falconer, a Chicago clubwoman and probation officer, to talk to them about it. Falconer arrived in early 1901, and according to another member of the College Settlement, her speech ignited the juvenile court movement in Los Angeles.[57] A little more than two years later, in April 1903, women activists throughout California claimed victory as state legislators enacted a juvenile court bill into law.[58] In Los Angeles, women's clubs followed the example of the Chicago Woman's Club by paying probation officers' salaries for the first three years, forming a juvenile court committee, and campaigning for the appointment of a woman judge (known as a "referee") to hear the cases of female youths.[59]

By 1909, twenty-two states had adopted the Illinois juvenile court bill in whole or in part, and women activists in the remaining states were pushing hard for the passage of similar measures.[60] Yet despite the success of the juvenile court movement, or perhaps because of it, the focus of female criminal justice reform during 1905–10 shifted away from the establishment of the court toward a search for ways to prevent women and children from becoming involved in crime and immorality, either as victims or as offenders. This shift occurred at different times in different cities, but in the early 1910s, it culminated in a nationwide movement for women police. Leaders of the new movement demanded that police departments hire women officers to perform two new related functions: the protection of women and children, and especially teenage girls, from the perceived moral dangers of the city; and the investigation of the social causes of crime. In time, these functions became the basis for the female-gendered model of police work, the crime prevention model.

Women and Crime Prevention

The seeds for the crime prevention model germinated first in private protective associations for women and children. Although these organizations provided a variety of social services, the focus here will be on their investigations into environmental causes of crime and immorality and their attempts to reduce the vulnerability of teenage girls and young women to sexual exploitation, which they thought encompassed virtually all instances of premarital sex. A few of these organizations, such as the Women's Protective Association, the Travelers' Aid Society, and the Girls' Protective League, were national federations. Others, such as the Women's Society for the Prevention of Crime organized in 1910 in New York City, were strictly local associations. Whether national or local, private protective associations formed part of the emerging network of professional social work agencies.[61]

A few private protective associations for women and children existed before 1900, but they sprang up everywhere in urban America during the Progressive Era. White native-born middle-class women dominated the membership of most associations. African American women established and ran separate associations. In general, the members of private protective associations hoped to make their cities safe for women and children. "Safe" in this context meant the absence of social conditions believed to be conducive to both crime and immorality. In the minds of members of private protective associations, crime and immorality were virtually identical. Thus they worried just as much, if not more, about transgressions of the moral code as they did about violations of the criminal law. They found it particularly disturbing that they could not count on the police to protect women and children from violations of vice laws because the police had notorious and well-deserved reputations for protecting vice (illegal liquor sales, prostitution, and gambling).[62] Members of private protective associations referred to their own efforts to protect women and children from crime and immorality as "crime prevention."[63]

In Chicago and Los Angeles, the same women who had spearheaded the establishment of juvenile courts in their respective states soon organized juvenile protective associations to work "upstream" from the court. They vowed to protect children's rights by identifying and eliminating the social conditions that they believed impelled children toward delinquency and dependency. The Juvenile Protective Association of Chicago, for example, undertook surveys of city neighborhoods, noting such features as the brightness of street lamps, the number of playgrounds and parks, the presence or absence of policemen, the number of saloons, pool rooms, dance halls, and other commercial amusement places, and signs of gambling or prostitution. It then used these findings to demand action from city authorities.[64]

The idea of preventing juvenile crime through manipulation of the environment reflected the fervent belief of most urban reformers in the Progressive Era that they could cure most social ills and transform city life by tearing down old tenements and making space for parks and playgrounds.[65] In many cities and towns, the same women who led the juvenile court movement also led the local playground movement. In Los Angeles, Bessie Stoddart served on the Juvenile Court Committee, the Juvenile Protective Association, and the Playground Committee.[66]

The sudden proliferation of private protective associations in the Progressive Era attests to middle-class women's escalating concern over the morals and physical well-being of urban women and children, especially teenage girls. They felt that urban life as a whole had grown boisterously beyond their understanding and control. It is easy to understand their point of view, for urban life had changed dramatically over the previous twenty-five years, and it was continuing to change at a dizzying rate. Beginning in the 1880s, an ever-widening flood of immigrants from eastern and southern Europe poured into northern cities, along with a steady stream of blacks from the rural South; the distinctive cultures and sexual mores of these disparate groups seriously alarmed the native-born white middle class. The turn of the century also witnessed increasingly bold styles of dance and dress among working-class young women, the beginnings of the modern mass consumer culture, a growing popularity of new commercial places of amusement, a burgeoning urban sexual commerce, and a record number of women working outside the home in both paid and volunteer positions.[67]

In a speech given to a Canadian audience in January 1913, pioneer policewoman Alice Stebbins Wells summarized what these changes meant to middle-class women like herself. "The world is now made up of men, women and children," she reflected. "At one time the public was composed almost entirely of men."[68] In an important sense, she was right: the ideological and cultural walls separating the private feminine sphere from the public masculine sphere had visibly broken down. The benefits of this breakdown seemed clear to many women reformers, because they believed that the public world of business and government sorely needed women's values. Yet the dangers of a sexually integrated public space sometimes appeared to outweigh the advantages. These dangers stemmed in part from the fear that women's presence in the public sphere would result in their debasement. Rather than women conquering the world, the world would conquer women. This fear, which lay at the heart of much crime prevention work, found its most dramatic expression in the white slavery scare of 1905–15.

Stories about white slavery first appeared in nativist propaganda pamphlets published at the turn of the century. According to these pamphlets, hundreds, perhaps thousands, of innocent white teenage girls and young women were kidnapped and forced into prostitution every year by swarthy-skinned foreigners ("white slavers"). By 1910, films, plays, novels, and magazine articles about white slavery were bombarding the public from all sides. These stories, many of them purporting to be case histories, usually featured a crowded urban setting, a young woman in public on her own, and an abduction scene. Some Americans became so fearful and angry about white slavery that they demanded laws regulating morals and the workplaces of immigrants. In 1910, Congress passed the most well-known of these laws, the White Slave Traffic Act, also known as the Mann Act. This law made it a felony to transport females across state lines for "immoral purposes."[69]

On the surface, the white slavery scare concerned the brutal sexual exploitation of virginal young women. Most historians of sexuality doubt, however, that the abduction and sale of girls and women were as widespread and organized as contemporary accounts claimed. They argue that the white slavery scare was part of the reaction of the native-born white middle class to unsettling social changes in the late nineteenth and early twentieth centuries, especially the massive immigration from southern and eastern Europe, the rise in female employment outside the home, and most important, the rapidly changing sexual behavior and values of young people. Urban sexual culture changed so rapidly and completely among youth that some scholars have labeled the changes a revolution. Working-class young women and girls were at the forefront of the changes, for many of them overtly rebelled against parental and middle-class ideas of respectability. Some were labeled "charity girls," a term that referred to their practice of bartering sexual favors for an evening's entertainment on the town. Others stopped short of premarital sex, but in the slang of the day, they "put on style" by dressing and acting in ways that shocked the moral sensibilities of their elders and the middle class.[70] Still others used sexual intimacy as a strategy to "keep" a steady boyfriend or to induce a man to propose marriage. Not surprisingly, the incidence of premarital pregnancy soared, rising from 12.6 percent of all pregnancies between 1841 and 1880 to 24.4 percent between 1881 and 1910. [71]

After the turn of the century, the revolution in sexual culture spread to the white middle class, ushering in the era of sexual liberalism. The transition from Victorian sexual values to those of sexual liberalism entailed much confusion and conflict, especially with respect to adolescent female sexuality. Between 1900 and 1930, middle-class parents watched and worried as their teenage daughters created self-conscious social and sexual identities. Following the example of working-class female youth, middle-class teenage girls and young women wore conspicuous make-up, dressed and danced provocatively, smoked cigarettes and drank alcohol in public, patronized dance halls and other commercial places of amusement, and experimented with premarital sex.[72]

Against the backdrop of these changes in female sexual attitudes and behavior loomed the disapproval of many parents, clergymen, women activists, and other concerned citizens. During the Progressive Era, middle-class social workers and reformers devised a new term—the "girl problem"—to refer to the ongoing sexual rebellion of female youth. Discussions of the girl problem took place at countless conferences of social workers, settlement workers, sex educators, and pioneer policewomen in the 1910s and 1920s. Most of the participants at these conferences agreed that parents were at least partly to blame for the misbehavior of teenage girls. If parents supervised their daughters more closely and gave them moral guidance, the reasoning went, their daughters would have neither the inclination nor the opportunity to misbehave.[73] Yet even though "lax parenting" figured as one of the major causes of the girl problem, discussions of female sexual rebellion often merged with discussions of white slavery. The white slavery scare of 1905–15 therefore provided a forum for middle-class Americans to express alarm and propose remedies for the ongoing revolution in sexual culture.

In many cities during the Progressive Era, doctors, lawyers, businessmen, and college professors responded to the revolution in sexual culture by forming commissions to investigate prostitution. These so-called vice commissions found prostitutes nearly everywhere they looked: in stores, cabarets, dance halls, public parks, penny arcades, skating rinks, lodging houses, railway stations, and nickel movie theaters.[74] Social purity reformers and women's organizations, particularly the WCTU, used the findings of vice commissions to campaign more fervently than ever for the closing of segregated districts (the areas of cities where prostitution was legal). Women activists also stepped up their efforts to raise the age at which a female was considered legally capable of giving her consent to sexual intercourse.[75] If a male had sexual intercourse with a female below this age, he was guilty of statutory rape. Between the late 1880s, when social purity activists first began their organized efforts to raise the age of consent, and the late 1910s, the age of consent in most states rose from ten or twelve years to sixteen or eighteen years.[76]

The publicized reports of vice commissions, the shocking tales of white slavery, the debates over segregated districts and age-of-consent legislation, and the bold sexual practices of some adolescent girls and women created a sense of crisis in the Progressive Era among urban middle-class citizens, male and female. These factors also fed the growth of private protective associations. Some of the associations, such as the Girls' Protective League, the Travelers' Aid Society, and the Women's Protective Association, set out to prevent the spread of prostitution by cutting down on the supply of new prostitutes. Reasoning that loneliness drove some young women to seek the companionship of untrustworthy strangers, private protective associations organized programs to befriend young women living or traveling alone in the city.

Some associations also undertook empirical investigations of female employment bureaus, working conditions, and rooming houses, seeking to discover if they were fronts for white slavery or other forms of prostitution. The Juvenile Protective Association of Chicago carried out what were perhaps the most exhaustive investigations of this kind in the nation. In the early 1910s, members of the association concluded that low wages, dreary jobs, and cheerless surroundings were the primary factors that drove some young women into sexual experimentation or prostitution. Like other women activists in crime prevention, the members of the Juvenile Protective Association of Chicago did not draw a clear distinction between sexual experimentation and prostitution, especially with respect to working-class teenage girls and young women.[77] To women in crime prevention, poverty and premarital sex were a lethal combination. They reasoned that once a poor girl lost her virtue, she more often than not came to view prostitution as an easy way to make money.

Even though women in crime prevention condemned premarital sex, they did not always or even necessarily condemn the young women and girls who engaged in it. Louise DeKoven Bowen, the president of the Juvenile Protective Association of Chicago, insisted that no one should blame single girls and young women for seeking fun and excitement at the end of the workday because their work in factories and stores was so dreary. She warned, however, that unless someone were on hand to watch over young women's search for excitement, the search would probably end in their victimization, for they well might spend their hours off work satisfying their sexual passions.[78]

Bowen's view, which was widely shared among women in crime prevention, helps to explain why many private protective associations kept a regular surveillance over dance halls, penny arcades, amusement parks, movie houses, and other commercial places of amusement. These establishments attracted working-class youth by the droves and so were the favorite haunts of all purveyors of vice. Self-appointed inspectors from protective agencies routinely patrolled these places, looking for signs of gambling, prostitution, the sale of liquor to minors, violations of child labor laws, the presence of truant schoolchildren, and erotic displays of any kind, such as sensual dancing, overt kissing and fondling, and obscene advertisements. All these investigations fell under the rubric of crime prevention.[79]

To modern eyes, the crime prevention work carried out by private protective associations denotes an obsessive preoccupation with morality, especially adolescent female sexuality. Indeed, Paul Boyer's observation about urban reform during the Progressive Era applies especially well to the surveillance of commercial places of amusement: it constituted an attempt to "re-create in the city the cohesive moral order of the village."[80] Crime prevention work also appears as a remarkably clear-cut example of class-based judgment and control. This is particularly the case with middle-class investigations of working-class commercial places of amusement. Yet these investigations were also acts of resistance against a sexual ethos that encouraged female expressiveness outside marriage. In this respect, women in crime prevention kept alive the ideas of the feminist contingent in the late nineteenth-century social purity movement, which railed against the separation of sexuality and reproduction.[81]

Like feminist social purity reformers, women in crime prevention believed that premarital sexual intercourse constituted sexual exploitation of women, even when women freely and enthusiastically chose to have premarital sex. To women in crime prevention, consent (and even enthusiasm) did not nullify the exploitative nature of premarital sex because premarital sex posed more dangers for women and teenage girls than it did for men and teenage boys, individually and collectively. Harm to an individual girl or woman allegedly came in the form of unwed pregnancy, severely damaged prospects of marriage, and especially among the working class, a probable "downward slide" into prostitution. Harm to the entire female sex came in the supposed weakening of women's claim to female moral authority, which reduced women's collective power relative to men.

The preoccupation of women in crime prevention with the hazards of premarital sex can easily obscure the fact that they acknowledged, and even occasionally celebrated, the existence of the female sexual drive. At the same time, however, they frequently portrayed the male sexual drive as an enemy to be conquered. Their view of men as ruthless sexual predators is the fundamental theme of *End of the Road*, a government movie they produced in 1918. This movie plainly tells adolescent girls and young women that most men cannot be trusted to restrain their sexual impulses. Refuse men's demands for premarital sex, the movie warns, or face a lifetime of regret.[82]

Women in crime prevention believed that the conquest of the male sexual drive came only through marriage and the establishment of a single (feminine) sexual standard that required men as well as women to remain chaste until marriage. In their view, young women who had sexual relations outside marriage harmed all women, not just themselves, because they had forsaken the single sexual standard. In a sense, sexually active unwed girls and women were traitors to their sex. Nevertheless, women in crime prevention often excused young women's treason by pointing to their age (adolescence was increasingly recognized in the 1910s as a time when the female sex instinct was particularly strong), the mind-numbing dreariness of their jobs, their supposedly inferior class, race, or ethnic backgrounds, and their alleged lack of adequate parental guidance.[83] Crime prevention work thus aimed to protect adolescent girls and young women, not only from the designs of white slavers and lusty men, but also from the alleged disadvantages of their youth and circumstances. And since women in crime prevention identified lax parenting as one of the chief disadvantages of modern young womanhood, they did not hesitate to try to take over from working-class parents the moral supervision of female youth. In sum, these women used their class privilege to exert influence over the younger members of their own sex in order to strengthen women's power relative to men and challenge the double sexual standard.[84]

The elitism of crime prevention work is undeniable; for the most part, the work represented an attempt by middle-aged women of the native-born middle class to impose their standards of morality on all women and girls. The pioneering generation of policewomen inherited this mission and worked hard to accomplish it. Yet despite the elitism, the underlying goal of crime prevention work—to reduce female vulnerability to the perceived dangers of male sexual license—aimed at empowering women. Moreover, women's desire to protect women from what they defined as sexual exploitation was shared across race lines. African American women, for example, worked diligently in local affiliates of the National Association of Colored Women to safeguard African American teenage girls and women from sexual predators of all races.[85] And like their white counterparts of the early twentieth century, black women social workers sought and obtained jobs with probation and police departments so that they could prevent crime and handle the cases of black women and girls accused of sexual offenses.[86]

It is important to note that women in crime prevention were not opposed to sexual relations per se, they were opposed to increased male access to women's bodies on what they defined as men's terms. They believed that female sexual activity outside marriage would lead only to increased exploitation of women sexually, economically, and politically. Given the woeful inadequacy and unavailability of contraceptive devices, their illegality in most states, and the economic and social hardships that usually accompanied unwed pregnancy, the idea that premarital sexual activity diminished, rather than improved, the quality of women's lives seems generally realistic. Of course, women in crime prevention consistently cast themselves in the role of protector and thereby revealed their class, cultural, and generational biases. In this respect they were typical women reformers of their class and era, viewing themselves as civic mothers and viewing working-class young women and girls as their daughters.[87] Pioneer policewomen shared this maternal self-image, often referring to themselves as "mothers" and "motherly."

After a few years in crime prevention work, members of some protective associations began to feel hampered by their lack of official authority. Describing the situation in Chicago in 1914, Louise DeKoven Bowen claimed that the Juvenile Protection Association needed "the police power which the city might vest in women trained for the work, giving them the authority to cope with certain dangerous situations with which private organizations have tried in vain to deal."[88] The question arises whether women in crime prevention wanted police power in order to enhance their authority over women and children, or to strengthen their hand when dealing with the owners of commercial places of amusement, whose animosity they repeatedly incited by their frequent investigations. In all likelihood, they wanted police power for both reasons. Additionally, their desire for official authority often reflected a self-conscious feminist goal to obtain public power as women.

In 1905, the members of the Travelers' Aid Society of the Portland, Oregon, chapter of the Young Women's Christian Association (YWCA) took a big step toward the appointment of women police officers. That year they asked city officials to confer police power on one of their employees, Lola Greene Baldwin, for the duration of the Lewis and Clark Centennial Exposition. They made this request because they feared that criminals who preyed on women and girls, such as white slavers, would be among the one million people expected to visit Portland in the summer and autumn of 1905. After due consideration, city officials granted Baldwin limited authority to oversee the safety of all girls and women at the Exposition. Baldwin and her band of women volunteers apparently did their job well, for three years later, the city created the "Women's Auxiliary to the Police Department for the Protection of Girls" and appointed Baldwin its first director. Despite Baldwin's impressive new title and official status, she did not get an office at the police station, nor did her daily work at the Travelers' Aid Society change for several years.[89]

Alice Stebbins Wells had probably heard of Baldwin's protective work when she asked Los Angeles officials to appoint her to the city police force in the summer of 1910. Although she never spoke publicly about the specific circumstances surrounding her decision to join the police department, the municipal election of December 1909 doubtlessly also played a role. That election swept twenty-three candidates from the progressive Good Government League into every elective municipal office. The only major issue in the campaign was the control of vice, particularly prostitution.

During the first decade of the twentieth century Los Angeles had a geographically small but thriving segregated district, the section where prostitution was legal. In 1908 a county grand jury reported that it had found one hundred brothels in operation. This figure seemed extraordinarily high to many Angelenos because the population of Los Angeles in 1910 was only 319,198; in comparison, the city of Oakland, California, had a population of approximately 200,000 in 1912, but it reportedly had only thirty-one brothels in its segregated district.[90]

Prostitution was a hot political issue in Los Angeles in 1909–10 because of recent changes in the city's ethos and demographic profile. Between 1850 and 1870, Los Angeles had a notorious reputation as a rough and lawless town, but as Carey McWilliams has pointed out, after 1900 it grew into "the most priggish community in America."[91] McWilliams and other contemporary observers attributed the change in the city's character to a massive influx of people from small towns in the Midwest. In 1913, Willard Huntington Wright sneered at the "hyper-morality" of migrant Midwestern "yokels" to Los Angeles. According to him, the city was "overrun with militant moralists . . . [who] brought with them a complete stock of rural beliefs, pieties, superstitions, and habits." The recent passage and enforcement of vice laws reflected "a good old medieval superstition afloat in Los Angeles that all those things which charm by their grace and beauty are wiles of the devil, and only those things are decent which are depressing." Wright identified the women of Los Angeles as a particularly strong moralistic force: "They are the leaders of most of the 'movements.' They vote, storm the curbstone tables to sign petitions of protest against immoral trafficking, attend citizens meetings, lecture on proposed ordinances and organize political clubs."[92]

When Angelenos read Wright's views in *Smart Set*, they vehemently denounced him—there was even talk of lynching him if he ever again set foot in California.[93] Angelenos were angry, of course, because Wright had spoken the truth about the moralistic fervor gripping their city at the turn of the century. He had also spoken the truth about the extraordinarily high level of women's social and political activism in Los Angeles and the power they wielded.

When the new Good Government administration came into power in 1909 pledging to abolish the segregated district, Wells must have thought that the time was right for a woman to obtain police power. She also must have thought that she was the right woman, because in her role as assistant pastor at a local church, she had been investigating commercial places of amusement in and around the segregated district for a long time. To her delight, the Good Government administration agreed with her, unanimously approving her petition to join the police force.[94]

Once on the LAPD, Wells immediately set up an office inside the downtown station where she plunged into work similar to the work of private protective associations. She routinely inspected dance halls, penny arcades, movie theaters, and other commercial amusement places, looking for evidence of immorality and violations of city ordinances, such as the ordinance against admitting children under the age of fourteen who were unaccompanied by a parent or guardian. "I have my hands pretty full with the inspection of moving-picture theatres," she confessed to an audience in 1913. Whenever she came across teenage girls and young women in public whom she perceived as sexually vulnerable or sexually promiscuous, she would ask them to step aside privately with her for a few minutes, then she would lecture them on the dangers of premarital sex. As a founder and vice president of the Los Angeles Social Hygiene Society, she firmly believed in sex education.[95]

As the pioneering woman officer of the LAPD, Wells encountered many obstacles, some of which she found farcical. For example, streetcar conductors frequently refused to grant her the free ride that they always gave to policemen because they refused to believe she was a LAPD officer. Once, when she was compelled to prove her identity by showing her badge to a conductor, he accused her of stealing it from her husband.[96] Other obstacles that she and other pioneer policewomen encountered were not trivial, as subsequent chapters reveal. In confronting and sometimes overcoming these obstacles, Wells and the pioneering generation of women police invented their own jobs in police departments. As individuals and as a group, they made the transition from voluntary social activism to paid public service. This transition characterized their generation of women, born in the quarter century following the Civil War and marked by an abundance of reform energy.

Female criminal justice reform underwent a remarkable evolution between 1882, when the Chicago Woman's Club joined the WCTU campaign for jail matrons, and 1910, when Wells took the swearing-in oath of the LAPD. First, the number of women interested and active in criminal justice reform soared, thanks largely to the mass appeal of the juvenile court among organized middle-class women. The success these women enjoyed in establishing the court in states throughout the nation gave them confidence in their collective power to infuse the criminal justice system with "feminine" or maternalist values. Consequently, when they heard of the appointment of a woman police officer in Los Angeles, most wanted to know immediately how to get women officers hired in their own cities and towns. Their vociferous demands for information made Wells a well-traveled and nationally known public speaker.

Second, the white slavery scare fused and focused the various elements of middle-class fears about the "girl problem" and the dangers of sexually integrated urban spaces. Private protective associations responded to these fears by attempting to reduce female vulnerability to all the perceived dangers of pre-marital sex. In practice, the investigations and surveillance activities of women in crime prevention constituted nothing less than an attempt to police the city. On one hand, this attempt can be seen as an extension of middle-class women's traditional role, for they had long claimed a position as the moral stewards of their communities. On the other hand, supervision of public safety and public order had always been a male prerogative. In this respect, women's crime prevention work subverted gender hierarchy and challenged men's gender-based right to maintain social order and control public space. Like other maternalist social and political initiatives undertaken by middle-class women in the early twentieth century, crime prevention work defied and blurred traditional divisions between male public space and female private space in the physical and cultural landscape of the city.

In her speeches across the nation in the early 1910s, Alice Stebbins Wells linked her employment as a police officer to ongoing efforts spearheaded by women to supervise, regulate, and reform city life. In New York City in 1913, for example, she declared,

> All over the country there is a spirit of cleaning up. We are beginning to realize the needlessness of a hundred different things which we have for years been accustomed to. . . . Women have helped enormously in this cleaning up process. They have been studying social problems very sincerely for a long time. . . . One woman in the police department in every city can learn much concerning the need of changes. . . . Under our present conditions much of the remedy must be applied directly or indirectly by women.[97]

Throughout the 1910s, pioneer policewomen and their advocates usually tried to hide the subversive elements of their activities by emphasizing the ways policewomen's work extended women's traditional role in America as guardians of morality. However, the early success of the movement for women police depended nearly as much on deep-seated changes rocking police work and police administration during the 1910s as on the strategies women activists devised. Even before middle-class women took up the cause of crime prevention, urban police departments were undergoing a series of political attacks and internal crises that continued well into the 1930s. These crises both helped and hindered pioneer policewomen and their advocates. The disorganized state of American policing gave women activists an opening to press for the employment of women police, but pioneer policewomen had to carve out an occupational identity for themselves amid a climate of general uncertainty and turmoil. Moreover, as the 1910s and 1920s unfolded, the movement for women police and the presence of women on the police force created new dilemmas and tensions within police work and female criminal justice reform. These pressures led to strained relations between policemen and policewomen and pushed them both into highly defensive postures.

CHAPTER TWO

Preventive Justice: The Campaign for Women Police

On April 7, 1922, Lieutenant Mina C. Van Winkle, director of the Woman's Bureau, Metropolitan Police Department, Washington, D.C., went before the police trial board on the charge of insubordination. Two weeks earlier she had refused to comply immediately with an order to release two girls in her custody to two men purporting to be their fathers. The girls, one fourteen years old, the other fifteen, had run away from their homes in Brooklyn, New York, a few days earlier. While stranded in a train station in Washington, D.C., the girls wired their fathers of their whereabouts. Before the fathers arrived to claim their daughters, male police detectives picked up and interrogated the girls, then, at 1:30 A.M., turned them over to Van Winkle's night assistant at the detention home. Shortly past dawn the next morning, the fathers arrived at police headquarters. The head of the Detective Bureau ordered the night assistant to release the girls. Before complying, the night assistant telephoned Van Winkle at home to get her approval. Van Winkle refused to give it without first verifying the identities of the two men. Although Van Winkle soon released the girls, the fathers were furious at the delay and complained to their congressmen and to the chief of police. As a result, the chief charged Van Winkle with insubordination.[1]

In her defense, Van Winkle asserted that the Detective Bureau should never have been involved in the case at all. She cited an order issued by the chief of police on February 25, 1922, effective March 1, stating that "All matters relating to cases of lost children and cases of females of whatever age . . . will be handled by the Woman's Bureau exclusively and not by the Detective Bureau, as heretofore."[2]

Representatives of sixty-two organizations of women, drawn from all over the country, attended Van Winkle's trial before the police board. In the minds of many of these women, the issue at stake was not only Van Winkle's professional reputation but also the principles underlying the entire movement for the employment of women police. These women feared that if Van Winkle were found guilty, the work of women police would be severely undermined.[3] Their fear was well-founded because, as this chapter reveals, the movement for women police arose from the premise that women were the necessary and natural protectors of women and children, especially teenage girls. The charge against Van Winkle threatened to subvert this premise. That is, if the police trial board ruled that Van

Winkle had been insubordinate, then the position of women police everywhere might always be dependent on an individual policeman's whim, rather than on the recognition of policewomen's gender-based authority over all cases involving women and children. At the heart of Van Winkle's trial lay the contested territories of female gender identity and the role of women in police work.

This chapter provides an overview of the movement for women police by analyzing the gender issues raised in Van Winkle's trial and in police reform in general during the 1910s, 1920s, and early 1930s. The chapter begins with a discussion of how the disorganized state of policing in the United States gave different groups of middle-class reformers an opening to carry forward their respective models of police work. The chapter then turns to the central questions of how gender influenced the discourse, direction, and nature of police reform, and how women police developed the crime prevention model of police work. Because the gendered content of this model has gone unexamined, historians have undervalued its significance. Finally, the chapter examines some of the everyday hopes and hardships of pioneer policewomen, including the hostile relationship between policewomen and policemen.

Urban Police and Municipal Reform

During the last quarter of the nineteenth century, the era Vernon Parrington aptly labeled the Great Barbecue, urban police in the United States acquired a well-deserved reputation for sloth, brutality, and corruption. The source of their corruption lay primarily in their close ties with urban political machines. Urban political machines were associations of loosely affiliated ward organizations that garnered most of their support from working-class immigrant communities. In return for their votes, immigrant men received important favors, such as jobs on city payrolls. By the late nineteenth century, machines had taken over the operation of most big-city police, fire, and sanitation departments, as well as schools, courts, and civil service commissions. Under machine control, the police generally allowed con artists, pickpockets, burglars, and other thieves to operate freely, provided that the police and the machine received a share of the profits. Similar arrangements existed between the police, the machine, and the owners of saloons, gambling casinos, and houses of prostitution. To help insure the continuation of machine rule (and their own opportunities for graft), police officers routinely harassed and assaulted voters believed to be hostile to the machine. For the same reason, police officers often did nothing to stop supporters of the machine from casting several ballots each at election time.[4]

Crusades to sever the ties between the police and the machine began in the late 1880s. Historians have identified the leaders of the crusades as white native-born middle- and upper-class businessmen and professional men who feared and hated the power of the machine. As Robert Fogelson argues, these men believed that machine politicians and their allies on police departments were "out to destroy the prosperity, the security, and indeed the very soul of urban America."[5]

Formal efforts to break the power of the machine usually began with the appointment of special committees to investigate the links between the machine, the police, criminals, and organized vice. In city after city, these committees probed deeply into the internal affairs of police departments; a few of the investigations took years to complete. In some cities, investigators had a free hand to subpoena almost anyone they chose, including judges, merchants, prostitutes, police chiefs, and saloon owners. The police and the machine usually fought these investigations every step of the way. For example, in 1894, when the Republican-appointed Lexow Committee began its investigation of the Democratic-controlled New York Police Department, the police bribed some prospective witnesses to leave town and framed others. One witness even claimed that a municipal employee had forfeited his job and risked his life by appearing before the committee.[6]

When investigative committees published their findings, police chiefs and precinct captains frequently lost their jobs, but often their replacements became cronies of the machine, too. In a few departments, investigations divided officers into factions, ostensibly pro- and anti-reform, but in reality often merely pro-graft. Typically, the members of one faction gave investigators damaging information about members of another faction, hoping to curry favor and to force the resignation of key officers. When reformers rewarded informants with promotions, these purportedly pro-reform officers sometimes continued the corrupt practices of their predecessors until public scandal finally compelled them to resign.[7] Battles over political control of the police thus engendered what one historian has called "the dreary cycle of scandal, followed by reform, followed by more scandal."[8]

Ridding the police of machine control took decades to accomplish; in many cities, reformers did not realize success until the 1930s. Machine politics, however, was not the only issue in police reform during the early twentieth century. In the Progressive Era, the middle-class movement to reform the police developed many facets, including nativism, social purity, concern for social justice, feminism, the extension of state control over individual lives, and the quest for efficiency and rationality. Historians divide the participants of this reform movement into two broad categories, civic reformers and moral reformers. Civic reformers (sometimes called businessmen reformers) carried forward into the 1910s, 1920s, and 1930s the drive to get rid of machine politics. They argued that once police departments were free of the machine, policemen would become more efficient, particularly with respect to crimes against people and real property, such as robbery and burglary. Moral reformers also hated machine control, but they primarily wanted the police to enforce vice laws. In the early 1910s, most moral reformers became proponents of women police.[9]

The categories of civic reformer and moral reformer oversimplify matters by drawing precise lines where none existed. Police reform, like most Progressive reforms, attracted diverse groups of people for different and sometimes contradictory reasons. Yet the categories of civic reformer and moral reformer are useful because they distinguish two strains of thought about police work, one that emphasized efficiency, one that emphasized morality. An inquiry into these two strains of reformist thought reveals that civic and moral reformers, as well as policemen themselves, had gendered views of what police work should entail.

Gender and Civic and Moral Reform

Before proceeding, it should be noted that although views of police work were not strictly dichotomized between men and women, businessmen and professional men tended to favor civic reform, and women activists and the clergy tended to favor moral reform. As for policemen, their discussions about reform did not distinguish between civic and moral reform. Instead, they characterized all reform as feminine meddling into men's business. This was especially the case after 1910, when moral reform branched into the separate movement for women police and drew thousands more middle-class women into the cause.

Uncovering the role of gender in history poses difficulties because gender has often operated silently. Few overt references to gender appear, for example, in the literature produced by the leaders of civic reform. These men had little need to justify or explain their actions and beliefs by references to what they considered timeless truths about who they were and their right to speak out; the interlocking systems of class, gender, and race had already legitimized their voices and hence their power. Nevertheless, a close look at the broad outlines of their reform agenda reveals its male-gendered character.

In the early years of police reform, civic reformers did not have a unified vision of the reformed police department. Instead, conflicting ideas about what the police ought to do circulated for years, until political goals impelled civic reformers to think seriously about the structure and functions of police departments. Their thoughts about police work evolved piecemeal, out of their sometimes successful, sometimes thwarted attempts to take political control of the police. Gradually, civic reformers identified several major stumbling blocks to reform. They realized, for example, that the decentralized organization of the nineteenth-century police department allowed individual precinct captains to create their own fiefdoms within the department and to cut their own deals with the machine. To reduce the power of the machine, civic reformers decided to strengthen the chief and weaken the captains by creating positions between these ranks and permitting the chief to make the appointments to the intermediate positions. Civic reformers also narrowed the role of the police by winnowing out some duties that had little or nothing to do with criminal law enforcement, such as cleaning streets, inspecting fire escapes, and providing overnight shelter for homeless people.[10] Narrowing the functions of the police constituted part of reformers' effort to rationalize police work through application of the principles of "scientific management." The concept of "scientific management" obsessed many businessmen at the turn of the century because of its promise of high efficiency.[11]

By 1910, most civic reformers envisioned the reformed police department as a kind of business corporation or military body. As one civic reformer phrased it, the police were a "municipal army."[12] These corporate and military images invoked the competitive, male-dominated public worlds of business and war; they also reflected civic reformers' desire to introduce into police work certain salient features of corporations and military bodies, such as centralized authority and rationality. According to prevailing gender beliefs, centralized authority and rationality were masculine because they demanded a radical separation of the realm of cognition (associated with masculinity) from the realm of belief and feeling (associated with femininity). To paraphrase Joan Scott's observation about French discourse over class, civic reformers conceptualized police reform in terms that were not explicitly about gender but that nevertheless reproduced historically specific definitions of masculinity.[13]

In contrast to civic reformers, policemen peppered their speeches and correspondence with explicit and coded references to gender. In general, police officials invoked the binary opposition of masculinity and femininity to describe, legitimize, and naturalize conflicts between themselves and reformers. As might be expected, they associated their work with masculinity and reform with femininity. Referring to reformers, one police captain in 1924 claimed that "if these people had their own way police departments would be run by old women of both sexes."[14]

The frequency with which policemen employed gender symbols arose from their strong need to assert themselves during a time of uncertainty and change. Throughout the early twentieth century, police administration in many cities experienced upheaval every few years (or even every few months). By associating police work with masculinity, and reform with femininity, policemen expressed their belief about the "natural" relationship between police and reformers: reformers were, or ought to have been, subordinate to the police.

A speech given in 1916 by Chief of Police Walter Petersen of Oakland, California, provides an excellent example of how policemen drew on gender to attack reformers, defend themselves, and uphold the status quo. For most of the speech, Petersen described the woeful fate of the modern police chief. The modern chief, Petersen asserted, found himself constantly plagued by moralizing zealots who wanted him to clean up every vice condition in the city. He was "the butt of every reform club; every woman's organization whose ideas are born of emotionalism and immature sentiment." In every instance, according to Petersen, the hidden

force behind reformers was a professional agitator in the pay of the chief's political enemies. Acting on specific instructions, the agitator stirred up the emotions
of gullible women and their weak-minded male allies. In the typical city,

> *a hired agitator is secured who holds public meetings, high heaven is*
> *pierced with perfervid oratory and the city is stamped with the stigma*
> *of vice in all its varied forms. Womens clubs are formed, societies for*
> *the repression of prostitution and the protection of women and chil-*
> *dren are organized, and the Chief of Police . . . is damned up hill and*
> *down dale for the sins of society.*

Petersen lamented the fact that the agitator usually did his job so well that the
beleaguered chief lost his position. Occasionally, however, a city had the good fortune to have a police chief who stood up to reformers. In Petersen's words, "Now
and again a MAN arrives in the position of Chief of Police." This chief is the ideal
chief because, among other things, he shows no concern "if a crowd of hysterical
women denounce him or unsexed men abuse him."[15] With that telling phrase, Petersen made clear his view of reformers: They were feminine, regardless of their
sex. Specifically, both "hysterical" and "unsexed" allude to the anatomical other-
ness of the non-male. ("Hysterical" comes from the Greek *hystera,* meaning womb,
while "unsexed men" signifies men without sexual identity or sexual power.) The
phrase "hysterical women" was meant to emphasize the reputed emotional insta-
bility of women and help explain the ease with which politicians manipulated
them and their impotent male allies. Moreover, the phrase "unsexed men" provides a sharp contrast to the bold masculinity of "MAN" to describe the ideal police chief. Petersen could not have made the gendered representations of the police and the reformer more explicit or more oppositional.[16]

Like other speeches by policemen, Petersen's speech focused on moral reformers, not civic reformers. Policemen often characterized the actions of civic reformers as mere politics-as-usual; in fact, Petersen portrayed civic reformers as the
chief's political enemies who exploited moral reform as an issue just to get rid of
the chief. Yet despite Petersen's aggressive stance against moral reformers, the
record shows that during his tenure as chief he gave in to some of their demands
regarding the enforcement of vice laws in Oakland. For example, in 1913 moral reformers demanded the closing of the segregated district, and Petersen went along,
despite his firm conviction that segregated districts represented "the best means
of controlling prostitution."[17] That same year, he also bowed to the demands for
policewomen by local women's organizations. On December 8, 1913, Beatrice A.
McCall and Alice Richardson became the first women officers of Oakland.[18]

During the first decade of the twentieth century, moral reformers' vision of
the ideal police department was as unformed as that of early civic reformers; at
first, moral reformers simply wanted better enforcement of vice laws. But during

the early 1910s, as moral reform of the police became subsumed into the movement for women police, moral reformers conceived and articulated the female-
gendered crime prevention model of police work.

Events in Oakland during the early 1910s illustrate how moral reform
branched into the separate movement for women police. In 1912, one group of
moral reformers, led by a coalition of local women's organizations, demanded
that Chief Petersen immediately revoke the licenses of all saloons that knowingly
or unknowingly sold liquor to minors. Petersen refused, stating that he would
recommend revocation of a license only if he received proof that a saloon habit-
ually violated the law.[19] Shortly thereafter, Los Angeles policewoman Alice Stebbins Wells came to Oakland to speak to women's groups about her work.[20] Although no record of her speech survives, in all likelihood she made the same pitch
there that she made to audiences in many other cities during the early 1910s, emphasizing that women police helped to protect the morals and safety of children
by enforcing vice laws, especially liquor laws.[21] The following year, women's
groups in Oakland persuaded city authorities to appoint women officers.

Women's Entry into Police Work

The movement for women police was decentralized, localistic, and highly politicized. Police departments usually hired women officers reluctantly and in most
instances only because of political pressure from women's groups and organizations. In the early years of the movement (1910–15), women's groups often demanded the hiring of women police after inviting Alice Stebbins Wells or another
prominent pioneer policewoman to their city to speak. Visits by pioneer policewomen fired the demand for women police in cities as farflung as Chicago, Denver, and Syracuse, New York.

In most cities, the campaign for women police reflected middle-class
women's anxiety over the sexual rebellion of female youth, labeled the "girl problem," and the moral dangers that the urban environment posed to women and
children, such as white slavery and illegal liquor sales. According to proponents
of women police, moral dangers and bad social conditions were as much to blame
for the girl problem as lax parenting. To solve the girl problem and make cities
safer, proponents argued, police departments should hire female officers to enforce vice laws, identify bad social conditions, and perhaps most important, steer
individual teenage girls and young women away from moral dangers. In sum,
policewomen were expected to take on the multiple roles of public inspector,
public chaperon, and social worker.

Although discussions of the girl problem and moral dangers dominated the
campaign for women police, the idea that women should have a representative
of their own sex in the police department surfaced from time to time. Pioneer po-

licewomen often raised this issue in their talks with women's organizations and civic groups. They claimed that prior to their appointment to the police force, many troubled women delayed or completely avoided going to the police with a problem, such as a husband's desertion or abuse, for fear that a policeman would not be sympathetic. In cities where police departments had hired women officers, policewomen asserted, troubled women no longer hesitated to seek police assistance. In addition, policewomen argued that most women knew little about their rights under the law, and that it was up to policewomen to educate them. Pioneer policewoman Aletha Gilbert of Los Angeles took the educational aspect of her work seriously. In the mid-1910s, she arranged for a woman attorney to teach "a course in law for housewives" that focused on financial matters.[22]

In many cities, the campaign for the appointment of women police grew out of a larger campaign by moral reformers to rid the city of chronic vice conditions. In Oakland, the initial campaign had targeted the illegal sale of liquor to minors. In other cities, such as Boston, Seattle, Philadelphia, and Portland, Oregon, the announcement of a major public fair fueled the demand for women police. In these cities, moral reformers, led by women activists, claimed that fairs bred so much crime and immorality that women police were needed to watch over the safety of women and children. In Philadelphia, for example, the women's planning committee for the Sesquicentennial Exposition of 1926 felt certain that the event would attract "unscrupulous people" who would trick naïve young women and girls into a life of prostitution by offering them "fake" employment that sounded respectable. The women's committee also feared that the "brilliantly attractive articles" for sale at stands throughout the exposition would tempt children to steal. Familiar with policewomen's duties in other cities, the women's committee recommended that Philadelphia hire women officers to do crime prevention work at the exposition. City officials, including a police commissioner and a police captain, agreed to hire seven policewomen. The women's committee happily helped to select seven women, who were subsequently stationed at various locations on the exposition grounds.[23]

Occasionally, a single tragic incident involving a teenage girl or young woman sparked the cry for women police. In Cleveland, the murder of a sixteen-year-old girl by a man in 1915 galvanized women activists into forming the Women's Protective Association to press for the employment of a policewoman. The following year, women activists secured the appointment of a woman "Special Investigator" to work jointly with the police department and their own organization. In 1923 this position finally evolved into that of policewoman.[24]

Joint appointments for policewomen were common in the Progressive Era and, as in Cleveland, usually involved a private protective association.[25] Occasionally, the joint appointment lasted only a few weeks or months before it became a fulltime public position with the police department. In Chicago in 1912, the mayor gave police power to Mary Boyd of the Juvenile Protective Association shortly before the city council passed the "Women Police Ordinance." Once a full-time position with the Chicago Police Department became available, Boyd quit the Juvenile Protective Association and applied for the job. Her career with the city police force spanned over a dozen years.[26]

Joint appointments must have appealed to city administrators because private agencies frequently paid for them in whole or in part for years. Furthermore, private funding gave women officers an opportunity to demonstrate the value of protective work without first having to overcome the parsimony of city administrators reluctant to allocate public funds for a new municipal position. The years that Lola Baldwin spent working as a protective officer for the city of Portland, Oregon, while being paid by the Travelers' Aid Society, allowed her to prove herself indispensable. When she was granted police power for the duration of the Lewis and Clark Centennial Exposition in 1905, she organized a team of volunteers from the Travelers' Aid Society. She and the other women stationed themselves at various points on the fairgrounds to keep watch over girls and young women. When the exposition ended, the team of volunteers disbanded, but Baldwin continued for several years to work closely with policemen in vice investigations and to handle police cases involving young women and girls. During that time, the city of Portland paid nothing toward her salary. Eventually, the expense of her work proved too great for Travelers' Aid, so she launched a campaign for the city to pay her salary in full. By then she had proven herself; the city not only granted her request, it doubled her monthly salary. Her career with the Portland Police Department lasted until 1922.[27]

Although most pioneer policewomen with joint appointments worked for a private social agency, a few began their careers in policing in a private company. In Sacramento, California, the first woman with police power worked jointly for the Southern Pacific Railroad and the Young Women's Christian Association (YWCA). Although details about the circumstances of her hire have not survived, Southern Pacific probably employed her to improve the reputation of the downtown train station. During the nineteenth and early twentieth centuries, train stations were notorious as places where unsuspecting lone females encountered wily and unsavory strangers of both sexes. Private protective associations, particularly the Travelers' Aid departments of the YWCA, routinely sent representatives to urban train stations to identify and fend off people who seemed bent on harming gullible-looking women and girls. In Sacramento, Southern Pacific and the YWCA required their joint employee to patrol "both in the station and out." As a railroad police officer, she exercised the power of arrest, which gave her much more authority over troublemakers than the average representative of a private protective association.[28]

The fact that some pioneer policewomen did not initially have publicly funded appointments with police departments doubtlessly hurt the status of all pioneer policewomen by giving some weight to the sentiment that women were not (and could never be) "real" police officers. In some of the cities that paid policewomen from public funds, policewomen's salaries reflected this sentiment. According to one study, policewomen in San Francisco made $1,200 a year in the 1910s, while policemen earned $1,464. Similarly, the top annual salary for policewomen in Chicago in 1915 was $900, while Chicago policemen earned between $900 and $1,320 a year. Los Angeles pioneer policewomen fared better; beginning in 1918, they earned the same salary as patrolmen. Despite their equal pay, however, female officers in Los Angeles never had the same opportunities for advancement as male officers.[29]

Political upheavals or conservative chiefs in Philadelphia, Milwaukee, San Diego, and Norfolk, Virginia, among other cities, made the appointment of women to the police force an on-again, off-again experiment.[30] In Philadelphia, for example, the seven policewomen who patrolled the Sesquicentennial Exposition of 1926 lost their positions when the exposition ended. Women's groups fought hard on the seven's behalf but lacked the political clout necessary for victory. Women's groups did not give up, however. For ten years, from 1926 to 1936, they asked repeatedly for women on their police force. Officials finally granted their request in 1936.[31]

Although the timing of women's entry into municipal police work was determined by local circumstances, federal policies undertaken during World War I accelerated the movement for women police. Shortly after the United States entered the war, the federal government launched a vigorous program to safeguard soldiers and sailors from liquor, prostitutes, promiscuity, and venereal disease. This anti-vice program reflected the popular notion that American soldiers and sailors were unsophisticated youngsters from small towns and farms who needed protection from the evils of the city during their period of military training.[32] By October 1917, the federal agency in charge of the anti-vice program, the Commission on Training Camp Activities, had set up several subagencies, including the Committee on Protective Work for Girls (CPWG), under the direction of Maude E. Miner, a social worker.

Miner focused much of the work of the CPWG on providing sex education to adolescent girls, who allegedly needed it because large numbers of them had come down with "khaki fever" soon after the United States had entered the war overseas. "Khaki fever" referred to the reportedly high incidence of casual, premarital sex between young fighting men and female youth who were smitten with men in uniform. To combat khaki fever, the CPWG sent lecturers to cities across the nation to educate audiences about the dangers awaiting sexually active female youth. According to the lecturers, these dangers included venereal disease and men's volatile, and occasionally violent, sexual nature. To augment the work of visiting lecturers, the CPWG deployed six field agents to organize "protective bureaus" in several dozen communities nationwide and to train women "protective officers" to work in the bureaus. Each of the selected communities was in the vicinity of a military training camp or embarkation center.

Most of the 150 protective officers who eventually worked for the CPWG were employees of local social work agencies and private protective organizations. Their duties closely resembled those of pioneer policewomen; for example, they patrolled the streets around military establishments, searching for instances of prostitution, promiscuity, and the sale of liquor. (The government had banned alcohol from the vicinity of military bases.) Protective officers also did "personal work" with teenage girls and young women who seemed either sexually active or sexually vulnerable. Personal work encompassed home visits, counseling, sex education, and referrals to social work agencies and "wholesome" girls' clubs. The record is not clear regarding the extent of protective officers' police power; it probably varied from community to community, depending on the whim of local officials. A journalist who discussed the work of the CPWG in 1918 remarked that the typical protective officer "does not try to make a record of arrests. She is interested in preventing crime and helping girls, and of course, has no ground for an arrest unless [a] law has been violated."[33]

Miner probably patterned the work of protective officers after the work of pioneer policewomen. A strong proponent of women police and a former probation officer with the New York Probation and Protective Association, Miner envisioned the CPWG as a trailblazing national agency for the moral protection of teenage girls and young women. Miner's ideas did not prevail within the CPWG for long, however. In mid-1918, Raymond Fosdick, the head of the Commission on Training Camp Activities, reorganized the CPWG under the Law Enforcement Division of the Commission. He renamed it the "Section on Women and Girls" (SWG) and expanded the number of its protective officers to two hundred. He also redefined the duties of protective officers, whom he called field agents. Now, instead of providing a range of services intended to protect the morals of female youth, field agents focused on tracking down sexually active women and girls, questioning them, and if it seemed necessary, arranging for them to be tested for venereal disease. When tests came back positive, field agents made arrangements for lengthy, institutionalized treatment. These duties kept field agents busy. By the end of the war, they had arranged for the medical quarantine of thousands of teenage girls and women.

Field agents did not have police power, despite the fact that they worked under the Law Enforcement Division of the Committee on Training Camp Activities. Nor did field agents track down and help to institutionalize teenage boys and men with venereal disease. In a clear demonstration of the double sexual standard, the government did not require teenage boys and men with venereal disease to be quarantined but instead allowed them to be treated as outpatients.[34]

Women's work in the federal anti-vice program left a mixed legacy to the movement for women police. On one hand, their work helped to legitimize the movement because the federal government had charged them with some of the same duties that pioneer policewomen carried out every working day. By assigning women to street patrol and investigative work, the federal government showed that it recognized women's ability to act as law enforcement officers, even though it did not grant women agents full police power. Recognition by the federal government, together with the public's anxiety over "khaki fever" during World War I, helped spur a dramatic rise in the number of U.S. cities employing policewomen, from approximately 125 cities in 1916 to 220 cities in 1918.[35]

On the other hand, the work of SWG field agents undermined a basic idea of the movement for women police: female protective work. As mentioned earlier, the work of pioneer policewomen reflected middle-class women's anxiety over protecting women, adolescent females, and children from moral dangers. Miner shared this concern, but her supervisor, Raymond Fosdick, did not. Nor did this concern shape the work of the SWG; indeed, to Fosdick and the Commission on Training Camp Activities, females who engaged in illicit sexual relations were sources of filth, disease, and degeneracy. A lawyer for the commission, John G. Buchanan, even went so far as to suggest that a law should be passed that would "make it a felony for a woman to commit fornication with a soldier or sailor anywhere."[36] Because the original avowed purpose of the federal anti-vice program was to safeguard young servicemen from the evils of the city, it is not surprising that the program adopted a course of action that defined males as potential victims of female sexual predators. Nevertheless, many women activists scorned the notion that sexually active servicemen were victims of wily females. Some of the women who worked for the commission, including Maude Miner, also criticized the commission for its apparent indifference to the safety of women and girls. In April 1918, Miner resigned from her post over this issue.

Miner's short-lived career with the CPWG illustrates the difficulties encountered by many women activists during the Progressive Era when they tried to enact maternalist policies. During Miner's first few weeks as director, she threw herself wholeheartedly into the work, but she swiftly grew frustrated. She thought it highly unjust that teenage girls and women were commonly arrested for illicit sexual activity, but teenage boys and men were not. As she once told Raymond Fosdick, "Enforcement of laws against men responsible for impairing the morals of young girls or guilty of criminal assault is essential for the protection of girls."[37] Fosdick disagreed. His directives to Miner instructed her to focus the work of the CPWG exclusively on female sexuality. In April 1918, a month before Fosdick officially reorganized the CPWG, Miner quit. "I could not be satisfied," she said, "to see the girls' interests entirely subordinated to the interest of the soldier."[38] In her place, Fosdick appointed Jane Deeter Rippen, a settlement house worker. The

work of the SWG continued past the end of the war, despite the continued opposition of some leading female social workers, activists, and professionals in juvenile justice.[39]

SWG field agents wielded public power (if not police power), but the price
of that power was that they had to use it solely to regulate and punish female sexuality. For some women, including Rippen, this price was not excessive because
they placed a higher value on combating female sexual expressiveness (the "girl
problem") and venereal disease than on combating male sexual license, misog-
yny, and the double sexual standard. Maude Miner and many other women refused to pay this price.[40] Class dynamics were also at work because the federal
government empowered middle-class women to instruct, regulate, and ultimately in many instances, incarcerate women and girls who were predominantly
from the working class. This aspect of the work did not bother Miner, for like
other supporters of women police, she understood the role of maternal protector
in class-specific terms: By virtue of their middle-class status and privileges, Miner
and other advocates of women police believed that they knew better than
working-class women and girls what was best.

Miner's experience in the federal anti-vice program points up the multiple
tensions in the movement for women police and in pioneer policewomen's daily
work: the tensions between empowerment and repression, between the single
and the double sexual standards, between the sexual rebellion of working-class
female youth and the fading but not yet obsolete moral standards of the middle-
aged middle class, between male political power and female moral authority, and
between Progressive reformers' desire for social justice on one hand and their desire for social order on the other. Pioneer policewomen in Los Angeles struggled
with these same tensions, and like Miner, they learned the limits of their ability
to put their ideas into practice.

Ideology of the Movement for Women Police

Regardless of local circumstances surrounding the hiring of pioneer policewomen, proponents everywhere made the case for women police by using arguments from "nature" that stressed gender differences.[41] At the core of these
arguments lay the belief that women possessed certain inherent qualities,
unique to their sex, that made them better than men at preventing crime and protecting the safety and morals of women and children. Arguments based on gender differences were ideologically conservative insofar as they reprised traditional stereotypes, especially those concerning female nurturing. Yet if women
activists had stressed women's similarities to men rather than their differences,
it is doubtful they could have persuaded many city officials to hire women officers. Ideas about the binary opposition of masculinity and femininity held a

great deal of currency in the early twentieth century. Simply put, Americans would never have supported hiring a woman to perform police work, that quintessential "man's job," if proponents of women police had openly claimed that women could perform all aspects of policing as well as men did. Only by making arguments founded on women's unique feminine identity could women activists hope to gain a foothold for women in police departments as officers in charge of female and juvenile cases. As one advocate of women police remarked, "Paradoxically, women have been admitted to that male domain, police work, primarily *because they are women*."[42] More to the point, advocates of women police ardently believed in gender differences, in women's supposedly more compassionate and self-sacrificing nature.

The speeches that Alice Stebbins Wells gave during her speaking tours of the early 1910s illustrate how pioneer policewomen and their proponents used their belief in gender differences to carve out a place for women in police work. According to Wells, police departments needed women officers to handle the cases of women and children because troubled women and children required a woman's special brand of sympathy and wisdom. To make this argument persuasive, Wells often portrayed the women and children with whom she came in professional contact as victims of crime, not offenders. This portrayal cast her in the motherly role of caregiver, rather than in the unladylike role of arresting officer. She told an audience in Chicago in 1912 that her office at the Los Angeles Police Department was "open for women who have troubles, and there are many."

> *Women know so little about their rights. They know so little of the law. They have such a terrible fear of the police court. . . . So they come to me. They would not stop a stranger upon the street, no matter how kind her face would be, but they can come to me without any apology, because the city provides me in order they that they may come to me with their troubles and get whatever helpful advice I am able to give them.*[43]

Three months after her talk in Chicago she informed an audience in Ottawa that most of the troubled women who came to her for advice had been deserted or beaten by their husbands.[44] Similarly, she told a large crowd in New York City that worried parents frequently sought her advice on matters involving the possible victimization of their children. "I had one case of a mother whose daughter had been enticed by an evil-minded old man in the neighborhood," she recalled. "The mother hesitated to go to the police about such a matter but, finding a woman on the force, she came to me and told me the whole rather ugly situation in order that the man might not be a menace to the other young girls of the neighborhood."[45]

The idea that policewomen were inherently better suited than policemen to handle certain cases helped women enter police work, but it fostered occupational segregation based on sex. Until the late 1960s, police departments restricted most policewomen to handling female and juvenile cases. To early proponents of women police this focus was not a crippling limitation but a hard-won acknowledgment from city authorities that an all-male police department could not adequately serve the interests of women and children. As Wells bluntly told a convention of police chiefs in 1914, "Women and children have a right to a representation in the police department."[46] Louise DeKoven Bowen, the president of the Juvenile Protective Association of Chicago, agreed. In *Safeguards for City Youth at Work and at Play*, Bowen outlined the need for women police and women jurors whenever women were arrested and tried. She also recommended that women court officials hear juvenile court cases involving girls. Underlying all Bowen's recommendations in this regard was her belief that male hegemony over the criminal justice system oppressed women.

> *During our years of experience in the Juvenile Protective Association,*
> *it became increasingly evident that there was a certain steady, although*
> *perhaps unconscious discrimination against the women who are daily*
> *brought into the court. . . . From the time of the arrest of a woman to*
> *the final disposition of her case she is handicapped by being in the charge*
> *of men and surrounded by men, who naturally cannot be expected to be*
> *as sympathetic and understanding as one of her own sex.*[47]

In 1928, a newspaper editor applauding the appointment of policewomen in New Haven, Connecticut, used even stronger language to express the same opinion: "It seems unthinkable that for centuries the female delinquent has been cast wholly on the mercy of male law enforcement agencies. . . . Men have arrested her, men have prosecuted her, and men have jailed her. At no point . . . has she had the benefit of feminine counsel or understanding."[48] Proponents thus viewed the appointment of women police as public recognition of the importance of women's sororial bonds. "It takes a woman to understand a woman's problems," journalist Irene Vandyck declared in praise of the work of New York City policewomen in 1922.[49]

Advocates of women police consistently claimed that women officers would know better than male officers how to handle the cases of women and children. In addition, they argued that the appointment of women officers to the police department would make the department more responsive to the needs of women and children. Both of these claims implied that, with respect to some duties, policewomen were simply more efficient public servants than policemen. This line of reasoning may have been proponents' strongest because it reiterated gender stereotypes about women's "instinctive" knowledge of women and children while promising more efficiency in government at a time when the quest for efficient government underlay most political reforms.

Had pioneer policewomen and their proponents limited the case for women police to straightforward arguments about efficiency, they might not have incurred as much resistance from policemen as they did. But instead they argued with firm conviction that the presence of women on the police force would transform the nature of policing in gender-specific ways. Specifically, they claimed that female officers would lift the overall intelligence level of the police, infuse police work with values associated with women and social work, and create a police system that would prevent crime, not just detect it. This maternalist argument held great appeal for many middle-class women in the Progressive Era who championed public policies that had qualities they associated with women and mothering. Not surprisingly, however, the maternalist argument provoked lasting hostility from nearly all policemen because it constituted a thorough critique of prevailing police practices and philosophy. As such, it provided the basis for the female-gendered crime prevention model of police work. This model, built by pioneer policewomen and their supporters during the early 1910s, had three major tenets: police work developed to its highest form is social work; crime prevention is the most important function of the police; and women are inherently better than men at preventing crime.

Gender and Crime Prevention

The strong emphasis on crime prevention was part of the legacy of the private protective associations. Like the members of these associations, pioneer policewomen and their supporters fervently believed that the causes of crime and immorality in a given neighborhood could be identified and eliminated. They expressed this belief succinctly in their motto, "Preventive Justice," which was inscribed on the cover of the *Policewoman's International Bulletin*.

Supporters of women police were confident that by reason of gender, education, and "social background" (by which they meant class), policemen could never be as effective as policewomen in undertaking crime prevention. One group of researchers concluded that,

> *with regard to the investigation and correction of social conditions which make for delinquency or more serious crimes on the part of both adults and children, most of the men in most police departments are inclined to be indifferent; nothing in their previous experience, in the curriculum of the training school, or in their experience as police officers gives them the needed social background or social interest necessary for intelligent investigation of the cause and prevention of bad social conditions. It is therefore generally found expedient   to bring to bear the point of view of social service workers and particularly of women employed as police officers.*[50]

Throughout the 1910s and 1920s, policewomen on patrol actively searched their communities for dark streets and "blind pigs" (places where people bought and drank liquor illegally), as well as for other social conditions that supposedly hid or encouraged crime. "Coming naturally under the domain of the woman officer are the places of amusement where the young gather—dance halls, skating rinks, picture shows, penny arcades, amusement parks, etc." explained Alice Stebbins Wells as early as 1913.[51] Mary E. Hamilton, a policewoman in New York City, went so far as to claim that "all popular public places," including parks, beaches, train stations, taxicab stands, and commercial amusement places, were "the very breeding places of crime and hence the logical domain over which the policewoman should have control."[52] Other leading pioneer policewomen agreed with her.

While searching out bad social conditions, pioneer policewomen also routinely looked for evidence of offenses against middle-class moral standards, such as the sale of obscene literature, erotic styles of dancing, and overt fondling and kissing in public. In this respect, pioneer policewomen, like the members of private protective associations, were public chaperons.[53] This role endeared them to their middle-class, and probably middle-aged, women supporters. But, as Chapter Three discusses in detail, the role of public chaperon often got them into trouble with powerful men because policewomen wanted to apply a single standard of morality to both sexes. They especially wanted to enforce laws against men who, in the parlance of the day, "led girls astray." As Maude Miner remarked in 1917, "Too often girls are placed under arrest and the men who have caused their delinquency are allowed to go free."[54]

Pioneer policewomen's focus on crime prevention occasionally impelled them to engage directly in municipal political activity. In Portland, Oregon, for example, Lola Baldwin successfully lobbied municipal licensing authorities in 1911 to prohibit girls under the age of eighteen from working in shooting galleries. According to Baldwin, any "respectable" female who worked in such a place would invariably "be subjected to the severest insult and temptation." Baldwin pushed for passage of the law after she interviewed the proprietors of shooting galleries and found out that they employed teenage girls and young women only for the purpose of attracting men.[55] Similarly, in 1915, Los Angeles policewomen helped to obtain the passage of city ordinances making jitney buses safe for lone female passengers (see Chapter Three).[56]

But other political projects fell short of success. In the late 1920s, policewomen in Los Angeles conducted a survey to discover the causes of juvenile delinquency in their city. Among other things, the survey showed that Los Angeles had very few public playgrounds. Acting on the commonly held belief that children with no place to play were more likely to become juvenile delinquents, policewomen petitioned the city council to place a $1.5 million bond measure on the next ballot to build playgrounds. The petition failed.[57]

The idea that the police ought to be involved in crime prevention had long been a theme among U.S. prison reformers, but before the turn of the century, police administrators themselves rarely considered it.[58] As the Progressive Era advanced, however, faith in the new social sciences, together with the general climate of positivist opinion, infiltrated some police departments. Beginning in the early 1910s, a few male police reformers, notably August Vollmer, enthusiastically took up the idea that the causes of crime could be discovered and eliminated through social-scientific police work. The annual conventions of police chiefs became forums for pronouncements on the importance of crime prevention. In 1911, Michael J. Regan, chief of police in Buffalo, New York, declared that "the primary effort of a Police Force properly conducted should be to prevent crime." "Many Police Officers," he continued, "labor under the mistaken idea that their first duty is to arrest the criminal and see that he is properly punished."[59] The next year, Chief Joseph M. Quigley of Rochester, New York, made the same point: "The first duty of the police is to prevent crime; the second the detection and apprehension of criminals if crime has been committed."[60] In 1915, Chief of Police James L. Beavers of Atlanta, Georgia, proclaimed that "the first duty of a police department is the prevention of crime." Even Chief Petersen of Oakland, California, took up the theme. He argued that the new emphasis on crime prevention was part of a "broad, sympathetic spirit of humanity" overtaking the country. He also explained in unvarnished detail how this new spirit necessarily entailed changes in police methods: "We police chiefs must in great measure forget the thumb screw, the illegal third degree, the too ready use of force of an unlawful kind in the conduct of our departments."[61]

Despite some police chiefs' new-found enthusiasm for crime prevention, few translated their words into action. Of these few, Chief August Vollmer of Berkeley, California, stands out. His draconian approach to preventing crime earned him a national reputation during the 1910s and 1920s as a forward-looking "modern" chief. Early in his career as a police chief, Vollmer defined crime prevention solely in terms of aggressive police intervention into citizens' everyday behavior. He accordingly exhorted patrolmen to become familiar with the daily routines of all the people on their beats so that they might readily identify and investigate any behavioral irregularities or suspicious movements. Then, in 1919, after a decade as chief, Vollmer seized on the idea that police officers could also prevent crime by using social casework methods.[62] He presented this idea as if it were brand-new in a paper entitled "The Policeman as a Social Worker."[63] Vollmer made no mention of policewomen in this paper; in fact, he exhibited antipathy to the idea of women police, stoutly maintaining that "wayward girls may be saved from taking the final plunge into a life of evil, and many homes saved from disgrace and sadness, by the kindly counsel of the policeman."[64] He successfully resisted appointing a policewoman in Berkeley until July 1925.[65]

Vollmer was not alone in ignoring policewomen. In the two decades before 1930, when the first generation of women were entering police work as crime prevention specialists, few police chiefs referred to women police when they talked at their annual meetings about what a police department could do to prevent crime.[66] Overall, the chiefs' silence constituted a denial of policewomen's gender-based claim to legitimacy, for throughout those years, proponents of the movement for women police repeatedly invoked women's gender identity to justify their employment in crime prevention. For example, a journalist sympathetic to women police argued in 1912 that "women will work harder than men to protect and save and will think less of punishment in dealing with those who are destroying themselves and others."[67] In 1913, another reporter observed, "The appointment of women in the police force . . . throws the emphasis upon sympathy and understanding instead of upon mere muscle."[68]

These comments are unusually explicit examples of the legitimizing function of gender. Proponents of women police did not ordinarily spell out the links between gender characteristics and specific missions or functions of the police, other than to make the obvious point that women officers should handle female and juvenile cases. Instead, proponents took for granted the public's knowledge of gender roles and built their case for policewomen's crime prevention function accordingly. In 1913 Alice Stebbins Wells told the City Club of New York that "the woman officer is an emphasis upon the prevention spirit of police work." Twenty-two years later, Dorothy Thomas, a journalist, made a similar observation about women's capacity to stop crime: "Preventive work, is the crying need—and it is a field in which women may most effectively serve." Martha Strayer, a writer who attended a regional conference of policewomen in 1927, likewise reported, "Protective and preventive work is the police function of their sex, everybody agreed." The next year, a male advocate of women police insisted that "in preventive work women police are more successful than men." Policewoman Mary E. Hamilton said it even more succinctly in 1924: "Policewomen stand for Prevention of crime."[69]

Examples abound of this kind of abbreviated reference to a correlation between women and crime prevention based on women's presumably more compassionate and tender nature, their finer moral sensibilities, and the "maternal instinct" that gave them greater affinity with children. These references are particularly plentiful in discussions of "predelinquents," children whose behavior allegedly predisposed them to a life of crime. For instance, in 1926, the year following the long-delayed appointment of the first policewoman in Berkeley, California, August Vollmer claimed that "inherent qualities possessed by women only peculiarly fit them for service among the pre-delinquents."[70]

Proponents of women police repeatedly portrayed policewomen's handling of

female juvenile cases as surrogate motherhood. Irene Vandyck took this character-
ization to its limit in an article published in the early 1920s entitled "No Man's Land
in Police Work." She begins her article by describing a hypothetical case that "happened a few years back when there was no organized policewomen in New York
[City] to mother the wayward girl." The hypothetical case involves Minnie, a
sixteen-year-old runaway who "fell prey to some unscrupulous 'lounge lizard' of
the underworld." Just as Minnie began to realize she had made a dreadful mistake,
a patrolman came across her, recognized her as a runaway, and rescued her before
"it was too late." Minnie felt very repentant, but without proper moral guidance,
she soon became restless again, ran away a second time, landed in jail, and eventually suffered a wretched fate as a convicted prostitute. According to Vandyck, a
policewoman could have prevented Minnie's downfall. If a policewoman had been
on hand the first time Minnie ran away, she could have "mothered" Minnie. Physical rescue by a patrolman was all very well, Vandyck argues, but it is not enough
to save "the Minnies of the world": "Minnie needed a mother. She needed her at
the moment she was found by the patrolman. The one thing a policeman cannot do,
no matter how much he may want to, is to 'mother' a girl in Minnie's predicament.
. . . What Minnie needed was a policewoman to mother her."[71]

So close was the match between the idealized policewoman and the idealized
mother that some descriptions of policewomen's crime prevention work could
easily be mistaken for an excerpt from nineteenth-century prescriptive literature
on the responsibilities of motherhood. August Vollmer proclaimed, for example,
that a policewoman could render invaluable services to predelinquent children by
"correcting bad habits, changing the disposition when this is necessary, develop-
ing the right sort of attitudes, cultivating wholesome tastes, strengthening the conscience, and inculcating personal, social and religious ideals, [and] creating desirable virtues and sentiments."[72] Vollmer's lack of faith in the ability of parents of
"predelinquent" children to perform these duties mirrored the opinion of many
juvenile court judges, social workers, and police officers, who blamed lax parents
and "broken homes" for the existence of juvenile delinquency.[73]

Although arguments for policewomen's role in crime prevention stressed
women's maternal role, they drew on other ideas about gender identity as well.
Rhoda J. Miliken, a pioneer policewoman, argues in "We Don't Carry Nightsticks!" that compared to policemen, policewomen have "*a greater unwillingness
to become cogs in a machine which sometimes causes more wreckage than it gives protection to a community.*" Drawing on the belief that women are inherently less interested than men in abstract principles, and more interested in particularities,
she continues, "It is not, I think, claiming too much for them to say that the
women have been more concerned with the methods of doing their job in so far
as those methods affect the people involved in the process of enforcing the
law."[74]

As Miliken's remarks illustrate, discourse over the employment of women police stretched some female gender role stereotypes even as it endorsed them. In this respect, arguments for women police typified much of the rhetoric used to justify women's increasing involvement in civic affairs during the late nineteenth and early twentieth centuries. During the Progressive Era especially, women activists liked to portray the city as an extension or larger version of the home. This portrayal justified female participation in municipal politics because it allowed women activists to characterize their participation as a form of housekeeping. In 1927, Police Commissioner Louis Brownlow of the District of Columbia took the analogy to absurd lengths. He opens a discussion of the merits of policewomen with the comment, "The policewoman after all is a woman and she believes in house cleaning." He then discusses modern ways of cleaning a house, asserting that women buy vacuum cleaners when they grow tired of nagging their husbands to beat carpets. He then compares policewomen with vacuum cleaners.

> *Women have been nagging at men for lo! these many years to do some cleaning up around town. The best they could do was to stir the comfort-loving critters into a spasmodic effort at reform every once in a while, after which they would relapse into the even enjoyment of their ways. Tired of that, the women have taken heart from the vacuum cleaner experience and have put in policewomen to keep the town clean right along.*
>
> *The way they go at it is different from the spasmodic raiding, haling into court and wholesale fining that the policemen used to do, as is the action of the vacuum cleaner on the living room rugs from the way father used to lambast the carpet in the backyard with a baseball bat.*[75]

Brownlow's humorous analogy underscores the general agreement among proponents of women police that policewomen's methodology, as well as their mission, was substantially different from that of policemen. While the popular image of policemen depicted brawny, thick-skinned, and thick-headed brutes making frequent arrests through application of muscle and official power, policewomen cultivated a public image of themselves as intelligent, sympathetic caseworkers, finding noncoercive solutions to the problems of crime. In a comparison of their different methods of work, a newspaper editor remarked, "The policewoman wants to advise, to aid, to find employment for those thrown into her hands, and she has an acute realization that often an actual arrest is the most destructive possible step."[76] In the early 1910s, Josephine Roche, a pioneer policewoman in Denver, attributed her successful use of noncoercive methods to the public's perception of gender roles: "Just because a woman is a woman and disassociated from the idea of force, she can frequently enforce the law with more ease than a man."[77]

In theory, policewomen's methods were shaped as much by acquired attributes, such as their training in social casework, as by their "inherent" gender attributes, such as their maternal instinct, womanly compassion, sense of disinterested service to others, and flair for detail. Descriptions of policewomen's work published from the 1910s through 1940 generally portray policewomen as indefatigable public servants who engaged almost exclusively in interpersonal, relational work. On a typical workday, their duties demanded a high level of affectivity and empathy, attention to detail, and cooperation with others.[78] They specialized in comforting lost children, answering letters of inquiry about missing persons, interviewing female and juvenile victims of crime (especially sex crimes), making referrals to social work agencies, giving advice to parents about troublesome children, handling domestic relations cases, and arresting women and girls. Prior to the hiring of policewomen, policemen had performed these tasks. Thus, policewomen not only carved out a new area of police work in crime prevention, claiming that they were by nature better suited than men to prevent crime, but they also took over from men the kinds of police duties that allegedly required a woman's sympathetic touch. As a result, the gendered representation of police work changed. That is, the entry of women into police work transformed policing from an occupation that was presumed to be sex-specific to men, to an occupation with an array of gender-linked functions.

An examination of the ways that proponents of women police presented their arguments sheds light on how the gendered transformation of police work took place. Implicit in their speeches and writings was an expanded but bifurcated definition of police work: men are best suited for the detection of crime and the arrest of criminals, and women are best suited for the prevention of crime and the protection of women and children. This new definition challenged the old by introducing a new pair of oppositions. Hence, beneath the surface of public discourse on women police (which included police chiefs' silence on policewomen's crime prevention work), two contests were taking place: a contest over a new role for women in the public sphere, and a contest over the meaning and direction of police reform. While proponents of women police fought hard to introduce a new meaning of police work, many male administrators and reformers fought just as hard to retain control.[79]

Seen in the context of a battle over the meaning of police work, police chiefs' persistent refusal to engage in a dialogue about policewomen makes sense. After all, most chiefs hired women officers only in response to outside pressure from women activists. Police chiefs' silence about policewomen also sprang, however, from their own frequently repeated acknowledgment during the 1910s and early 1920s that crime prevention was the primary duty of police departments. Even if this acknowledgment was only lip service given in a fit of reform sentiment, the chiefs drew the line between giving lip service to the importance of crime prevention and discussing among themselves the contribution women were making toward preventing crime. The stakes were simply too high. If preventing crime were indeed the primary duty of the police, and if women were indeed inherently better than men at crime prevention, then men would automatically be consigned to second-rate status within the police department.

Policewomen understood the threat they posed to policemen. Leading policewomen repeatedly stressed that policewomen did not intend to take over any police function that policemen already ably performed. In the first speech by a policewoman before the International Association of Chiefs of Police (IACP), Alice Stebbins Wells underlined this point.

> We should understand thoroughly that the policewoman is not going to take the place of the policeman. She is not going to antagonize him in any way or to displace him. She is not going to do any work that the policeman can do as well or better, but to do those things he should not be expected to do but which he now does the best he can.[80]

The same point was belabored in nearly every speech policewomen gave to the assembled chiefs in the 1910s and 1920s. It also showed up in countless journal articles about policewomen. In 1927, the authors of an extensive study of policewomen concluded, "There is a considerable field in which women can do better police work than men. There is another—and larger—field in which men can do better police work than women."[81] An editorial published in the *Policewoman's International Bulletin* that same year repeats the argument: "It was a long time before police officials realized that women were not competing with men—that as policewomen they were making a contribution to police service such as men were not making, namely, the program of preventive-protective work."[82]

Despite policewomen's claims that they were only trying to augment the work of policemen, some leading policewomen and their supporters had in mind a far more ambitious goal: to redirect police work through their own daily example from a narrow concentration on detection and arrest to a broad commitment to identifying and eliminating the causes of crime in a given community. "While demonstrating the possibilities of preventive police work, we expect the spirit of the policewomen's efforts to permeate the whole force," a public official wrote when his city first hired policewomen in 1927.[83] In a similar vein, a Minnesota clubwoman declared, "May our policewomen reinfect the whole of the police department with the social ideal, make the work constructive so that the activities may develop along the lines of protection and prevention!"[84] Speaking before a national convention of probation officers in 1926 about policewomen, another proponent proclaimed, "We hope and predict that the use of trained women, experienced in social case work, will act as a leaven within the police department itself . . . [and] lead to a better supervision and control of neighborhood conditions."[85]

Mina C. Van Winkle, controversial head of the Woman's Bureau in Washington, D.C., was confident of policewomen's potential to transform police work along "social" lines, but she knew that it would be a hard struggle to change policemen's attitudes. "It must be remembered," she observed, "that the police are a part of the whole system of criminal justice steeped in false tradition which obliges them to consider crime instead of criminals."[86] Van Winkle proclaimed that although the road to positive change within police work was hard, policewomen would eventually succeed. Moreover, they would transform not only the police, but the entire criminal justice system and how it was perceived.

> *By insisting upon the social protection of women, children and the community, rather than upon the vindication of "rights" which are presumed to inhere in the individual and the state, [policewomen] are introducing into the administration of criminal justice a social viewpoint which should influence a change of attitude on the part of the courts and the public toward those accused of delinquency and crime.[87]*

Woman's Bureaus

Policewomen were eager to distinguish their work from that of policemen. In city after city, proponents of women police urged city authorities to appoint not just one policewoman but several and to consolidate policewomen's work within a separate woman's bureau. The organization of woman's bureaus in police departments during the 1910s and early 1920s marks a high point in separate female institution building.[88]

In 1914, Aletha Gilbert of the Los Angeles Police Department (LAPD) organized one of the longest-lived separate bureaus of policewomen in the world, the City Mother's Bureau. It survived as part of the LAPD until 1964. Gilbert established the bureau primarily because she wanted to be able to offer confidential advice to troubled women and their teenage daughters. (Gilbert's work as City Mother is the topic of Chapter Three.) The Woman's Bureau of the New York City Police Department, established in 1925, had a similar purpose: "to provide a central office, where women and girls seeking aid, advice and assistance relating to police service may apply and discuss their problems and troubles with women officers."[89]

The unspoken assumption behind the establishment of woman's bureaus was that women and children would voluntarily go to policewomen for help in personal matters. To make it easier for those seeking advice, policewomen in a few large cities convinced administrators to locate the woman's bureau in a building outside the police station. As Aletha Gilbert explained in 1914, "I am purposely establishing headquarters away from the police station . . . [because] so many women and girls object to calling there."[90] A writer for the *Journal of Social Hygiene* praised the location of the Los Angeles City Mother's Bureau "away from the other departments of the city administration . . . [where it was] practically as quiet and unobtrusive as a private home."[91] In New York City, the Women's Precinct operated for a short time in an abandoned police station that police-women redecorated with "colorful curtains at the windows, and colorful cush-ions and easy chairs and couches."[92] They hoped that their efforts made their office look less like a police department and more like a private home. A photo-graph of the interior of the Los Angeles City Mother's Bureau shows a similarly homey atmosphere created by large wicker chairs with flowered seat cushions and a vase of fresh flowers on a small desk.[93]

Leading policewomen believed that women and children would feel more comfortable in a homelike setting than a bureaucratic or institutional one. Mary E. Hamilton, director of the Women's Precinct of New York Police Department, once explained that "in removing from the Women's Precinct all the earmarks of a regular police station it at once became a center where a woman could seek in-formation, advice or aid from those of her own sex without fear of being subjected to the grim atmosphere of the average police desk."[94] Mina Van Winkle thought she had found the ideal setting for a woman's bureau when she visited the Netherlands in 1923.

> When we reached Amsterdam we came to a realization of almost per-
> fection in the housing of the policewomen. Their work was done in a pri-
> vate dwelling house. Nice curtains were at the windows, good furni-
> ture, flowers on the desk, and over all a fine spirit. There was plenty of
> light, sunshine and fresh air. The windows were clean and large. . . . To
> us it seemed as though we had arrived at some religious shrine by con-
> trast with some of the American headquarters which are unsuitable and
> badly kept.[95]

The physical separation of woman's bureaus from police stations, as well as the deliberate recreation of a homelike atmosphere, attests to pioneer police-women's desire to distance themselves from the work and workplace of police-men. It also suggests that policewomen were aware, however subliminally, that by contriving to make woman's bureaus look like private homes, they were recre-ating in the public sphere middle-class women's traditional base of power. More-over, Van Winkle's comparison of the woman's bureau in Amsterdam to a reli-gious shrine underscores the continued vitality of the idealization of the home as a physical and spiritual refuge from the outside world. In the view of pioneer po-licewomen and their supporters, woman's bureaus provided a temporary refuge for the city's troubled women and children, a place where women could find sup-port and advice open to them twenty-four hours. In sum, pioneer policewoman intended woman's bureaus to extend the idealized female world of nurture into the criminal justice system.

Policewomen and their supporters succeeded in establishing woman's bureaus under the direction of a woman supervisor in comparatively few cities.
According to a statement by the secretary of the International Association of Policewomen, only fifteen to twenty cities in 1925 had "regularly organized policewomen's bureaus."[96] In most cities, policewomen were scattered throughout the
precincts or were answerable to a male supervisor other than the chief. Leading
policewomen and their advocates disliked these practices and advised against
them at every opportunity. They claimed that scattering policewomen throughout the city lessened the chances that policewomen could effectively carry out
their special duties.[97] They also claimed that policemen made poor supervisors of
policewomen. In a study published in 1925, for example, Chloe Owings argues
for the establishment of female-headed woman's bureaus. She quotes from a
study that concluded that the woman's bureaus in Detroit and Washington, D.C.,
were successful because their female directors were free to select their own personnel and implement their own programs of preventive work. In contrast, she
suggests, a purely punitive police department is one that lacks a female-headed
woman's bureau: "In the United States each community must decide for itself
whether or not it desires to see its police department remain a purely punitive
agency or develop into a social instrument for the prevention of delinquency."[98]

Van Winkle also discussed the need for female-headed woman's bureaus. In
a speech before the annual convention of police chiefs in 1926, she marshalled
negative female stereotypes to argue for the appointment of female supervisors.

> *It is much easier for women to put women to work. Men are a little bit*
> *gallant; they are a little bit polite even to policewomen. Women are*
> *very hard to manage. Each one, especially if she has been married, is a*
> *sort of law unto herself, and it takes a woman to break down that sort*
> *of attitude and break a woman into service and make her function.*
> *Then, too, a policewoman can't deceive another woman as she can a*
> *man. . . . Another woman knows the other person, the other female, just*
> *like each man knows the other fellow. They can't deceive each other. A*
> *policewoman can't get by a woman as she can a man without working*
> *for a living in the department. . . . It is a hard thing . . . for the women*
> *to learn not to look in the shop window, not to have her [sic] thoughts*
> *turn inward and think about herself, but to think about the job."[99]*

Four years earlier, in another speech to the assembled chiefs, Van Winkle had discussed the reasons for giving women supervisors more authority. Referring to
her own experience as a police lieutenant, she confided, "I like the rank. I tell you,
I can make some of those young couples on the street corners do things, when I
have the rank. I even make them do things that they don't want to do. . . . I tell
you it pays to give the policewoman, the Director, the rank."[100]

In both of these speeches before a male audience, Van Winkle adopted a masculine stance; in 1926 she invoked a common male view of women, and in 1922 she bragged about her use of coercion through rank. Her masculine posturing and use of demeaning stereotypes about women were the calculated result of her beliefs about how her conservative male audience viewed women. By basing her argument for female-headed woman's bureaus on men's prejudices, she probably hoped to nullify in advance their objections to the idea of women supervising women. This tactic could have easily backfired.[101]

Van Winkle's affirmation of her police power ("I even make them do things that they don't want to do") strikes a discordant note in the discourse over women police. Most proponents minimized policewomen's power to intimidate and arrest. The officers of the Los Angeles City Mother's Bureau, for example, had police authority, but they refrained from using it "except when absolutely necessary," according to Aletha Gilbert. Los Angeles policewomen, she said in 1922, always try to "awaken" citizens (especially parents) to their social responsibilities "through love, sympathy, encouragement, and personal interest."[102] That same year, a journalist pointed out that policewomen in New York City did not arrest runaway girls but instead tried "to protect and foster-mother them back to normal, healthy womanhood."[103] Over two decades later, another journalist noted that the typical policewoman "leans over backward . . . not to arrest the young people she finds in trouble. She will do everything she can to avoid making formal charges against a minor."[104] In 1926, Valeria H. Parker, a member of the American Social Hygiene Association, had found "the rapid rise of [the] policewoman . . . gratifying evidence of her usefulness in the welfare efforts, as distinguished from the detective and arresting activities, of police departments."[105]

As the following chapters reveal, limitations placed on pioneer policewomen ensured that they made fewer arrests than policemen. These limitations notwithstanding, policewomen's supposed reluctance to arrest people formed a vital part of their bifurcated, gender-based definition of police work. Specifically, policewomen's feminine identity gave them a scale different from that of policemen by which to gauge their performance on the job. As Virginia M. Murray, director of the Women's Division of the Detroit Police Department, declared in 1921, "The unit by which policewomen measure their success should not be the number of arrests made, but rather the number of arrests prevented."[106] Irma Buwalda of the Metropolitan Police Department of Washington, D.C., made the same point: "A Policewoman's success is attested by the number of cases she keeps out of court rather than by the number that she sends there. It has been found possible in nine cases out of ten to adjust the case without a court experience."[107] In 1930, a Minnesota clubwoman drew an even sharper contrast between the work of policemen and policewomen by alluding to gender stereotypes about men's large appetite for personal glory and women's self-effacing desire to serve their community.

*The policemen and the detectives weigh their success by the number of
arrests they make. It is their presumed duty to spy, pursue, and arrest
for which they may receive medals, promotion, honorable mention, and
even publicity on their prowess in the public press. The women of the
police department balance their success silently on the other arm of the
scales with the number of arrests they make unnecessary.[108]*

The Question of Uniforms

Nowhere is the link between female gender identity and the movement for
women police more apparent than in the discourse over uniforms. For the first
quarter century that women worked as police officers, nearly all U.S. police departments forbade policewomen to wear uniforms. Pioneer policewomen and
their supporters agreed with this policy, but despite the consensus of opinion, the
idea of a woman wearing a police uniform generated scornful comment and car-
icature throughout the 1910s, 1920s, and early 1930s. According to Alice Stebbins
Wells, cartoonists responded to her appointment to the Los Angeles Police Department in 1910 by depicting a large, brawny woman with her hair pulled tightly
back, wearing a severely cut uniform, and brandishing a huge club over the head
of a small, cowering man. During the next quarter century, as hundreds of
women entered police work, similar cartoons of policewomen wearing paramil-
itary costumes appeared from time to time in newspapers and magazines. One
advocate of women police, Clarence B. Smith of the New York Bureau of Municipal Research, claimed in 1922 that cartoonists who lampooned policewomen had
seriously impeded the movement for women police in the United States. "Nevertheless," he averred, "it should be noted that these thoughtless critics were un-
erring in their instinctive ridicule of the uniformed policewoman." Referring to
the recent dismissal of policewomen from the London Metropolitan Police, Smith
continued, "It may therefore be the very fact that women patrols of London wear
the police uniform, together with other outward signs and badges of authority,
[that] influenced the Parliamentary Committee in its far-reaching conclusion."[109]

   Smith's reference to the "outward signs and badges of authority" worn by London policewomen was not an allusion to weapons. Neither American nor British
policewomen routinely carried billy clubs or guns during the 1910s, 1920s, and
early 1930s, although cartoons of uniformed policewomen sometimes portrayed
them as fully armed. Unlike uniforms, weaponry did not become an issue for
women police until the mid-1930s, when a few departments began issuing guns to
some female officers. During the 1910s and 1920s, the thought of routinely arming
a woman apparently seemed so absurd that it did not generate controversy or discussion. Uniforms were a different matter, however, because they did not denote
masculinity and raw power as unambiguously as did guns and clubs. Moreover,

no one seriously proposed dressing a policewoman exactly like a policeman, in regulation trousers and shirt; even the cartoons of uniformed policewomen generally depicted them wearing tailored dresses. Nevertheless, just this hint of masculinity in women's attire excited a great deal of negative comment because of the symbolic importance of dress in maintaining gender distinctions and gender hierarchy.

The discourse over policewomen's uniforms reflected two levels of opposition, one widely recognized and discussed, the other seldom openly acknowledged. The first involved the kind of work policewomen did. Unlike a policeman on his beat, a policewoman was supposed to patrol public areas inconspicuously. According to policewoman Helen D. Pigeon, policewomen in plain clothes were often able to "secure evidence hidden from the man in uniform."[110] Mary E. Hamilton of the New York Police Department agreed: "In not wearing a uniform, women officers have an advantage over uniformed patrolmen, for they may mingle with the crowd without arousing suspicion and thereby detect conditions that would never exist while a bluecoat were in sight."[111] In this respect, policewomen's duties resembled those of male plainclothes detectives. Additionally, whenever policewomen in public interceded in the lives of women or children, they were expected to do so without drawing undue attention to the matter. Decades before sociologists devised labeling theory, policewomen and their supporters claimed that the experience of being arrested and transported to jail was so stigmatizing (especially to women and children) that it frequently led to a massive loss of self-esteem and the beginnings of a criminal career. As Van Winkle once explained, "I do not believe in humiliating the woman I have arrested by forcing her to accompany a uniformed official through the streets, showing the world that she is under arrest and on her way to jail."[112]

Pioneer policewomen and their supporters also shunned uniforms because they knew that police uniforms commonly provoked resentment and fear. Mary Jane Spurlin, a former juvenile court judge in Portland, Oregon, asserted in 1935 that policewomen in street dress had an advantage over uniformed patrolmen in gaining the confidence of parents of troublesome children.[113] Van Winkle, who owned but rarely wore a uniform, shared Spurlin's point of view. "There is a peculiar psychology connected with the uniform," Van Winkle commented, "that in a large number of cases inspires fear and distrust, and I find I am better able to . . . discharge my duties conscientiously when I am dressed as an ordinary business woman." Her belief that she could not perform her work as conscientiously in uniform as in plainclothes illustrates how potent a symbol of power and coercion the uniform was. Because Van Winkle, like other pioneer policewomen, defined policewomen's work as preventive and protective, rather than detective and coercive, she did not feel she was being altogether true to her ideals when she wore the outward symbol of coercion. She also admitted that when she was dressed in ordinary clothes, she obtained confessions more easily than when she was in uniform.[114]

The second level of opposition to uniforms for policewomen involved female gender identity. Police uniforms were and are a universally understood symbol of the coercive power of the state over life, liberty, and property.[115] For many Americans, the idea of a woman wearing a police uniform subverted the purpose of the uniform and kindled doubts about gender roles. Moreover, as the unflattering cartoons and caricatures of policewomen attest, the appearance of uniformed policewomen aroused anxiety about the ways women on the force challenged gender hierarchy and disrupted fixed notions of how women should appear in public. The threat posed by uniformed policewomen to the stability of gender roles can be inferred from the remarks made by the chief of police of Chicago in 1928. Speaking of Europe, he sneered, "Over there they put their women in uniform and send them out on beats just like the men. That's ridiculous! You might just as soon send out so many children."[116] Perhaps his contempt for uniformed policewomen masked a fear that policewomen might perform some police functions as well as policemen performed them.

Policewomen's rejection of uniforms formed part of their attempt to create an occupational identity separate from that of policemen. It also reflected their fervent wish to avoid appearing as if they were competing with policemen. In this respect, however, policewomen's opposition to uniforms may have inadvertently provoked policemen's resentment because the most sought-after position in police departments, that of detective, did not and does not require the routine wearing of a uniform.[117]

By the mid-1920s, a few police departments required policewomen to wear uniforms on certain ceremonial occasions, such as parades. Usually these early uniforms were not a feminine version of the men's uniforms; that is, they were not made of the same blue or black fabric, nor were they decorated with the same kind of buttons and insignia. For example, the first uniforms worn by Los Angeles policewomen were plain, white dresses similar to nurses' uniforms.[118] Since few occupations have been as sex-linked as nursing, or as rigidly subordinate to a male-dominated profession, policewomen's new uniforms sent a clear message about Los Angeles policewomen's subordinate status within the department.

Police administrators well understood the power of the uniform. They also understood how to use uniforms to maintain social hierarchy. In summer 1935, for example, the New York Police Department issued uniforms to some of its policewomen for the first time, but it allowed policewomen to wear the uniforms only "around prisons and occasionally on Coney Island beach patrol, where an agglomeration of foreign elements makes visible authority desirable."[119] In sum, the race, class, and ethnic characteristics of prisoners and "foreign elements" made permissible the temporary empowerment by uniform of some policewomen on public patrol.

Policewomen–Policemen Relations

When women officers dressed in uniforms, their outward appearance bore the unmistakable stamp of police authority, and they no longer looked like social workers. Nevertheless, because of their gender, class, education, experience, and professed goals, most pioneer policewomen continued to think of themselves, and were still thought of by policemen, as social workers. Thus, the movement for women police was more than a sustained campaign by women to invade and transform a male institution; it was also an intrusion by members of one occupation into the daily working lives of the members of another occupation. This aspect of the movement distinguishes it from most historical instances of female entry into male occupations because in most instances women who entered an all-male field of work did not try to retain a distinctly different occupational identity from men. Nor in most instances did women entering a male occupation try, as pioneer policewomen did, to graft the goals and methods of their occupation onto the men's different occupation.

Understandably, most policemen resented, and to some extent even feared, the invasion of social workers. In 1921, the Executive Committee of the International Association of Chiefs of Police (IACP) warned U.S. police departments that unless they improved their performance, social workers might take over police work.[120] How seriously this warning was meant or heeded is difficult to say. In the late 1910s and early 1920s, struggles over reforming and professionalizing the police raged across the United States, and job security for any police officer, from the police chief down to the patrolman, did not exist. In nearly every major city, a municipal election could bring a complete change in police administration. At the same time, the number of social workers grew. From a policeman's point of view, it may well have seemed possible in 1921 that his job could someday be taken over by a social worker.

Even when considered in the light of separate occupational identities, however, dynamics of gender intrude into policewomen-policemen relations because the occupations of police officer and social worker were (and to a large degree still are) strongly sex-linked. Most police officers were men, and most social workers were women. Thus, when the Executive Committee of the IACP warned policemen to improve their performance or face possible replacement by social workers, policemen understood the gendered subtext of the admonition: improve your performance or you might be replaced by women. Even if no policemen took this warning to heart, they knew that over the preceding three decades women had successfully moved into many arenas of public life, such as electoral politics, that formerly were male preserves. Because this movement by women was unprecedented, no one knew where it would stop. Uncertainty over women's "place" in society strained gender relations everywhere, including police departments.

The thorny relationship between policemen and policewomen involved differences in social class, too. Most pioneer policewomen came from the middle and lower middle classes, although a few of them, such as Mina C. Van Winkle, were from the upper middle class. Some held college and advanced degrees, but many did not.[121] The personal backgrounds of pioneer policewomen in Los Angeles were probably typical of those of most pioneer policewomen (see Table 1). In contrast, policemen were predominantly members of the working class whose formal education stopped short of high school.[122] In Los Angeles, 64 percent of the police force in the mid-1920s had never reached the ninth grade (see Table 2.) These marked differences in class between policemen and policewomen correlated and fused with gender and occupational differences, creating a gulf of discord between male and female officers.[123]

Overt references to class occasionally appear in the literature from the movement for women police. "First of all," Van Winkle told a journalist in 1928, "the policewoman must be a lady. She must be born as well as made for her job. From her background she must draw innate refinement, innate tact and a finely adjusted sense of values that can be had only from early training of the right

TABLE 1.   PERSONAL BACKGROUNDS OF TEN LAPD PIONEER POLICEWOMEN

Name/ Lifespan	Years with the LAPD	Birthplace	Level of Education	Former Activity or Occupation
Lorel Boyles 1881–1969	1913–1930s	Los Angeles, Calif.	High school	—
Marguerite Curley 1887–?	1920–1930s	—	—	PTA president
Juanita Edwards 1898–1957	1929–49	New Orleans, La.	—	Stenographer
Elizabeth Feeley 1874–1927	1905–1920s	Providence, R.I.	—	Social worker
Elizabeth Fiske 1895–?	1929–64	Woodland, Calif.	Some college	Social worker
Aletha Gilbert 1870–1931	1902–29	El Monte, Calif.	Some high school	Traveling saleswoman
Anna Hamm 1869–51	1912–19	King City, Calif.	High school	—
Georgia Robinson 1879–1961	1916–29	Opelousas, La.	High school	Social worker, governess
Lucille Shelton 1885–1940	1925– late 1930s	Carterville, Ga.	—	—
Alice Wells 1873–1947	1910–40	Manhattan, Kans.	Graduate school	Assistant pastor, social worker

TABLE 2.   FORMAL EDUCATION OF 1,954 LAPD OFFICERS, 1923

Grade Reached	Number of Officers
Ungraded	126
3rd	4
4th	45
5th	65
6th	133
7th	221
8th	666
9th	171
10th	177
11th	107
12th	99
College	
1 year	75
2 years	36
3 years	12
4 years	17

Source: Compiled from August Vollmer, "Supplementary Table Showing Alpha Score Averaged by School Grade," *Survey of the Los Angeles Police Force, 1923–24,* in Woods, "Progressives and the Police," p. 184. The survey included approximately twenty-five policewomen.

kind."[124] Van Winkle sometimes alluded to her own elite status and personal wealth. In a speech she gave to a convention of police chiefs in 1926, for example, she asked her audience to complain to Congress about a recent rollback in salaries for police officers in Washington, D.C. (Congress voted on all appropriations for police in the District of Columbia.) She hastened to tell the chiefs that she was not asking for money for herself, declaring, "I have no financial advantage to gain. I don't need the money I get but give it back."[125] Her audience may well have resented her noblesse oblige.

Alice Stebbins Wells's speeches had a decided air of condescension toward policemen: "None of us sitting here care to be police officers," she announced to the City Club of Chicago in 1912, temporarily ignoring the fact that she was a police officer. "We feel that . . . [policemen] are not of our caliber or our character. . . . But what do we expect of these men who enter this department? We give them no social recognition; we do not invite them to our receptions, to any of our gatherings." These remarks, which Wells made at the beginning of her talk, established the class backgrounds of "we" (the middle- and upper-middle class audience, with whom Wells clearly identified) and "them" (working-class policemen).[126]

To many policemen, women's entry into police work must have formed part of the hated middle-class movement to reform the police, for policemen could not have missed the class bias inherent in the demand that police departments hire only trained social workers (preferably college graduates) as policewomen. In fact, middle-class women's entry into police work—a working-class men's occupation—owed much of its success to class dynamics. Had police work been a middle-class men's occupation, such as accounting, middle-class women would have encountered many more difficulties than they did in entering police departments. But because most policewomen came from a socioeconomic class superior to that of most policemen, they had some psychological leverage over policemen.[127]

Given their many differences, no wonder mutual hostility flourished between male and female officers. Occasionally, antagonism was expressed in gender-specific terms. In 1923, Chief Jacob Graul responded to the appointment of the first woman officer to the Cleveland Police Department with the simple statement, "There is no place in police work for a woman."[128] On the other side, a proponent of women police claimed in 1928 that because every policeman was first and foremost a man, he could not avoid treating female suspects brutally: "Not that the policeman was deliberately brutal; but . . . he partook of the inevitable attributes of mere man and was incorrigibly blind."[129]

Overall, however, antagonism between male and female officers involved a tangle of criticism and prejudices about ethnicity, education, experience, class background, occupational standards, and competing beliefs about gender roles. Often the criticism was veiled, but it always carried the speaker's sense of superiority. For instance, Van Winkle once claimed that wherever woman's bureaus existed, they brought about "a better and more intelligent attitude on the part of policemen."[130] In a similar vein, Edith Abbott warned that "the work of the policewoman certainly cannot be adequately performed by persons who have no more education than most of the men now filling positions in the police department."[131] A study undertaken in 1927 by the Bureau of Public Personnel Administration in Washington, D.C., which solicited information from policewomen and their advocates, concluded that policewomen "come from a higher intellectual stratum than the average run of policemen. They have better educational equipment, and more often better technical training."[132]

Policemen returned the attack by suggesting that college-educated policewomen were eggheads. "We may not have any university educated women in our department," a St. Louis police chief acknowledged in 1930, "but we have real trained police women who possess good common horse sense." He added that he consistently resisted pressure to place a woman in charge of the St. Louis Woman's Bureau because he wanted his policewomen "to continue doing real police duty, and it is doubtful if a social worker could supplant a trained and experienced policeman and obtain results as satisfactory."[133] In 1935, a veteran policeman in New York City minced no words in expressing his hostility toward policewomen. After learning that New York Police Department women officers were starting to wear uniforms on beach patrol, he exclaimed, "They were no bargain in civies, and they'll be worth less rigged out in blue."[134]

Van Winkle occasionally made direct references to policemen's hostility toward women officers. In a speech to a convention of police chiefs in 1920, she remarked, "I have seen with my own eyes how women can be persecuted inside of police departments." Six years later, at another convention, she informed the assembled chiefs, "We seem to be welcomed here, and we were not always welcome in the police chiefs' group. In the early days we had to tread on the male prejudice against women in this kind of occupation."[135] In 1928, while president of the International Association of Policewomen, Van Winkle complained to a reporter that policewomen existed on sufferance nearly everywhere. She lamented that in many cities policewomen sat idle and silent, "and the more silent they are, the more popular they become."[136]

Other women, from inside and outside the criminal justice system, referred to policewomen's difficulties in obtaining acceptance from policemen. In an address to the annual convention of the International Association of Chiefs of Police in 1930, Sarah V. Dunn, a lawyer, reminded the audience of the hostile reception their group gave to pioneer policewoman Alice Stebbins Wells in 1914. "I just hope nobody present here today is going to suggest, as was suggested before Mrs. Wells spoke at that meeting, to call the patrol." She later observed, "There are still a great many policemen who question the wisdom of police women, and as a matter of fact, there are some officials who go so far as to question the value of a woman as a factor in police work at all."[137]

As Dunn's remarks suggest, women's place in police work was still not secure in 1930. Many Americans, male and female, continued to believe that police work was no job for a woman. In their view, police work was corrupt and dangerous. What respectable woman, they wondered, would choose to rub elbows with prostitutes and other criminals? This question continues to plague policewomen today.

Despite the insecure status of women in police departments, thousands of "respectable" middle-class women chose policing as a career in the 1910s and 1920s. Their presence in police departments angered most policemen, who agreed with Chief Jacob Graul of Cleveland that there was "no place in police work for a woman." Until the early 1910s, there was indeed no place for women in police work because normative standards of gender had always excluded them. Of course, a few cities, such as Chicago and Portland, Oregon, had granted police power to a woman or two before 1910, but the mass hiring of women as police officers did not get under way until the early 1910s. At that time, women's organizations across the country saw the appointment of women police as a solution to an array of closely related problems—the regulation of adolescent female sexuality (the "girl problem"), urban moral hazards, and bad social conditions.

As this chapter documents, the leaders of the campaign for women conceived and articulated their arguments in gender-specific terms. By directly and consciously resisting male hegemony of law enforcement, advocates of women police broke with the tradition that held that policing was a public matter under the exclusive control of men. The maintenance of a moral social order, they said, depended on the actions and wisdom of city mothers, as well as (or even in the place of) the actions and wisdom of city fathers. Most policemen and civic police reformers probably ridiculed this argument. But its maternalist premise appealed to middle-class women during the 1910s and early 1920s because it corresponded with their belief that as a sex, they could make gender-specific contributions to public life through the prevention of crime and immorality.

Pioneer policewomen encountered many difficulties as they tried to put the ideals of preventive justice into practice. Some of these difficulties were inherent in the crime prevention model of police work itself. According to the model's chief architects, women and children needed protection from crime and the moral hazards of city life. But once women had police power, they often "protected" women and children by arresting them. For all its emphasis on protection, the crime prevention model still required the discretionary use of coercive state power over individual lives. In this respect, it did not differ from other models of police work. Moreover, arrest statistics reveal that working-class female youth comprised the majority of people whom policewomen "protected" through arrest. To a greater extent than other maternalist reforms of the early twentieth century, the crime prevention model of police work placed middle-class white women in charge of working-class women and children, including working-class women and children of color.

As we see in the following chapters, the experience of women officers in the Los Angeles Police Department during the early twentieth century throws light on how pioneer policewomen in America interpreted their crime prevention mission and attempted to put its ideals into practice. Perhaps in no other city in the United States did women police have a more promising start than Los Angeles, or, in retrospect, a more thorough defeat.

PART TWO

WOMEN POLICE
IN LOS ANGELES

Mrs. Wells is not what one would imagine a police officer

to be, but is the essence of femininity.

Riverside (California) Press
May 24, 1911

CHAPTER THREE

"Just Mothers to Everybody": The City Mother's Bureau of Los Angeles, 1914–29

In early summer 1927, Mary Lockyer repeatedly forbade her sixteen-year-old daughter, Nancy, from attending certain "wild" parties. Much to her distress, her daughter defied her authority and went to the parties anyway. Worried that she had lost control over Nancy, Mary Lockyer turned to the Los Angeles City Mother's Bureau for advice. The bureau, established thirteen years earlier, was a branch of the Los Angeles Police Department (LAPD). Staffed entirely by police-women, the bureau enjoyed an international reputation for its crime prevention work. For a period of fifty years (1914–64), the City Mother and her assistants gave material aid and advice to thousands of Angelenos on matters such as disobedi-ent children, spousal support, abusive husbands, alcoholism, immigration and cit-izenship, neighborhood quarrels, adultery, unemployment, and adoptions. Under the direction of Aletha Gilbert, the founder of the bureau who served as City Mother until 1929, the bureau also ran a low-cost day nursery for the children of working mothers, sponsored weekly municipal dances, placed children in foster homes, and provided baby-sitters on election days. Gilbert undertook all these projects, and many more, in the firm belief that they helped to prevent crime.[1]

This chapter explores the work of separate woman's bureaus by taking a close look at how Aletha Gilbert came to head the City Mother's Bureau and how she in-terpreted her role. It also analyzes the kinds of support she enjoyed, the opposition she faced, and the compromises she made. Unfortunately, the paucity of evidence about individual pioneer policewomen makes it impossible to determine the extent to which Gilbert was representative of the group as a whole. Nevertheless, her ca-reer provides a window into the world of women police during the 1910s and 1920s by illustrating three aspects of pioneer policewomen's work: their efforts to protect female youth from the perceived moral dangers of the urban environment, their role as social caseworkers, and some of the limits they encountered when they entered the politicized world of urban police departments.

Aletha Gilbert: Police Matron and Policewoman, 1902–14

Gilbert joined the LAPD in March 1902 as an assistant to her sixty-two-year-old mother, Lucy Uthera Gray, the department's first jail matron. The preceding December, Gray had asked Chief John Elton for an assistant, pointing out that the population of the city, and hence the women's jail, had more than doubled since her date of hire in autumn 1888. Statistics support her claim; according to the federal census, the population of Los Angeles grew by 103 percent during the final decade of the nineteenth century, reaching 102,479 in 1900.[2] Gray particularly wanted her daughter Aletha as her assistant because her position required her to live in two small rooms in the jail, and she disliked the prospect of sharing her living quarters with a stranger. In addition, Gray trusted Aletha to do a good job because Aletha had already assisted her in an unofficial, unpaid capacity for years.[3]

Elton assented to Gray's request, but he had to obtain approval and money for the new position from the notoriously tight-fisted city council. In an eloquent appeal to the councilmen, he claimed that Gray "lived from one end of the year to another, shut up in the jail, in cheerless and unsanitary quarters." He then urged the council to provide funding for an assistant to the matron on the grounds of humanity and justice. "Otherwise," he warned, "we are very liable to kill with overwork an old and faithful public servant." The council immediately gave its unanimous approval.[4]

Gilbert was a thirty-two-year-old single mother when she became assistant matron. She was born Aletha Theora Maxey on January 17, 1870, in El Monte (Los Angeles County), the seventh child of Warren and Lucy Maxey. Her father died in 1875, when she was five. Soon afterward, her mother moved the family to a squatter's cabin in nearby Azusa and for several years farmed the land with the help of her eight children, who ranged in age from less than one year to sixteen. In 1880 the family moved to Los Angeles, where Gilbert's mother married Thomas R. Gray, a rancher in his late fifties. The rancher died in 1882, when Gilbert was twelve. Four years after her stepfather's death, Gilbert married Thomas M. Gilbert. Little is known about her husband. According to one account, he was an engineer with the first electric railway in Los Angeles; according to a later account, he owned a local restaurant and nightclub in Venice, a beach resort famous for its popular amusements.[5]

In 1889, at age nineteen, Gilbert bore her only child, Hilda Beatrice. Her marriage did not last. In 1897, she divorced her husband for reasons that remain obscure, and she obtained custody of Hilda. Although Gilbert was only twenty-seven at the time of her divorce, she never married again. Immediately after the divorce, she went to work for a wholesale grocery business as a traveling saleswoman. In later years she claimed that she was one of the first traveling saleswomen in California. Gilbert held this job until March 1902, when she officially became her mother's assistant at the jail.[6]

Considered together, these facts suggest that Gilbert came from the lower margins of the middle class. Marrying at sixteen, she may not have finished high school. More important, the facts indicate that male authority figures did not have a lasting presence in her personal life. Her father and her stepfather died before she was thirteen, and her marriage ended in divorce before she was twenty-eight. Yet if her father, stepfather, and husband were transitory figures in her life, her mother, the redoubtable Matron Gray of the LAPD, was not. She provided Gilbert with a remarkably strong female role model, an example of female independence, resourcefulness, and courage that contradicted Victorian gender stereotypes about women's dependent and vacillating nature. In addition to raising nine children for many years without the help of a husband or other adult in the household, Gray took on the challenge of being the sole person in charge of women prisoners in the city jail, where she was on call twenty-four hours. At the time of her appointment in 1888, she was forty-seven years old, with a five-year-old son and seven-year-old daughter. Although only five feet tall and weighing less than one hundred pounds, she rapidly earned a reputation as a stalwart member of the LAPD. Throughout the 1890s and early 1900s, Los Angeles newspapers carried stories of her perilous but successful encounters with violent and insane prisoners. These stories did not surprise her children, for according to family lore, an unarmed, ten-year-old Gray, traveling with her family to the California goldfields, had once successfully defied four Apache men raiding the family's temporary camp outside Tucson, Arizona.[7]

When Gray died of pneumonia in 1904, Gilbert took over as chief matron. She served in this position until 1912. Little evidence survives regarding her policies while matron, but an interview she gave in 1911 to a local newspaper reporter reveals her belief that most female crime arose from social conditions, rather than from biological causes or innate depravity. In the interview, Gilbert claimed that approximately two-thirds of the female inmates of the Los Angeles City Jail turned to crime because of the low wages paid to women workers. Gilbert singled out women's work as sales clerks as particularly ill-paid, asserting that many of the prisoners "had tried the stores and found they could not live on their wages." Her opinions matched those of most female charity and corrections workers in the Progressive Era.[8]

The publication of Gilbert's views did not stir up controversy in Los Angeles, although her remarks probably annoyed a few merchants. After she left the chief matron position in 1912 and became a policewoman, however, she gradually learned that she dared not discuss certain topics in public if she valued her career. She learned that she had entered the politicized world of male police work.

Ironically, the circumstances surrounding her promotion from chief matron to policewoman in 1912 involved the same issue that would later repeatedly get her in trouble with police and city officials: the protection of girls and women from the perceived moral dangers of the urban environment. Gilbert's promotion can be traced to an incident in April 1911 that left her frustrated with her status as a jail matron. While walking along the street one Friday evening in downtown

Los Angeles, Gilbert came upon "flashily dressed" young men ogling and physically accosting women and girls. "My fingers itched to grab them," she remarked the following day, "but I was afraid my police power [as matron] did not give me the right to make arrests." She refrained from collaring the men but took the matter straight to the newly appointed LAPD chief Charles E. Sebastian, asking him outright for the power of arrest. "I'd just love to drag one of those miserable brutes into court," she declared. Sebastian soon granted her request, for he was that rarity in police circles, a chief who supported the employment of women police. Although it took nine months, he eventually cleared the matter with the city council, then appointed Gilbert to the LAPD Juvenile Bureau, thereby conferring upon her full police powers.[9]

The timing of this incident is significant because it occurred only seven months after Alice Stebbins Wells joined the LAPD as the first woman police officer. Gilbert probably envied Wells her power to make arrests. In fact, Gilbert's remark that she was afraid that her own police powers did not extend to the right to make arrests was disingenuous because she knew very well that she could not legally arrest anyone. Perhaps she thought that if she introduced a note of doubt into the matter, she would more easily attain what she wanted.

At the time of Gilbert's promotion, the Juvenile Bureau employed three policewomen, including Wells, and their supervisor, Leo W. Marden. Before Wells was hired, Marden had been the sole officer assigned to the unit. As Chapter Four discusses, Gilbert helped to establish the Juvenile Bureau in 1909. By July 1914, the number of juvenile officers had increased to nine, all women except for Marden.[10]

The first few weeks of Gilbert's career with the Juvenile Bureau passed quietly. Within six months, however, she and Leo Marden incurred the wrath of police and city officials by speaking out about the sexual dangers that they believed daily threatened women and girls on the streets of Los Angeles. Specifically, they made the error of discussing how the existence of prostitution in Los Angeles adversely affected all women and girls who lived in or near the city. Their remarks, made to San Diego policemen in late 1912, were extremely ill-advised because Chief Sebastian had finally succeeded in shutting down the local red-light district, and both he and Los Angeles Mayor George Alexander refused to tolerate any suggestion that they had not completely eradicated the "social evil" in their city.

In theory, Los Angeles had been a "closed" city since the reform election of 1902 in which voters ratified an amendment to the city charter prohibiting prostitution and gambling within city limits. But according to LAPD historian Joseph Gerald Woods, the passage of the amendment in 1902 inaugurated "an era of corruption unexampled in the city's previous experience. The sale of protection forged a bond between politician, vice dealer, and policeman. A few individual [police] officers grew richer but the majority languished in apathy, penury, and infamy."[11] Woods believes that the era of corruption stretched from 1902 to 1938 with only one brief interruption, the years between 1911 and 1915 when Charles Sebastian headed the LAPD. Whereas other so-called reform police chiefs only made a show of closing down the vice district, Sebastian, with the successive backing of Mayors George Alexander and Fred Rose, made an honest attempt to do so.[12]

Gilbert probably thought in 1911 that the time for meaningful reform had finally come. As a member of the LAPD since 1902, she had seen seven police chiefs come and go; during 1902–9 alone, five chiefs had left in disgrace because of scandals directly linking them to organized commercial vice. Arthur Kern, for example, began his career as LAPD chief in 1906 by joining the mayor and police commissioners in reaping profits from local gambling and prostitution operations. When an exposé forced all of them out of office in 1909, the new chief, former Vice Squad Captain Thomas Broadhead, took over police graft. Broadhead lasted three months before a scandal forced him to resign. In 1911, after two more chiefs who condoned vice conditions had come and gone, reformers once again cleaned house and appointed Sebastian to the top post. Sebastian's past was hardly spotless—while assigned to the Vice Squad in 1908–9 he had been named as one of three couriers who delivered vice payoffs to Chiefs Kern and Broadhead. He survived that scandal, Woods has surmised, probably because the reformers considered him "a hapless tool of corrupt superiors." Despite, or perhaps because of this background, Sebastian ran a closed city during his tenure as chief.[13]

Much to the dismay of Gilbert, Marden, and others, Sebastian's strict enforcement of vice laws neither eradicated prostitution nor reduced the incidence of venereal disease in the city. Instead, it moved prostitution out of the brothels and into the streets, making it more dangerous for the prostitutes and more visible to the general public. Prostitutes who once had worked for a madam in the tenderloin found their way into "respectable" neighborhoods, restaurants, hotels, and stores. The shift from brothels to the streets took place not just in Los Angeles but everywhere in urban America during the early twentieth century, as moral reformers shut down red-light districts.[14]

To Gilbert and Marden, the strict enforcement of vice laws was a disaster for the women and girls of Los Angeles. Their opinion came to light in October 1912, when they traveled together to San Diego to bring back a teenage girl who allegedly had been abducted from Los Angeles over two months before. While in town, Gilbert and Marden complained to San Diego police that the closing of the segregated district in Los Angeles had scattered prostitutes throughout the city, and that as a result, "unprincipled men" were propositioning girls and women in every part of town. Gilbert and Marden then darkly claimed that teenage girls who previously had not even known of the existence of prostitution had suddenly become the objects of prurient speculation and outright commercial solicitation. When the entire city is a red-light district, the officers implied, every woman and girl is vulnerable to insult, or worse. A San Diego newspaper reporter

quoted Gilbert as saying, "There are more fallen women, more young girls coming before our juvenile courts for delinquency, and more disgusting disease in
Los Angeles than was ever the case when we had a restricted district." Marden
added, "You may walk down any street in the city and pick out a dozen fallen
women any night in the week, and at almost any hour of the day."[15]

When the officers returned to Los Angeles, Sebastian and Alexander were
seething with anger over the officers' public criticism of official policy. The chief
and mayor had read the officers' remarks in the *San Diego Union* and demanded
an immediate, full explanation. Sebastian threatened to charge Gilbert and Marden with violating a departmental rule that forbade police officers "from discussing the acts and policies of their superior officers and of the administration."
At a hearing held the next day, Gilbert and Marden defended themselves by claiming that they had talked to San Diego police about the work of the LAPD Juvenile
Bureau while seated in a car in front of the San Diego police station. According to
them, no newspaper reporters were present, so one of the San Diego officers had
to have leaked the story to the press. In response, Sebastian and Alexander requested that the San Diego officers be deposed. The depositions must have satisfied all concerned, for the issue died in the local newspapers, and the LAPD retained the services of both Gilbert and Marden for many years thereafter.[16]

The Birth of the City Mother's Bureau

During summer 1914, Gilbert approached Chief Sebastian with the idea of creating the City Mother's Bureau, a separate unit of policewomen that would operate primarily as a counseling agency for "wayward girls" and their mothers. By
"wayward girls," Gilbert did not mean young women whom the juvenile court
had already labeled delinquent; Gilbert did not expect to handle, nor did she handle, cases involving girls and young women who had already been before the juvenile court. Instead, she planned to offer confidential advice to mothers who suspected their daughters of forbidden sexual activity. She also planned to offer
advice directly to teenage girls themselves. She hoped that through counseling
mothers and "wayward" daughters, she could keep teenage girls and young
women from ever having to appear before the juvenile court on the charge of sex
delinquency.[17]

During the early twentieth century the charge of sex delinquency meant premarital heterosexual intercourse. Because of the double sexual standard, teenage
boys and young men rarely faced this charge. Statistics show, however, that sex
delinquency was the most common grounds for the arrest and incarceration of
teenage girls and young women throughout the country and that the charges often originated in the girls' families.[18] In Los Angeles, for example, 63 percent of the
female youths appearing before the juvenile court in 1920 faced the charge of sex

delinquency; nearly half (47 percent) of these petitions named a parent or other family member as the source of the complaint.[19] Gilbert believed that parents usually turned to the juvenile court as a last, desperate measure to exercise control over their daughters' sexuality. She further believed that if parents (especially mothers) sought help when their daughters first began to rebel, most would never need to take the drastic step of taking their daughters to court. She therefore intended the City Mother's Bureau to be an agency of first resort for troubled parents, a place where they could seek confidential advice from a sympathetic expert.

During summer and early autumn 1914, Gilbert talked about her plans for the bureau to several newspaper reporters. In these conversations she frequently emphasized the necessity of locating the bureau "away from the depressing atmosphere of Police Headquarters." A separate location was necessary, she asserted, because she wanted the bureau to offer complete confidentiality to mothers and daughters. The delicate nature of their problems demanded nothing less: "I will be dealing with cases that have not reached the publicity stage and it will be my great aim to keep them from ever reaching it."[20] She argued that if she were forced to locate the bureau in or near a police station, her promise of confidentiality would be worthless, because police stations were notoriously crowded places where secrets could easily be overheard.[21]

In making the case for a separate location, Gilbert always spoke in terms of clients' needs. She did not draw attention to the fact that a separate location would allow her a large measure of independence from direct police supervision. The prospect of running her own show must have powerfully appealed to her, however. As a woman who had had neither father nor stepfather since she was twelve, who had divorced her husband fourteen years earlier and had never remarried, who had raised her daughter for many years with only the help of her mother, and who had enjoyed a great deal of autonomy during a ten-year career as chief matron, Gilbert by 1914 was not accustomed to subordinating herself to anyone. Called autocratic by some, she had strong opinions and a strong will. Luckily for her, once she became City Mother she never again had to work under anyone's immediate supervision. As City Mother, she had only to make reports to the chief from time to time.[22]

In late September 1914, the finance committee of the city council responded to Gilbert's request for a separate location by diverting four hundred dollars from the police fund to refurbish rooms in the abandoned State Normal School building for Gilbert's use.[23] This location earned the bureau much favorable press. One journalist approvingly described it as a "haven for troubled mothers and erring or ignorant girls who need advice . . . [but who] fear . . . publicity."[24] During the opening ceremonies for the bureau, Judge Thomas P. White captured the general enthusiasm for the bureau's separate location in a statement widely quoted in newspapers throughout California.

> *From this time on no girl will have to pass through the doors of the po-*
> *lice station, before the eyes of a morbidly curious crowd, to tell her piti-*
> *ful story to officers there. Instead, she will confide in a big-hearted city*
> *mother, either in the bureau's office or in the privacy of her home. She*
> *will not be haled into court, but will be advised and cared for.*[25]

Gilbert, of course, concurred: "My bureau will try to reduce the work of the ju-venile court by saving girls after they have gone only a short distance in the wrong direction."[26]

Gilbert's plan to "save girls" directly addressed middle-class anxiety over ongoing changes in sexual culture. This anxiety had been simmering for years, but it came to a boil during the 1910s, as the middle class gradually abandoned late Victorian sexual values and began to adopt the values of sexual liberalism. Like many other Progressive reformers, Gilbert associated underlying changes in sexual culture with changes in the social landscape of city life. According to her, modern features of urban living, such as "easy communication, swift travel, and diversified amusements," constituted "nothing less than menaces to morality" because they tempted female youth to stray farther and farther from the home cir-cle and thereby made female youth vulnerable to sexual exploitation.[27] Her plan to "save girls" from sexual exploitation and all the moral hazards of the city had several closely related meanings.

First and most obviously, Gilbert's plan to save girls meant steering them away from premarital sex. Gilbert believed that under ideal conditions, mothers gave moral instruction to their daughters. But if mothers could not educate their daughters, or if they would not, Gilbert planned to take their place.[28] She saw her-self as a surrogate mother to ignorant female youth, and she therefore intended to give most of her advice to girls and young women privately. Just as a mother would sit down at the kitchen table for a serious talk with her daughter, so, too, would Gilbert sit down with a teenage girl or young woman. Gilbert explained that through sympathetic but candid discussions she hoped to instill "a desire for right—the higher ideals of life—and the responsibilities of womanhood."[29] She called her approach "moral suasion," and she thought it would work because she had a high opinion of the "modern girl": "I find the modern girl most interesting and as a rule she is very independent, self-reliant, and capable of doing her own thinking even though her thoughts do not coincide with her parents or we elders; but as a whole she is amenable to reason if approached in the right manner."[30] Gilbert remained optimistic about the power of moral suasion throughout her ca-reer as City Mother.

A second component of Gilbert's plan to "save girls" involved protecting them from venereal disease through sex education. Venereal disease emerged as a key social issue in the Progressive Era thanks largely to the determined efforts of doctors and social reformers to break the public silence about its prevalence. According to doctors' surveys taken in the early 1900s, the incidence of syphilis and gonorrhea in the United States had reached epidemic proportions. In 1901, one influential doctor and social reformer, Prince Albert Morrow, estimated that eighty out of one hundred adult males in New York City had gonorrhea. Although this estimate struck many doctors as absurdly high, few doubted that syphilis and gonorrhea constituted a serious health problem. In 1914, when Gilbert established the City Mother's Bureau, the first effective treatment for syphilis, Salvarsan, was gaining widespread acceptance. No cure for gonorrhea existed, although painful and useless treatments abounded. After decades of declaring gonorrhea a relatively benign disease in women, physicians in the late nineteenth and early twentieth centuries changed their minds when presented with evidence that it caused sterility. The grave consequences of gonorrhea, together with the absence of a cure, made "saving girls" from venereal disease a high priority among pioneer policewomen across the nation.[31] In Los Angeles, Gilbert's concern for the well-being of sexually active female youth had a solid foundation: in 1920, 53 percent of all female youth charged with sex delinquency in the juvenile court tested positive for venereal disease.[32]

A third, much-publicized aspect of the plan to "save girls" involved protecting them from white slavery. Stories about white slavery circulated in Los Angeles repeatedly throughout the early 1910s, inspiring several police investigations. One of these investigations played a role in the founding of the City Mother's Bureau in 1914. Interestingly, this investigation started in 1913, only a few months after Gilbert and Marden's impolitic remarks in San Diego about the continued existence of prostitution in Los Angeles. A few weeks after this investigation began, Chief Charles Sebastian talked to newspaper reporters about his plans to involve local women activists in the citywide hunt for white slavers. Specifically, Sebastian claimed that eradicating white slavery was the kind of work "that only women can do." He told reporters that he intended to ask the city council at its next meeting to pass an emergency ordinance creating positions for twenty-five female "special appointees." By "special appointees," Sebastian explained, he meant women who would serve as police officers without pay. He also noted that he was going to ask the council for five more regularly appointed policewomen. Once the council approved these recommendations and the women's white slavery squad formed, Sebastian planned to place the squad under the supervision of Aletha Gilbert, who already had "an active part in the white slave cases." Sebastian closed his interview by giving reporters a copy of a letter he had sent the day before to the Friday Morning Club, the most prestigious women's organization in the city.[33]

In his letter, reprinted in full in the *Los Angeles Examiner*, Sebastian asked club members to take an "active part" in the police investigation of white slavery. Because they were women, he reminded them, they had the power to "mold public opinion and strengthen the moral fiber" of Los Angeles. He then pleaded for their assistance: "I therefore urge that the members of your club take the initiative in this matter toward the end that an auxiliary investigation committee be created, to be composed of the women of the various clubs and organizations of the city, who shall be invested with special police power by this department." Sebastian concluded the letter by expressing his hope that if clubwomen took up the cause, "the young girls of the city will be protected in a far greater degree than they are at present."[34]

Sebastian's interview with reporters represents an extremely rare example of a police chief's public support for women police. As discussed in Chapter Two, pioneer policewomen typically had to struggle against overt hostility from the rank and file of policemen throughout the 1910s, 1920s, and 1930s. In contrast to most Progressive Era policewomen, the women officers of the LAPD during the early 1910s had a chief whose zeal for their work at times matched that of their strongest female allies. Yet the significance of Sebastian's actions lies deeper than his support for policewomen; it lies in his public recognition of female moral authority. He could not have made his regard for female moral authority more clear or more public than when he told reporters that the eradication of white slavery was the kind of work that only women could do. His announcement of his plans was akin to giving women activists the moral keys to the city. Like a frontier sheriff calling for deputies to form a posse to help catch bank robbers, Sebastian called for female volunteers to form a posse to help investigate vice conditions. His proposal to form a female posse and place it under the direct supervision of Aletha Gilbert must have stunned a lot of people in Los Angeles.

The city council did not rush to endorse Sebastian's recommendations. Council members had an impressive record for enacting political reform legislation, but few shared Sebastian's enthusiasm for women police. And so, instead of immediately approving an emergency ordinance, as Sebastian hoped, the council referred the proposal to the budget and supply committees. Whether the proposal would have survived the committees will never be known, because soon after committee members received the proposal, they lost their positions as councilmen through the massive recall campaign of June 1913. This campaign was engineered by a disparate group of local power brokers who had long supported political reform in Los Angeles but who opposed even the mildest social reform. In their eyes, the mayor and the city councilmen had given far too much support to social reform measures. With one notable exception, all members of the city administration lost their positions in June 1913. The exception was Chief Sebastian. But although he kept his job, Sebastian did not get the ordinances he requested regarding hiring of "special appointees" and five policewomen.[35]

Despite these setbacks, neither Sebastian nor Gilbert abandoned the idea of involving clubwomen in police work. Approximately eighteen months later, they obtained permission from police commissioners and the city council to create an all-female board of advisors to the new City Mother's Bureau. Members of the new board did not have police power, and so they never acted as a female posse. However, on the day of the opening ceremonies for the bureau, they received an outward symbol of police power: regulation police badges inscribed with the words "City Mother."

The first women to wear "City Mother" badges represented nine civic and women's organizations, including the Friday Morning Club, the Million Club, the Parent-Teachers Association, and the Florence Crittenton Home (a local affiliate of a nationwide network of homes for unwed mothers). In later years, representatives came from the Big Sisters League, the Young Women's Christian Association, and the Red Cross. No African American women's clubs or organizations had representatives on the board, even though by 1914 African American women had built strong local organizations, such as the Sojourner Truth Industrial Club.[36]

The creation of an outside board of women advisors was a master stroke, because the advisors provided an invaluable link between the bureau and the local female activist community. This community, although extremely young compared to those in the Northeast, had by 1914 achieved several key social welfare reforms. In 1897, for example, the local College Women's Settlement Club succeeded in making Los Angeles the first city in the nation to employ a public nurse. Women activists also pushed for the appointment of Matron Lucy Gray at the LAPD (1888), the establishment of the Los Angeles County Juvenile Court (1903), and the hiring of pioneer policewoman Alice Stebbins Wells (1910). Under Gilbert's leadership in the mid-1910s, they successfully campaigned for the appointment of a woman judge to hear female cases in the juvenile court. "We need a woman judge more than we have ever needed anything in juvenile work in Los Angeles," Gilbert told women's clubs during autumn 1914. "No man can do the work that a woman could do." The first woman judge of the Los Angeles County Juvenile Court, Orfa Jean Shontz, obtained her appointment in 1915. The following year, women activists oversaw the establishment of a separate court for adult female offenders. This court, known simply as the Women's Court, had a female judge, who barred men from its proceedings. Policewomen acted as bailiffs.[37]

Women activists in Los Angeles did not, of course, realize all their aims, but they wielded considerable influence during the 1910s and 1920s, as Willard Huntington Wright snidely but accurately noted. In an article published in Smart Set in March 1913, Wright observed that "women in Los Angeles . . . are the leaders of most of the 'movements.' . . . Many of them hold public offices. Their pictures appear in the daily papers, labeled 'leading citizens.' Their support is sought by politicians. They bristle with genuine importance. They are a public factor to be reckoned with. Docility is not one of their virtues."[38]

Women activists' support of the City Mother's Bureau during times of institutional crisis substantiate Wright's remarks about their lack of docility. In 1919 and again in 1929, women activists successfully protested moves by LAPD chiefs to abolish the bureau's semi-autonomous status. In 1919, Chief George K. Home sought to move the bureau into a police station. His plan met immediate, heavy opposition from women's organizations.[39] In autumn 1929, Chief James E. Davis tried to do the same thing. He took advantage of Gilbert's retirement a few months earlier to try to place the bureau, as he candidly phrased it, "under the rule and regulation of the police department." In addition to relocating the bureau, he sought to transfer the bureau's files to the LAPD Records Division. Women activists launched a counterattack by submitting a petition to the city council urging it to pass an ordinance "relieving the city mother's bureau from any subordinate position under the police department." The council did not pass such an ordinance, but neither did it approve Davis's plan.[40]

Newspaper reporters interviewed Gilbert and all advisory board members when the bureau opened in October 1914. These interviews reveal a surprising amount of dissatisfaction with the local juvenile court, particularly its treatment of teenage girls. As one advisor explained, "This City Mother's Bureau is to be the greatest thing ever instituted by the city. It will keep young girls out of the courts."[41] Gilbert and her advisors wanted to keep teenage girls out of juvenile court because they believed that the experience of being in court harmed them. "We do not want girls to be dragged even through the juvenile courts. Often the poor things are not the least culpable," Gilbert told a news reporter.[42] At the opening ceremonies for the bureau, Chief Sebastian expressed similar sentiments: "The matter is clear to any observer. In many instances children who go wrong really are not to blame. . . . We want to keep children out of the courts. The influence of the court is bad for them, and the fact of having been there fastens a certain stigma upon a boy or girl."[43]

Significantly, both Gilbert and Sebastian explained their intent to keep children out of juvenile court by noting that many children were not to blame for their alleged misdeeds. They thus implied that the juvenile court, or at least the Los Angeles County Juvenile Court, had a reputation for holding children culpable. This kind of reputation contradicted the ideals expressed by the court's founders, who a decade earlier had repeatedly insisted that the court would neither hold children responsible for their alleged misconduct nor accuse a child of committing a crime.[44] As Grace Abbott, chief of the U.S. Children's Bureau, once asserted, the juvenile court was established specifically to remove the child "from the domination of the ideas and practices of the old criminal law."[45] In the eyes of Sebastian, Gilbert, and others, the Los Angeles County Juvenile Court fell short of this ideal.

Throughout her tenure as City Mother, Gilbert had two policewomen assistants, Lorel Boyles (her younger half-sister) and Deanne Harris. Boyles, the tenth child of Lucy Gray, joined the LAPD in November 1913 as a policewoman with the Juvenile Bureau. Hers was the only position that the new city council of late 1913 approved. When Boyles transferred to the City Mother's Bureau in 1914, she took the title "chief investigator." Harris, who eventually became the assistant City Mother, entered police service in late 1915, after having worked with Gilbert as a volunteer for nearly a year. Unlike Gilbert, who actively sought public notice, Boyles and Harris received little publicity for their work in the City Mother's Bureau.[46]

Social Casework with "Wayward Girls"

Gilbert devised several strategies to implement her ideas in her first year as City Mother, but the heart of her plan involved counseling wayward girls and their mothers at critical junctures in their lives. She identified three scenarios in which these counseling sessions would take place: Mothers would directly seek her advice about how to exercise control over their daughters; she or her assistants would go to the homes of children whose misbehavior had been reported to the bureau by a friend, neighbor, or schoolteacher; and, a child or young adult who felt bewildered, lonely, or afraid would come to the bureau to be "mothered." As one journalist explained this concept in 1914, "Girls and boys, away from the influences of their homes, are invited to call whenever they feel the need of a guiding hand. Everything that a mother would do for her child will be done for the youth of Los Angeles and done quietly without recourse to courts."[47] Mrs. James Westpheling, an advisor to the bureau, said it more succinctly: "We are going to be just mothers to everybody."[48]

Gilbert never doubted that hundreds of mothers would voluntarily seek her help in matters of child care. Today, the prospect of large numbers of people besieging the police for advice on parenting seems unlikely. But Gilbert claimed that prior to the founding of the bureau, a "long line of worried parents" had constantly appealed to Los Angeles police for aid in controlling their children.[49] Lest her comment appear self-serving, it should be remembered that throughout the second half of the nineteenth century, poor and working-class people often turned to the police in circumstances they no longer do today. The police gave poor people food, medical aid, assistance in job hunting, and overnight lodging in the corridors and jails of the police stations. The police also sheltered lost children. Providing advice and material aid was an essential part of the mission of the nineteenth-century police to manage the so-called dangerous classes. Although the police function of class control helped to perpetuate an unjust power structure, poor people derived some small benefits from the arrangement. Eric Monkkonen even argues that from the point of view of the homeless poor, the nineteenth-century police function of class control was far superior to twentieth-century police functions, because it created situations where the poor and the police sometimes had positive encounters. Monkkonen believes that once the police stopped providing welfare services, they lost familiarity with the daily problems of the poor, and all police interactions with the poor occurred in negative, conflict-ridden circumstances.[50]

During the mid-1910s, when Gilbert first headed the City Mother's Bureau, police in Los Angeles still provided many traditional services and had even added new ones. According to the 1916–17 LAPD *Annual Report,* the department had, in the previous year, found jobs for over 100 men and 37 women, operated an "inebriate farm" for 170 male alcoholics "who admit their inability to resist drink and who express a desire to conquer the habit," provided lodging for 817 men and 26 women, and fed 294 hungry people.[51] This list excluded services provided by the City Mother's Bureau. To a significant extent, Gilbert owed her success in establishing the City Mother's Bureau to the continued vitality of the nineteenth-century mission of the police, which allowed the police to function as welfare service providers.[52] Gilbert and her advisors redefined this mission to embrace the methods and goals of social work. Whereas nineteenth-century (male) social welfare policing aimed primarily to provide relief in the form of food, overnight lodging, and work for destitute men, the City Mother's Bureau aimed primarily to resolve familial conflict and instill or strengthen middle-class moral values in individual adolescent girls and their parents. In its focus on the perceived needs of mothers and daughters, the City Mother's Bureau exemplified the female-gendered character of social-welfare policing envisioned by pioneer policewomen and their advocates. Like other maternalist reformers, Gilbert and her staff directed their energies to improving the lives of women and children. The social-welfare policing provided by men in the nineteenth and early twentieth centuries lacked this focus.

What specifically did Gilbert and her staff do every working day to "save girls"? Analysis of the daily operations of the City Mother's Bureau poses difficulties for the historian because the LAPD long ago destroyed all the bureau's internal records. To make matters worse, the chief source of information about the LAPD during most of the relevant years, the *Annual Reports,* contains very little data about the bureau. Fortunately, however, for three years, from July 1924 to June 1927, the LAPD published information about the national, ethnic, or racial identity of Gilbert's clients. This information provides valuable clues to the mystery of who sought Gilbert's advice (see Table 3).

During the mid-1920s Latinos and African Americans went to the bureau in numbers roughly proportionate to their percentage in the city's population. African Americans in Los Angeles composed 2.6 percent of the population in 1920 and 3.1 percent in 1930. The number of Mexicans, Mexican Americans, and other Latinos in Los Angeles in the 1920s is difficult to ascertain precisely; estimates

TABLE 3. NATIONAL, ETHNIC, OR RACIAL BACKGROUND OF CLIENTS OF CITY MOTHER'S BUREAU, JULY 1924–JUNE 1927

	Mexican (%)	Colored (%)	Jewish (%)	Italian (%)	Russian (%)	Other (%)	American (%)
1924–25	6.4	2.8	3.3	1.5	1.5	5.1	79.4
1925–26	10.3	2.6	2.8	2.0	2.5	3.9	75.9
1926–27	8.4	3.0	1.8	2.4	1.4	3.7	79.2

Source: LAPD, *Annual Report*, fiscal years 1924–25, 1925–26, and 1926–27.

Note: The nomenclature in this table is the same as that used by the LAPD; "American" probably referred to native-born whites of northwest European ancestry. (Percentages may not total 100 because of rounding.)

range from 3.5 percent to 12 percent of the total population. Significantly, the LAPD did not single out people of Asian descent in its statistics, even though the number of people of Asian descent in Los Angeles during the mid-1920s nearly equaled that of people of African descent. Apparently so few people of Asian descent sought Gilbert's help that the LAPD categorized them with other unspecified minority groups under the catchall heading "Other."[53]

Despite the LAPD's wholesale destruction of the bureau's records, a few documents survive thanks to Gilbert's descendants. Although these documents are too few and fragmentary to allow extensive analysis of Gilbert's social casework, they furnish a glimpse into the ways she and her assistants handled individual cases of "wayward girls." A surviving case record summary for all cases opened in July 1927 is particularly useful. This document contains brief descriptions of six instances wherein parents (five mothers and one stepfather) consulted Gilbert about their teenage daughters' alleged sexual misconduct. Gilbert classified all six cases under the category "In Danger." "In Danger" was a term Gilbert and her assistants usually applied to unwed female adolescents who engaged in, or who were suspected of engaging in, sexual activity or sexually provocative behavior. Occasionally, the term referred to battered wives, rape victims, and neglected or abused children.

All six "In Danger" cases of July 1927 discussed below involved persons of western European descent because none has the notation "Colored," which Gilbert and her assistants used to indicate African American clients, and all the surnames of the principals (including boyfriends) suggest Dutch, English, German, or Scottish ancestry.[54] In this respect, the cases are representative of the bureau's caseload during July 1927, for of the 130 cases handled by the bureau that month, only 8 cases (6 percent) involved people with Hispanic surnames, 1 involved a person with a Japanese surname, and 1 involved an African American. Unfortunately, with one exception, the case of Margaret O'Donnell, the case record summary does not contain information indicating the socioeconomic class of the clients or other principals in the case, such as occupation, level of education, or annual income.

In the first case, Dorothy Manning told Gilbert that she feared her sixteen-year-old daughter, Gertrude, was pregnant because the teenager's behavior had changed in alarming ways: her menstrual period was late, she had asked "unusual questions," she was infatuated with a young man, and she had been found with five quinine tablets in her possession. (Quinine had a reputation as an abortifacient.) Gilbert advised Dorothy Manning to have her daughter undergo a "medical" (i.e., pelvic) examination. When Gilbert learned that the examination showed Gertrude to be a virgin, she closed the case with the comment, "Mother appears to be mentally afflicted to the extent that she is very imaginative pertaining to her daughter's virtue."[55]

In another case, Mary Lockyer took her sixteen-year-old daughter, Nancy, to the bureau because she feared that Nancy was becoming a "delinquent." Upon questioning, Nancy admitted that she had committed "very flagrant [sexual] indiscretions." Gilbert gave Nancy a "severe warning" about the consequences of her behavior. The details of the lecture are not recorded, but Gilbert doubtlessly painted a grim picture of the fate of sexually active teenage girls. Gilbert concluded the interview by placing Nancy on "probation" to her mother.[56]

Parental probation was a tactic without official teeth. It did not require any involvement or supervision by the police or probation departments, so it had no force or effect beyond an individual parent's ability to discipline a child. However, it did throw the weight of the City Mother's Bureau (and by the extension, the LAPD) behind a parent's demand for obedience. Gilbert worked out the terms of parental probation with both the parent and the child, specifying in detail the daily duties and obligations each owed to the other. According to Gilbert, parental probation improved communication between parent and child. In her view, better communication led to improved family relations because most children disobeyed their parents through a lack of mutual understanding. Gilbert hoped that by her setting forth the terms of probation to both parent and child, each would know what to expect from each other.[57]

In a third case, Charles Becker went to the bureau to discuss his eighteen-year-old stepdaughter, Margaret O'Donnell, whom he described as living away from home with a group of "careless girls." He wanted Gilbert to help him persuade Margaret to return home. Gilbert contacted Margaret, who agreed to come into the bureau for questioning. During the questioning session, Margaret admitted to having sexual relations with Clarence, a twenty-year-old student at the University of Southern California. Margaret claimed that Clarence fully intended to marry her, and to prove it she showed Gilbert four letters from him in which he proposed marriage. Margaret further claimed that the only obstacle to the marriage was the disapproval of Clarence's mother. Gilbert contacted Clarence's parents and asked them to bring him into the bureau. When they refused, Gilbert warned them that if they did not bring him, he might be charged with contributing to the delinquency of a minor. Although they then agreed, they went to see Gilbert without him. During their interview they told Gilbert bluntly that they disliked Margaret and that Clarence was on vacation. The case record summary does not mention the reason, if they gave one, for their dislike. Perhaps they condemned Margaret because they knew or suspected that she and their son engaged in premarital sex. Or perhaps Margaret was from the working class, and they were socially ambitious for Clarence, hoping he would make a more advantageous marriage.

Believing that Clarence's parents had sent their son out of state to avoid prosecution, Gilbert "ordered" them to bring him back. Meanwhile, Margaret had undergone a pelvic examination, which found she was pregnant. Shortly thereafter, Margaret and her mother went to the bureau to tell Gilbert that Margaret had just married Henry, a young man who knew of her condition and "felt sorry for her." Gilbert dropped the idea of bringing charges against Clarence, and she closed the case.[58]

Another case concerned fourteen-year-old Celeste. According to her mother, Beatrice Walker, Celeste often stayed out all night with a nineteen-year-old young man named Steven. When Gilbert questioned Celeste about Steven, Celeste admitted that she had had "numerous experiences of sexual intercourse" with him. Gilbert then asked Steven to come into the bureau, which he did. As soon as he confirmed Celeste's story, Gilbert turned him over to an officer from the Juvenile Bureau, who promptly arrested and jailed him, then released him on police probation. This type of release meant that Steven had agreed to report regularly to a policeman in the Juvenile Bureau. The LAPD routinely offered police probation to first-time juvenile offenders as a way to avoid a court record. No charges were brought against Celeste. Soon thereafter, Celeste discovered she was pregnant, so "through the collaboration of the various departments," Steven and Celeste were allowed to marry. Gilbert closed the case after their wedding.[59]

In the final two, unrelated cases, underaged daughters had eloped with young men. In both instances, the daughters' parents disapproved of the young men and wanted to have the marriages annulled. Gilbert interviewed all parties, found the young couples to be "very much in love," and advised the parents to drop the idea of annulment.[60]

Although no general conclusions about Gilbert's handling of "In Danger" cases can be drawn from such a tiny sampling, in these six cases, Gilbert fulfilled her promise to try to keep teenage girls out of juvenile court. But she seems to have had a different attitude about teenage boys. These same records show that Gilbert arranged for the arrest of the boyfriend of one pregnant teenager and held the threat of an arrest over the boyfriend of another pregnant teenager. In another case involving a teenage girl, however, Gilbert advised a mother to take her daughter to court. This case involved fourteen-year-old Barbara Burton, who, unlike the six teenage girls discussed above, is described in the case record summary as "Incorrigible," rather than "In Danger."

According to the record, Barbara's mother was "in despair" over her daughter's behavior. Unfortunately, no specific allegations of misconduct appear in the records, except for the comment that Barbara smoked and drank. Smoking and drinking were common activities among rebellious teenagers, and by themselves did not usually provide grounds for a referral to juvenile court. Still, the fact that Gilbert did not classify Barbara "In Danger" strongly suggests that Barbara's misbehavior involved something other than sexual activity. Gilbert had no advice for Barbara's mother other than to encourage her to file a petition in juvenile court, which the mother reportedly did. Barbara's case proves that Gilbert was willing to advise some parents to take their teenage daughters to court, but it does not offer any clues about her reasons for this decision.[61]

On the most basic level, these cases document that Gilbert was correct in her assumption that some parents would seek her advice about their disobedient daughters. The cases also corroborate Linda Gordon's conclusion that people often sought services from social work agencies in order to gain power for themselves within their families.[62] Yet, as Gordon has pointed out, not all clients of social work agencies got what they wanted. The cases discussed above suggest two reasons why social workers sometimes did not give the kind of help their clients wanted.

In some instances, social workers disagreed with clients' aims or with clients' interpretation of family conflicts. This explanation fits Gilbert's handling of the two elopement cases, in which Gilbert displayed a surprising degree of respect for the daughters' rights to autonomy. Had Gilbert's interest lay only or even primarily in upholding parental authority, she would have supported the parents' wishes for annulment. This explanation also fits the case of Gertrude Manning; once a doctor declared that Gertrude was a virgin, Gilbert saw no reason to chastise her or to place her on parental probation. In sum, Gilbert rejected Dorothy Manning's interpretation of Gertrude's behavior.

In other instances, circumstances forced social work agencies to act in ways that did not meet clients' initial expectations. For example, the discovery that fourteen-year-old Celeste Walker was pregnant changed nearly everything about her case. Rather than place Celeste on parental probation, Gilbert expedited the bureaucratic process that allowed Celeste to marry Steven. Gilbert probably disliked this course of action because she disapproved of most early marriages. "There should be a law that no girl may marry before she is 17 or 18," Gilbert proclaimed in the mid-1910s. "The marriages urged often by the Juvenile Courts I do not always approve. . . . What if through consent of the parents, the marriage is permitted? What right have they to choose as husband for their little daughter a man who has already harmed her?[63]

Celeste's mother, Beatrice Walker, could have easily blocked Celeste's marriage to Steven. She could have asked for Gilbert's help in placing her daughter in an institution for unwed mothers, such as the Florence Crittenton Home or the Truelove Home. Many parents of unwed, pregnant daughters went to Gilbert with this request. But Beatrice Walker chose to allow her daughter to marry the father of her baby, and in so doing, she lost all legal authority over her daughter. This was probably not an outcome she wanted when she first went to the City Mother's Bureau.

Celeste's case also illustrates a key point about Gilbert's social casework as City Mother: the relationship between the City Mother's Bureau, its clients, and the clients' children was interactive. In Celeste's case, her marriage to Steven was a solution worked out by Gilbert and all the parties named in the case record summary.

Sexual Dangers in Los Angeles

In addition to counseling mothers and daughters, Gilbert attempted during the 1910s to keep adolescent girls and young women out of juvenile court by publicly disseminating information about the sexual dangers she believed surrounded them in Los Angeles. In early 1915, the City Mother's Bureau published a list aptly titled "Don'ts for Girls." Gilbert and her board of advisors compiled this list after they received numerous complaints from teenage girls and young women about their experiences aboard jitney buses. According to these complaints, young women traveling alone on crowded buses often received improper and unwelcome suggestions from men. At other times, young women became victims of men who lured women into their private cars or trucks by pretending to be jitney drivers. Apparently some of these men carried signs in their private vehicles that falsely claimed the vehicles to be public transportation. The men hid the signs until they saw a girl or young woman waiting for a bus, and then they brought out the signs to entice her to ride with them. "Generally the sign contains letters so faint that the girl cannot read it," explained Mrs. Jefferson D. Gibbs, an advisor to the bureau. "The driver will stop and ask her fare. He will agree to go where she desires and the usual things follow." The list of "Don'ts for Girls" included the following tips: "Don't get into a jitney bus unless the sign upon the car front clearly indicates that it is a passenger carrying vehicle. Don't stay in a supposed jitney bus if you see that upon the dash board there is no city license. . . . Don't get in a jitney bus late at night if you are not escorted by a man or an older woman."[64]

Gilbert and her advisors also urged LAPD officials to ask the city council to pass an ordinance setting a maximum number of passengers for jitney buses. According to Gilbert and her advisors, the limit placed on the number of passengers would put a halt to "the practice of crowding women in with the men." This revealing phrase points up the sense of unease Gilbert and her advisors felt toward the sexual integration of public space. Gilbert and the advisors also wanted lights placed over the rear seats of jitney buses; thanks to their advocacy, the city council passed an ordinance mandating the placement of these lights.[65]

Gilbert decided in late 1914 to get the public schools involved with "saving girls." She therefore organized the Committee of City Mothers and School Women, a group that included Gilbert, three of her advisors, and fifteen female school administrators. In January 1915, the committee composed a letter "To the Mothers of Los Angeles." They sent it to the homes of all female students at Los Angeles city schools and, to guarantee the widest possible audience, to local newspapers as well. The purpose of the letter was to alert mothers to the new "moral menaces" surrounding female youth. "The dangers to girls have multiplied a hundred fold in the last twenty-five years," the letter began. Yet even if the world had changed, "girl nature" had not: "It has the same trustfulness, the same love of admiration, the same inexperience, and the same susceptibility to masculine appeal." Unfortunately, however, "society is just as merciless in case of a mistake, and mankind just as indifferent." It was therefore the responsibility of women everywhere to protect their daughters: "The welfare of the girl is woman's problem, and chiefly the mother's." To safeguard her daughter, a mother had to exercise constant vigilance. All mothers must, at all times, "no matter what the cost to them in time and effort . . . know where their daughters are, what their daughters are doing and with whom they are associating." After all, "overconfidence on the part of the mothers is responsible for much disaster to girls."[66]

The open letter to the "Mothers of Los Angeles" illustrates Progressive reformers' common assumption that lax parenting, and especially lax mothering, was largely to blame for the "girl problem." Gilbert often added her voice to the chorus of those condemning parents for laxity, but she vacillated between accusing parents of outright selfishness (including emotional selfishness or detachment) and finding excuses for them. In one speech she claimed that parents had their priorities wrong, making it clear that she had middle-class parents, as well as working-class parents, in mind: "'I haven't the time' is the excuse offered by the average father and mother. . . . Many mothers can find time for bridge and beauty lectures; fathers for clubs and golf. But are any of these more important than a little time spent in studying child welfare or child psychology?"[67] At other times, Gilbert absolved parents of purposefully neglecting their children. Most parents are not negligent, she declared in a speech she gave frequently, they are simply caught off-guard by all the changes taking place in U.S. society that adversely affect teenage girls: "Through the world all conditions, either social or economical, are in a stage of rapid growth. . . . This changed environment is the cause for those perplexing problems a girl must face today and too often without the proper guidance of her parents because they have not kept abreast with the times."[68] The letter to the "Mothers of Los Angeles" aimed to educate both kinds of parents she described, the ones who were too busy for their children and the ones who were asleep to the dangers of the "changed environment."

For a few months in 1915, Gilbert turned to another, more dramatic medium for advising parents, the "real-life" story published in local newspapers. In these stories, Gilbert gave first-person accounts of cases she handled as City Mother. According to the newspapers, she gave fictitious names for all persons concerned (except police personnel), and she omitted details that would make identification possible. In one story, she warned parents of the danger of emotionally alienating their children. This story, published in August 1915, "Afraid to Tell; Hides Her Shame," begins, "This is the story of the girl who came too late—no, I must not say that—but you mothers of Los Angeles and you fathers with growing sons, here is something for you to think about!" The story concerned unmarried, seventeen-year-old Linda, who stumbled into the City Mother's Bureau a scant hour or so before the birth of her stillborn son. Linda had met the young man who became her lover at work; he, too, was only seventeen years old. She had sexual relations with him, she told Gilbert, because she thought they would soon marry. She hid her pregnancy from her family, friends, and co-workers by lacing herself tightly. (Gilbert thought the tight lacing probably led to fetal death.) Then, nearly fainting from labor pains, Linda sought out the City Mother, who rushed her to the hospital and comforted her when the baby was born dead. "This girl faced the greatest ordeal of a woman's life, befriended by a stranger," Gilbert sadly informed her readers. "Think of this, you parents. She was AFRAID TO TELL HER OWN MOTHER! Is YOUR daughter afraid to tell YOU if misfortune overtakes her?"[69]

The details of Linda's story tally with the findings of historians who have examined the lives of young working-class women in the Progressive Era. Like Linda, most of the single working-class young women who were sexually active chose men of their own age and class for sexual partners, and many young women first became acquainted with their lovers at their place of work. The only atypical aspect of the story is Gilbert's choice of moral. Gilbert did not, as historians of moral reform might expect, take Linda's parents to task for failing to instill "proper" notions of conduct in her, or for manifestly failing to supervise her social life. Instead, Gilbert bewailed the fact that Linda did not feel emotionally close enough to her mother to confide in her and to seek her help. The moral of the story is: Do not alienate your children, lest they turn to a stranger in a time of need.

In writing another "real-life" story for the *Los Angeles Record*, Gilbert allowed her zeal to protect young women and girls from sexual dangers to cloud her judgment, for this story, entitled "Batter Down Door; Save Girl," alluded to white slavery in Los Angeles. Its publication in November 1915 landed Gilbert once again in deep trouble with city and police officials. "Batter Down Door; Save Girl" related the case of sixteen-year-old Edith, whose mother allowed her to go to the theater one evening with a young man whom Edith had met only a short time before. When Edith had not returned by midnight (two hours late), her mother telephoned Gilbert at home, frantic with worry. Gilbert asked the mother for a description of the young man, and upon hearing it, realized there was no time to lose. As she told her readers, "The sickening suspicion that leaped to my mind grew to a positive certainty." Gilbert recognized the young man as a known male procurer "of the worst type." She telephoned the chief of police, who ordered two male detectives to help her find Edith. Afraid that her readers might falsely conclude that the chief assigned two men to the case because women officers lacked police powers, Gilbert added, "The city mother and her aides are clothed with full police authority, but I felt that this was a case where able-bodied men were needed." She thus implied not only that it was her idea to deploy the male detectives but also that she retained control over the investigation. A short time later, after she and the two policemen had questioned the patrons of various cafes and learned that Edith and her companion had gone with another couple to a "notorious roadhouse," Gilbert and the detectives sped "in a high-powered automobile" to the rescue. "It didn't seem melodramatic to me then," Gilbert reflected. "All I was thinking of was that little girl with those beasts. I was excited, yes, but ready to fight to the last ditch." The police had barely arrived at the roadhouse when they heard a muffled scream from upstairs. All three raced to the second floor, where they found "little Edith cowering in a corner, her clothes torn, her hair disarranged, her face white with terror." While Gilbert comforted Edith, the detectives arrested her male companion. Gilbert ended her story by demanding, "HOW MANY LOS ANGELES MOTHERS KNOW AS MUCH AS THEY SHOULD ABOUT THEIR DAUGHTER'S CALLERS? AND WHAT IS A FATHER'S DUTY TO HIS DAUGHTER?"[70]

Except for the leading role played by a policewoman, Edith's story is virtually indistinguishable from other white slavery accounts. It features a young naïve female, described as a "little girl," to whom it attaches no blame, it has the typical male "beast" as its villain, and it has a sophisticated urban setting. Yet despite the standard plot, its publication in the autumn of 1915 caused a small furor, because it implied that Los Angeles police officers (including Gilbert) knew two things that they were not supposed to know: the identity of at least one procurer and the location of at least one place of ill-repute. More specifically, it implied that officers had this knowledge prior to Edith's abduction but did not act upon it until circumstances forced them. The implication that the "social evil" still existed in Los Angeles and that it enjoyed police protection enraged police and city officials, because it was true.

As Woods has documented, the brief era of genuine attempts by the LAPD to suppress commercialized vice ended in 1915. The event triggering the return of "politics as usual" was the election in June 1915 of reform-minded LAPD Chief Charles Sebastian to the mayor's seat. On July 16, 1915, Sebastian officially resigned his post as chief to take up his new, ultimately short-lived political career as mayor. While he was chief of police (1911–15), Sebastian had waged a sincere and successful war against vice and corruption. His stand against vice made him a favorite among women activists and greatly contributed to the reputation of Los Angeles in the early 1910s as a morally puritanical city. But once Sebastian became mayor, he no longer pursued reform, probably because his own reputation had been permanently smeared.

Sebastian's reputation began to sink when rumors circulated that he was having an adulterous affair and that he was tool of the underworld. These rumors plagued him throughout his campaign for the mayor's seat in early 1915 and eventually proved his political undoing. According to the rumors, Sebastian, a married man, was having an affair with Mrs. Lillian Pratt; even worse, he was conducting the affair in the presence of Pratt's sixteen-year-old sister, who lived with Pratt at the Arizona Rooming House in downtown Los Angeles. At the height of the mayoral campaign, Pratt's sister confirmed the rumors, prompting the district attorney to charge Sebastian with contributing to the delinquency of a minor. A sensational trial followed. Outside the courtroom clubwomen and members of the Woman's Christian Temperance Union (WCTU) paraded with banners proclaiming their belief in Sebastian's innocence. A jury acquitted Sebastian of the charge just before the election, but questions about his character followed him into the mayor's office. In 1916, the *Record* proved the rumors of his affair were true by publishing some of Sebastian's indiscreet correspondence with Pratt, which Sebastian's wife had discovered and given to the *Record*. The published evidence of his guilt, together with other, unproven allegations about criminal activity, forced Sebastian out of office in October 1916.[71]

In the meantime, Sebastian's successor at the LAPD, Clarence Snively, showed little interest in running a "clean" city. After Snively became chief, vice operators once again began to set up shop, intending to bring back what some Angelenos called the "good old days" of "gambling, girls, and liquor."[72] As mayor, Sebastian kept a low profile. Commercialized vice had begun to reappear in downtown Los Angeles in autumn 1915, when the *Record* published Edith's story. Its publication angered many police and city officials because it opened up the possibility of yet another round of vice scandals that might cost them their jobs and illicit profits.

The day after Edith's story appeared, Gilbert told the *Record* that she would no longer write stories for publication. This news so infuriated the editor that he immediately fired off an editorial in which he theorized that Gilbert had lost her nerve. Gilbert, he said, had wilted under the political heat that city authorities placed on anyone who tried to tell the sordid truth about criminal activity and police corruption in Los Angeles.

> *The Record understood that if the truth were told, some toes would be stepped on, some criticism aroused, some high political influence used and some editorial pressure brought to bear, but The Record didn't worry about these things. It was part of the fight. Mrs. Gilbert, apparently, is more tender-hearted.*
>
> *YOU CANNOT CLEAN STABLES WITHOUT GETTING MUSSED.*
>
> *If Mrs. Gilbert will publish what she knows this town will be a cleaner, safer, better city. . . .*
>
> *And while we are on the subject, The Record will remark right here THAT OF COURSE THE OFFICIALS KNOW THERE ARE PROCURERS AND HOUSES OF ILL-REPUTE. . . . MORE THAN THAT, THEY ARE PROTECTED. . . .*
>
> *Those who fight with The Record need something more than a sweet smile and a bottle of smelling salts. They need Christian courage enough to go ALL the way for the common good.*
>
> *At that, The Record doesn't blame Mrs. Gilbert. She had to stand up under a lot of pressure to tell such truth as she told. We are merely sorry the public must be kept in ignorance.*[73]

The language of this passage reflects the condescension with which many men viewed policewomen (and by extension, of course, all women). With the remark that "those who fight with The Record need something more than a sweet smile and a bottle of smelling salts," the editor damned Gilbert as a faint-hearted incompetent who seemingly began a fight armed only with those feminine accouterments, and he implicitly mocked her earlier boast that she was "ready to fight to the last ditch." His suggestion, however, that Gilbert was too tender-hearted to continue writing stories for publication was illogical. Toward whom did Gilbert allegedly feel tenderhearted? The editor did not say because it was irrelevant to his argument. He made the allegation simply to create a link between tenderheartedness—a feminine trait—and Gilbert's supposed cowardice, euphemistically referred to as her quintessentially feminine dislike of getting "mussed." He later conceded that Gilbert withstood a great deal of political pressure before giving in, but by that time he had already conveyed the message that a fight against crime and corruption was a masculine undertaking. Tender hearts, sweet smiles, and bottles of smelling salts were feminine (that is, useless) substitutes for "courage enough to go ALL the way for the common good."

There is no evidence to substantiate the editorial's implication that Gilbert wrote Edith's story because she wanted to blow the whistle on police protection of prostitution. Motivations are difficult to ascertain, but it seems likely that Gilbert wrote Edith's story for the same reason she composed the list of "Don'ts for Girls" and the open letter to mothers: to warn parents and their daughters about the sexual dangers that she believed threatened the female youth of Los Angeles. Even though Gilbert must have deplored the return of "the good old days," she probably did not knowingly risk her job by writing an exposé of police protection of vice. Moreover, Edith's story casts Gilbert herself in a negative light by portraying her as having knowledge of illegal vice operations. Gilbert was a proud woman, well-known in Los Angeles for taking moral stands. It seems doubtful that she would purposely portray herself as tolerant of any open vice conditions.

Whatever Gilbert's motives were for writing the story, her eagerness to show off her own leading role in the fight against vice led her to make two mistakes. The first mistake was specificity. Whereas the list of "Don'ts for Girls" and the open letter to mothers contain only general warnings about sexual dangers, Edith's story reveals the existence of a well-known procurer and a "notorious" roadhouse. The second mistake was the assignment of responsibility. In the list of "Don'ts for Girls" and the open letter, Gilbert plainly tells women and girls that they are responsible for their moral and physical safety; although Edith's story carries this message, too, it also implies that if the police were doing their job, well-known procurers would be in jail and well-known commercial vice operations would not exist. Consequently, in Edith's story, the issue of sexual danger—a "woman's" issue—spilled over into the issue of police corruption. To ensure that it would not happen again, Gilbert quit writing stories for publication, probably at the demand of her superiors, as the editor of the *Record* surmised.

The incident in San Diego in 1912 and the circumstances surrounding the publication of Edith's story in 1915 together illustrate the limits placed on pioneer policewomen when they entered the politicized world of male police work. They also illustrate the kind of compromise policewomen made when they found themselves no longer outside the institution they wished to change.[74] Once women carved a place for themselves in police work, their efforts at crime prevention necessarily took on a specific institutional character. Thus, Gilbert learned that Los Angeles police and city officials would not tolerate public discussion by police officers of the existence of prostitution because such talk endangered the positions and profits of powerful men. In 1912, officials hid behind a departmental regulation forbidding police officers from discussing LAPD policies, and in 1915 they probably pressured Gilbert to discontinue her stream of stories to newspapers. Thereafter, whenever Gilbert publicly warned parents of the various dangers threatening youth, she never mentioned the existence of the "social evil" in Los Angeles. It was part of the price she paid to keep her job.

Municipal Dances

After her withdrawal of "real-life" stories from newspapers in November 1915, Gilbert concentrated her efforts on other ways to protect the morals of female youth. Among her projects during the 1910s were the City Mother's municipal dances, held weekly each winter. Gilbert organized the first series of municipal dances in the winter of 1914–15. She hoped that by offering teenagers their favorite ragtime music and by charging only twenty-five cents (which included nonalcoholic beverages and checkroom privileges), she could lure young Angelenos away from "rough" commercial dance halls, such as the Silver Swan, the Belvedere, and Solomon's. As she phrased it, she intended the municipal dances "to cover the necessary breach between the undesirable so-called public dance and the often unattainable society dance."[75]

By "undesirable so-called public dance," Gilbert meant commercial dance halls. As her choice of phrase makes plain, she deplored the existence of commercial dance halls, believing them to be immoral places where teenage girls and boys lost their inhibitions through liquor and unsupervised, sensual dancing. When she was with the Juvenile Bureau, she had frequently investigated dance halls for infringements of the middle-class moral code and violations of the law. These investigations, like those carried out elsewhere by pioneer policewomen and private protective associations, were by intent and practice repressive to the working class. Nevertheless, Gilbert and other investigators were right to associate dance halls with the undermining of middle-class moral standards. As contemporary accounts reveal, dance halls and other commercialized amusements fostered a permissive sexual ethic among working-class youth; this ethic challenged the middle-class moral code—just as middle-class reformers feared.[76]

Like other women in crime prevention, Gilbert disapproved of the new sexual ethic and linked it to the atmosphere of commercialized pleasure in dance halls. She did not disapprove of dancing itself, however. On the contrary, she frequently defended young people's desire to dance. "Dancing is natural to young people," she wrote in 1915. "They love music and the rhythm of music." A member of her advisory board agreed: "It is just as natural for a girl to want to dance as for a bird to sing." On one occasion, Gilbert helped to defeat the passage of a city ordinance barring people under eighteen from commercial dance "academies." (At that time, the owners of dance halls could circumvent local laws regarding minors by offering dancing lessons and thereby earn the right to call their establishments dance "academies.") "Restrict the young people from . . . dance places, and they will dance anyway. . . . They will stage clandestine 'parties' in cottages and barns, in fact, [in] any place in which they can dance if they are absolutely restricted," she argued. Her views directly contradicted those of Martha Law, the president of the Los Angeles branch of the WCTU. In a long speech in council chambers, Law pleaded for the passage of the ordinance and denounced modern dance steps as "obscene" and as "dangerous as fire."[77] Whereas Law's actions reveal her wish to eradicate the emerging ethic of sexual liberalism (symbolized in modern dance steps), Gilbert acknowledged both the futility and the potential harm of Law's approach. Through the municipal dances, Gilbert sought to modify and supervise the new sexual ethic, at least insofar as the ethic was manifested on a public dance floor.

The first municipal dance took place in a rented hall in downtown Los Angeles on February 19, 1915. More than one thousand people attended, which so thrilled Gilbert and her advisors that they decided to hold a dance every Saturday night. With her typical love of publicity, Gilbert discussed her ideas with a newspaper reporter. "If dances are conducted in the proper way, and well chaperoned," she declared, "they make a wholesome form of amusement for young people, and it is in this proper way, with refined surroundings and the spirit of 'home' that we are going to conduct our municipal dances."[78] She used the same adjectives—proper, wholesome, refined—repeatedly in 1915 whenever she publicly discussed municipal dances. Her use of these particular adjectives demonstrates her interest in making the dances completely respectable middle-class events and in assuaging any possible concerns about their propriety. Gilbert and her advisors acknowledged and addressed at least one of these concerns before the first municipal dance by promising that they would perform all necessary introductions between strangers. The huge attendance at the dance, however, must have made it impossible for them to keep their promise. Nor could they have kept it at subsequent dances, which attracted as many as fifteen hundred.

To help ensure that young working-class women would attend every dance, Gilbert went to the biggest local employers of women, the telephone company and downtown stores, to drum up interest. At each place of employment, she asked young female workers if they liked to dance; when, as expected, they said yes, she asked one of their number to organize them into a club to attend the next dance as a group.[79] Gilbert was careful, however, not to leave the impression that municipal dances were only for the working class. On the eve of the first dance she declared, "Our municipal dances [are] the kind that every young person of every class will be delighted to attend. Our dances are not for the working and business girls alone. Many school girls have signified their intention of attending."[80] Gilbert also told newspapers to stress the idea that evening dress was optional, and that people could wear "the clothes most convenient to them."[81]

After the first two or three dances, Gilbert and her supporters began to schedule special activities to take place during the dance, including card parties, prizes for the best dancers, and a grand march headed by Gilbert herself. They soon received complaints from teenagers and young adults who claimed that all they wanted was a chance to dance. Gilbert quickly dropped most of the extra activities, but she did not agree to everything young people wanted in order to keep them coming to the dances.[82] She banned dancing cheek-to-cheek, for example, asserting that "dancers may be able to steady themselves better during the dizzy whirls by leaning against each other's cheeks, as they claim, but just the same they ought to learn how to stand up." She also disapproved of the "bunny hop" and "shimmy," presumably on the grounds that they were sexually suggestive, or in the language of the day, "tough." Yet she did not go so far as to forbid popular dances. Instead, she hired women instructors to attend municipal dances and teach the "proper" way to perform the latest steps.[83] This assignment must have proved difficult, because nearly all the popular "tough" dance styles—the chicken glide, the grizzly bear, and the humpback rag, to name a few—required close bodily contact and repetitive pelvic motions.[84] Dance instructors who held their pupils at arms' length while performing these dances, or who drastically changed the movements, were not teaching the latest dance steps, they were modifying them to suit an older middle-class generation's standards of "respectable" conduct.

City Mother's municipal dances were not unique. In cities across the nation, social work agencies, private protective associations, and settlement houses sponsored public dances specifically for working-class youth. Like Gilbert, some of the sponsors hired instructors to teach young people the "proper" way to dance. Occasionally, sponsors put so many restrictions on dancing and music that few young people bothered to attend. These public dances were simply too sedate for teenagers' taste. At other times, sponsors failed to enforce their codes of behavior, so their dances became as rowdy as those at rough commercial dance halls. In Los Angeles, City Mother's municipal dances avoided both extremes. Gilbert's acceptance of ragtime music and tolerance of tame versions of popular dance steps made City Mother's municipal dances sufficiently attractive to young people, while the presence of policemen (occasionally even the chief of police himself) kept them from resembling evenings spent at Solomon's.[85]

City Mother's municipal dances remained popular throughout World War I. In a brilliant promotional move, Gilbert helped bolster dance attendance by arranging for the presence of stage and screen stars, such as Lillian Gish and Lily Langtry. A typical announcement for an upcoming dance listed thirty-eight movie stars who planned to attend and proclaimed that at the dance one "may meet and dance with one's favorite film beauty or hero."[86] What adolescent girl or young woman could resist attending this dance, especially if she was one of the thousands of starstruck hopefuls who migrated to southern California in the 1910s to try their luck in the burgeoning motion picture industry?[87] Far from ignoring or criticizing the popularity of motion pictures, the newest form of commercial amusement, Gilbert capitalized on the proximity of the City Mother's Bureau to Hollywood movie studios.

Sometime during the early 1920s, the bureau stopped sponsoring dances. Gilbert never publicly explained why. Cost was not a factor, because fraternal organizations usually volunteered the use of their halls and local orchestras performed at little or no charge; occasionally the police band provided the music. During the 1910s, the dances had brought in a small profit that went into the bureau's emergency fund for destitute clients. Yet when the bureau ceased its sponsorship, no other agency took its place. One likely explanation for the discontinuance of the dances lies in the gradual acceptance of commercial dance halls by the middle class in the 1920s. According to Russel B. Nye, most Americans by 1930 viewed the dance hall as a "desirable and useful social institution."[88] Attendance at City Mother's municipal dances probably dropped off as tolerance of commercial dance halls and cabarets grew. Ironically, City Mother's municipal dances helped to nourish the growth of this tolerance in Los Angeles. By sponsoring public dances, Gilbert implicitly acknowledged their intrinsic appeal and helped to make them respectable.

City Mother's municipal dances epitomize the goals and methods of pioneer policewomen's idealized approach to crime prevention. Rather than support attempts to bar minors from dance academies, Gilbert offered young people a genteel alternative. Her idea worked, but by the early 1920s, the dances had outlived their purpose. As Gilbert herself understood and intended, municipal dances bridged a gap in Los Angeles between the working-class commercial dance hall and the "unattainable" society dance of the elite. Gilbert could not have foreseen that this gap would gradually disappear as cabarets and other forms of commercial amusement gained middle-class approval and patronage in the late 1910s and 1920s, but in the mid-1910s she understood that nineteenth-century middle-class patterns of courtship and ideals of public behavior had disappeared. Through the municipal dances she had tried to accommodate, and not simply repress, the emerging sexual order.

The Changing Role of the City Mother, 1923–29

Although Gilbert greatly missed municipal dances and occasionally spoke of her desire to bring them back, in the mid-1920s the primary focus of her work began to shift away from "wayward girls" to cases of marital discord. The LAPD *Annual Reports* provide a rough guide to this change. For example, 24 percent of the cases opened by the bureau between July 1, 1916, and June 30, 1917, fell under the category "In Danger" (281 of 1,158 cases). This percentage gradually rose over the next few years to peak at 33 in 1921–22 (351 of 1,074 cases), and then it began to drop. During the period from July 1925 through June 1927, which covers the last years the LAPD published separate statistics for the bureau, the percentage of "In Danger" cases declined to under 17 (270 of 1,647 cases in 1925–26, and 292 of 1,742 cases in 1926–27).[89] Meanwhile, the percentage of marital discord cases steadily climbed. Between 1916 and 1921, the percentage of "Domestic Relations" cases hovered between 10 and 13, but by 1925–26, these cases composed nearly 24 percent of the bureau's workload (390 of 1,647 cases).[90]

Interviews and speeches Gilbert gave in the mid- and late 1920s help to document the changed nature of her caseload. She stopped writing instructive anecdotes about "wayward girls" and began writing stories about quarreling husbands and wives; she was no longer "saving girls," she was saving marriages. She even began to refer to the bureau as a "Domestic Relations Court," no longer mentioning, even in the most general terms, the sexual dangers of the urban environment. But Gilbert never lost her focus on preventing crime. Whenever she talked about her work in saving marriages, she mentioned that most juvenile delinquents came from "broken homes."

By locating the cause of juvenile delinquency in individual homes, rather than in the urban environment, Gilbert followed the trend in social policy during the 1920s, which increasingly discouraged broad-based reform. Moreover, her silence about sexual dangers in Los Angeles spared her the wrath of police and city officials at a time when, as Joseph Gerald Woods has documented, police and city officials were more deeply and more flagrantly involved than ever in commercial vice operations.[91] And so in her speeches and interviews, Gilbert avoided discussing the sexual dangers of the urban environment and instead gave married people tips on how to stay happily married. She also bragged about the number of marriages the bureau saved from divorce every year. Newspapers published her tips and the statistics about "saved marriages" without mentioning that Gilbert had divorced her own husband many years earlier.

In 1928, Gilbert made a remark that demonstrates how much her perception of her work had changed over the years. In an interview with a local journalist she boasted that over the preceding several years, "just as many husbands as wives" came to her for advice on how to avoid a divorce. Although no statistics survive to corroborate her claim, the case record summary for July 1927 reveals that one-third of the marital discord cases opened that month were initiated by men (thirteen of thirty-eight).[92] The image of the bureau as a counseling agency for troubled mothers and "wayward" daughters was fading fast.

The "revolution in morals and manners" of the 1920s helps to account for the dwindling number of "In Danger" cases during that decade. In urban areas especially, behavior once deemed a sure sign of female immorality, such as smoking cigarettes, wearing cosmetics, and dancing erotically, became accepted and commonplace.[93] Yet the advent of middle-class sexual liberalism does not completely account for the decrease in "In Danger" cases, because social taboos against premarital heterosexual relations remained strong. Elaine Tyler May has speculated that Americans' preoccupation with adolescent virginity may have even increased during the 1920s because young women's self-consciously sexy clothing and behavior made it more difficult than ever for Americans to determine whether an individual young woman was "chaste."[94] Moreover, the double standard of morality continued to prevail, so the social stigma and economic hardships attaching to unwed motherhood did not diminish. The decrease in the number of "In Danger" cases therefore does not signify an easy acceptance by the public or by parents of teenage girls' premarital sexual activity. Nor does the decrease reflect a lower level of premarital sexual activity. On the contrary, studies of sexual behavior undertaken in the 1950s reveal that the incidence of premarital intercourse increased significantly during the 1920s among middle-class girls and young women.[95] Why, then, did the percentage of "In Danger" cases decline so precipitously?

A definitive answer to this question is elusive for two reasons: the large number of social and cultural factors involved and the destruction of the bureau's internal records. Part of the answer, however, may lie in administrative changes in the LAPD. In August 1923, America's most well-known police chief, August Vollmer of Berkeley, California, went to Los Angeles to head the LAPD. During his one-year tenure as chief, he made many sweeping structural changes, including forming a new unit known as the Crime Prevention Division.[96] The Crime Prevention Division encompassed the City Mother's Bureau, the Juvenile Bureau, the Men's and Women's Parole Boards, and the Women's Probation Bureau. Although the City Mother's Bureau was administratively part of the new unit, Gilbert retained the separate physical location of the bureau and kept control of the bureau's records. She received orders, however, to refer all "criminal actions" involving juveniles to the Juvenile Bureau. This order meant that some cases formerly handled by the bureau as "In Danger" cases now went straight to the Juvenile Bureau. For example, if parents of an underaged daughter complained to Gilbert that their daughter was having premarital relations, then in theory Gilbert had to turn over the case to the Juvenile Bureau because the case involved an allegation of statutory rape. In practice, she did not always do so, as the case of fourteen-year-old Celeste Walker documents. In theory, Gilbert also had to refer to juvenile officers all cases involving the crimes of abortion and attempting abortion, contributing to the delinquency (or dependency) of a minor child, transporting a female across state lines for immoral purposes, "offering an immoral use of a vehicle or public lodging place" (a city ordinance), and rape. Even though Gilbert did not make all the referrals she was supposed to make, she probably did not completely ignore the new order. As a result, the order must have had an impact on the number and percentage of "In Danger" cases.[97]

The rise in the percentage of domestic relations cases during the mid-1920s is easier to explain than the concurrent decline in the percentage of "In Danger" cases. Between 1900 and 1930, the national divorce rate more than doubled, rising from 0.7 per thousand marriages in 1900 to 1.6 per thousand in 1930.[98] Historians have speculated that the rise in the divorce rate reflects changes in expectations about marital life. According to both contemporaries and historians, traditional ideas about marriage, emphasizing duties, shared sacrifices, and spiritual union, gave way in the 1910s and 1920s to new ideas that emphasized romance, emotional compatibility, and sexual pleasure.[99] The new expectations often led to disappointment and frustration, and in Los Angeles, helped to drive up the percentage of domestic relations cases handled by Gilbert and her staff. In addition, Gilbert probably referred relatively few unhappily married people to other units in the LAPD because, unlike "In Danger" cases, most marital discord cases did not involve the kind of criminal activity the police investigated.

Gilbert retired in 1929 at the age of fifty-nine because of a disabling injury to her knees. She died two years later in an automobile accident.[100] Her career as City Mother illustrates some of the achievements, frustrations, and defeats of pioneer policewomen. From the point of view of pioneer policewomen, Gilbert's finest achievement was probably her success in grafting the goals and methods of social work onto the LAPD; in fact, once she became City Mother she made extremely few, if any, arrests. In this respect, the City Mother's Bureau was unusual among separate policewomen's bureaus. In most cities with separate bureaus, such as Wichita, Washington, D.C., and Portland, Oregon, policewomen assigned to the bureaus routinely made arrests and filed petitions in juvenile court. In some cities, policewomen's bureaus even sent officers out on patrol. For example, Dorothy Henry, the head of the Cleveland Woman's Bureau, reported in 1928 that during the preceding year her officers had handled 373 cases that originated from their patrol duty.[101] But even though the women officers of other policewomen's bureaus made arrests, many of them shared Gilbert's views of policewomen's work. As Henry remarked, "Most of our work is preventive, keeping the girls out of courts."[102]

Gilbert achieved many social reforms in Los Angeles. She spearheaded the drive to have a woman judge hear the cases of girls and young women in juvenile court, and she organized the campaign for the establishment of the Women's Court. In 1919, she established a low-cost public day nursery for the children of working mothers. With funds raised by Gilbert and her board of advisors, the Municipal Day Nursery provided two nurses for the daily care of forty-five children. According to one source, the Municipal Day Nursery still existed in 1928.[103] Gilbert also played an instrumental role in the passage of several city ordinances, including the ordinance requiring jitney buses to carry a light over rear seats.

Still, Gilbert encountered many obstacles in her attempts to prevent crime and eradicate immorality. Over the years, she became very familiar with the limits of women's power to establish female moral authority in Los Angeles. Moreover, she learned that the boundaries of women's power did not remain static.

While Charles Sebastian was chief of police, women police and their supporters in moral reform had a strong ally. Shortly after Sebastian became mayor, however, he was shown to have feet of clay, and policewomen lost their champion.

Changing circumstances also adversely affected the heart of Gilbert's work with "wayward" girls. Despite her sustained attempts to "save girls" from the perceived hazards of premarital sex and male sexual license, the percentage of female youth who engaged in premarital sex rose during the 1920s. Yet even as Gilbert struggled to keep teenage girls and young women from going before the juvenile court on the charge of sex delinquency, other Los Angeles pioneer policewomen during the 1910s and 1920s were arresting female youth for sex delinquency and filing petitions on their behalf in juvenile court. To understand how these policewomen tried to reconcile their power of arrest with their promise to protect we turn to an examination of their work in the LAPD Juvenile Bureau.

CHAPTER FOUR

Double Lives: Policewomen of the LAPD Juvenile Bureau

In *My Double Life,* pioneer policewoman Mary Sullivan of the New York Police Department describes at length her exploits as an undercover detective on the Homicide and Bunco Squads. Throughout the 1910s and 1920s she spent days, and occasionally weeks, posing as a gangster's wife, a "greenhorn" immigrant, a habitué of speakeasies, or a representative of the Board of Health. She left no doubt that she took great delight in this kind of work: "I've found few things in the world more thrilling than the moment of revealing myself to a trapped and startled crook as a woman detective."[1] Her series of impersonations formed the basis of her claim that she led a "double life." But all pioneer policewomen could have made the same claim, whether, like Sullivan, they routinely carried out undercover investigations, or whether they spent most of their careers inspecting dance halls and handling female juvenile cases. Scorned by most policemen, who believed that no woman could perform "real" police work, pioneer policewomen shared a work identity layered with dualities more demanding and subtle than those required by undercover detective work. These dualities required pioneer policewomen to reconcile their state power to make arrests with their deep conviction that the judicious use of social casework methods was the best means to prevent crime and reduce immorality, particularly among young people. Pioneer policewomen accordingly spoke the language of protection instead of coercion, wore tailored dresses instead of regulation trousers and shirts, and hid their badges of authority in their handbags instead of pinning them to their chests. Called "women policemen" by the press, they were female social workers in what everyone agreed was the male world of law enforcement. Through their attempts to weave together the competing claims of their dual identity, pioneer policewomen invented their own jobs in police departments by using maternalist principles as a guide. In so doing, many of them carved out a rewarding professional niche for themselves, but they never fully shed the burdens of living a double life.

This chapter explores the double lives of pioneer policewomen in the Los Angeles Police Department (LAPD) Juvenile Bureau by examining the intertwining themes of discipline and protection in their work and work identity. Discipline refers broadly to pioneer policewomen's use of state power to make arrests, for although they stoutly rejected some authoritarian aspects of police work, such as wearing uniforms, they routinely used state power in coercive ways, just as policemen did. Protection refers broadly to pioneer policewomen's belief that they could prevent crime and lessen the sexual vulnerability of women and girls through the noncoercive methods of social casework. To examine how discipline and protection simultaneously shaped Los Angeles policewomen's work and work identity, this chapter draws primarily on two rich sources of information, the *Annual Reports* of the LAPD and the case files of the Los Angeles County Juvenile Court from the 1910s and 1920s. When analyzed together, the statistical data from the *Annual Reports* and selected case histories from the juvenile court show the kinds of juvenile cases pioneer policewomen most frequently handled, and the factors that influenced them to make an arrest or file a petition in juvenile court.

The chapter begins with an overview of policewomen's work as juvenile officers during the 1910s, showing how gender and the sexual division of labor restricted their range of action. It then traces dynamics of gender, class, race, family, and culture in female sex delinquency cases. Sex delinquency cases encompass the themes of discipline and protection more fully than other types of cases because the women officers of the Juvenile Bureau often "protected" a teenage girl by arresting her for sex delinquency. In fact, the charge of sex delinquency accounted for between 21 percent and 40 percent of all female juvenile arrests by the LAPD between 1926 and 1940. The chapter concludes with a discussion of how some women officers of the LAPD carried their role as social worker and police officer into their personal lives.

Sexual Division of Labor and Sexual Politics

The Juvenile Bureau of the LAPD came into existence in 1909, an unexceptional year in the turbulent political history of Progressive Era Los Angeles. In March, a local newspaper demanded and received the resignation of Mayor Arthur Harper, who was subsequently indicted for official malfeasance along with the chief of police, a former chief, and a former police commissioner. While in office, each of these men had enjoyed a lucrative relationship with vice operators. As Joseph Gerald Woods has pointed out, they "made a profitable enterprise of the gaming, whoring, and drinking establishments located in the tenderloin until the inevitable expose blackened their reputations and drove them from office."[2] Once the mayor resigned, the leaders of the Good Government League threw themselves into preparations for new municipal elections. The first election, held in April, chose a provisional mayor to serve in the interval before the second, regular elections were held in December. The issue of vice and its control dominated the political campaigns of both elections. Reform sentiment swirled around the city for months, finally culminating in the election of Good Government candidates to all city offices in December.[3]

Aletha Gilbert, chief matron of the Women's Jail, and Patrolman Leo W. Marden capitalized on the prevailing spirit of moral reform by proposing that a new unit be added to the LAPD to handle the cases of juveniles. Like moral reformers in other U.S. cities during the Progressive Era, Gilbert and Marden linked the issue of juvenile delinquency to the larger issue of vice and its control by arguing that exposure to vice influenced children and young teenagers to take up lives of immorality and crime. Moral reformers especially railed against the presence of unchaperoned children and young teenagers in saloons, cabarets, dance halls, movie theaters, and penny arcades, charging that these kinds of popular establishments were the favorite haunts of gamblers, prostitutes, white slavers, and other purveyors of vice. Studies of urban life lent some credence to reformers' views. In 1899, for example, W.E.B. DuBois reported that many prostitutes frequented dance halls in Philadelphia, and in the 1910s and 1920s, the Juvenile Protective Association of Chicago, headed by the ever-vigilant Louise DeKoven Bowen, documented hundreds of illegal acts in and around commercial places of amusement.[4]

During 1909, the twin issues of vice and juvenile delinquency in Los Angeles impelled women activists and their male allies in moral reform to organize and incorporate the Juvenile Protective Association, supplanting an unofficial organization that had existed for several years. Like its counterpart in Chicago, the Los Angeles Juvenile Protective Association zealously investigated dance halls, saloons, penny arcades, cafes, and movie houses, gathering evidence to use in lobbying for ordinances to govern the admittance of children. The association also pressured the police to enforce laws regarding curfew and the sale of salacious literature to children. The chief of the LAPD from April 1909 to January 1910, Edward Dishman, did not sympathize with the aims of the association. Like his predecessors at the LAPD, Dishman was not a reformer at heart, and he had no intention of interfering with commercialized amusements or shutting down vice operations (he once called opponents of segregated districts "fanatics"). But shortly before newly elected city officials fired him in January 1910, Dishman threw a sop to moral reformers by granting Gilbert and Marden's request for a Juvenile Bureau.[5]

No policewomen served on the LAPD in 1909, and so Marden took the title of Juvenile Officer. During his first year, he worked alone most of the time, although he occasionally called on Gilbert for help in handling cases of rape and other crimes involving girls and young women. In September 1910, he acquired a full-time assistant, newly hired Alice Stebbins Wells. According to Wells, Chief Alexander Galloway called her into his office on her first day of work and frankly told her he did not know how to use a woman officer. He then gave her the kit all rookies received—a badge, a book on first aid, a Gamewell patrol box key, and a book of rules—and assigned her to work with Marden. She remained in the Juvenile Bureau for most of her thirty-year career with the LAPD.[6]

By mid-1914, five officers were serving under Marden's command: Wells, Aletha Gilbert, Anna Hamm, Rachel Shatto, and Nell Tarbell. (Until the winter of 1915–16, Marden was the only man to work in the Juvenile Bureau.) In autumn 1914, Tarbell resigned from the LAPD, and Gilbert left the Juvenile Bureau to head the newly formed City Mother's Bureau, taking her half-sister, police-woman Lorel Boyles, with her. Boyles had joined the LAPD in November 1913 as a "Temporary Policewoman." In her case, "temporary" meant pending approval of funding for her position, which she received. A few other women officers came and went as members of the Juvenile Bureau throughout the early 1910s, but their number never exceeded six.[7]

Policewomen assigned to the LAPD Juvenile Bureau had four major duties in the early 1910s: to handle incoming complaints from or about female juveniles (girls and young women under the age of twenty-one) and boys under the age of eight; to carry out investigations and arrests of female witnesses, suspects, and victims of crime, both juveniles and adults; to inspect commercial places of amusement for signs of immorality and crime; and to escort home female youths they found in public and who they believed were in moral or physical danger. Outlining these duties in a 1914 report, Marden pointed out that because there was always a trained woman on desk duty, the bureau was able to "get reports of sexual crimes from women who would otherwise fail to report the same if they were obliged to detail the facts to a male officer." In addition, policewomen were doing "valuable work in the prevention of delinquency among young girls" through their inspections of public amusement places, "particularly in the late af-ternoon and night hours," through their "escorting [home] those who, by their conduct . . . are in danger of becoming delinquent," and through their "making reports to . . . parents with a proper warning."[8]

As Marden's report implies, the policewomen of the Juvenile Bureau primar-ily acted as agents of sexual regulation, a role they undertook with great enthusi-asm. "The policewoman, by patrolling the streets, has prevented many a tragedy to girlhood," boasted Nell Tarbell of the Juvenile Bureau in 1914.[9] By "tragedy," Tarbell alluded not only to the loss of sexual innocence and unwed motherhood but also to syphilis and gonorrhea, which were not uncommon among sexually ac-tive female youth during the early twentieth century. In 1920, 53 percent of the fe-male youths facing charges of sexual delinquency or "morally suspect behavior" in the Los Angeles County Juvenile Court tested positive for venereal disease.[10]

In 1913, Lorel Boyles bragged that policewomen's powers of persuasion had kept many teenage girls and young women chaste: "The motherly talk of the po-licewoman has put many a girl right. Encouragement, not humiliation, has been salutary."[11] The same year, while discussing adult men who "pick up" teenage girls, Aletha Gilbert expressed her desire to see "the squad of policewomen grow into an army of protection for the girl and the home."[12] The phrase "army of protection" captures the dual occupational impulses underlying pioneer police-women's work with female youth. Whereas "protection" brings to mind the empathetic image of the motherly social worker, "army" connotes the disciplinary and coercive aspects of state surveillance and control. The pioneer policewomen of the Juvenile Bureau used both of these approaches in their role as regulatory agents.[13]

In Los Angeles and elsewhere, pioneer policewomen's regulatory role did not affect all female youth equally; as arrest records and juvenile court records document, working-class female youth bore the brunt of policewomen's efforts to oversee and direct morality. The class dynamics underlying pioneer police-women's work had at least four sources: policewomen's class bias, the behavior of working-class female youth, the attitudes and actions of working-class parents, and the attitudes and actions of middle-class parents.

Pioneer policewomen's class bias reveals itself most clearly in their nearly constant search for ways to give moral instruction and "uplift" to working-class girls and young women. In a joint statement issued in 1914, the women officers of the Juvenile Bureau proclaimed that in their daily work with teenage girls, they always "emphasized the joy of right living and right thinking, and explained away the folly of the so-called good time that girls seek in cafes and dance halls."[14] Some of Aletha Gilbert's actions as City Mother, such as her establishment of the municipal dances, vividly illustrate pioneer policewomen's efforts to show working-class female youth the "joy of right living and right thinking."

Policewomen's class bias also shows in their belief that premarital sex posed more hazards to working-class teenage girls than to middle-class teenage girls. Policewomen thought that few working-class female youths could make enough money in lawful ways to survive, and they reasoned that once these girls lost their moral bearings through the practice of "treating" (accepting gifts in exchange for sexual favors) or through premarital sex with boyfriends, not much stood in the way of their eventually becoming prostitutes. "When a girl goes wrong, there is not much hope," Los Angeles policewoman Anna Hamm remarked sorrowfully in 1914.[15] In an interview with a journalist, Aletha Gilbert linked prostitution to low wages paid to women in industry and retail establishments. According to Gilbert, prostitutes began their lives of vice when "they found out, about two-thirds of them, that they could not make enough money under the present system to live honestly, then they lost heart, and began to slip down." To help solve this problem, Gilbert proposed vocational training for working-class girls: "A girl who realizes a life of useful labor awaits her . . . should be allowed to choose her occupation and then be trained to fill her chosen place." Gilbert chastised parents who did not arrange for their daughters to receive industrial training but instead made them into "kitchen drudges." "Housework is a splendid avocation, but a poor ultimate vocation," she averred.[16]

Many moral reformers and social workers held similar views about the desirability of vocational training for working-class girls, claiming that once an untrained poor girl strayed from the straight and narrow path, she unknowingly began a tragic journey down the "Road to Destruction." In 1913, Robert A. Woods and Albert J. Kennedy of the National Federation of Settlements took working-class parents to task for failing to train their daughters properly. "Little effort is made to prepare the daughter for the opportunities and dangers of her work in life," they observed.[17]

The behavior of working-class female youth undoubtedly played a key role in making them the primary focus of pioneer policewomen's attention. In general, working-class teenage girls rebelled against the moral codes of their parents and the middle class more flagrantly than did other teenage girls. In the vanguard of the reinvention of female adolescence in the late nineteenth century, working-class female youth grabbed the headlines of the revolution in sexual culture. Their behavior remained a focal point of middle-class moral reform for years. Not until the late 1920s did the "modern" idea that it was "natural" for a teenage girl to exhibit sexual feelings and enjoy some social autonomy take root in the middle class.[18]

Working-class parents responded to their daughters' rebellion with alarm, anger, and in some cases, harsh measures. Ruth Alexander has theorized that working-class parents probably opposed daughters' rebellion more than middle-class parents did because by the early twentieth century, middle-class families had a more child-centered, democratic structure than did working-class families.[19] Working-class parents' anger toward their daughters often prompted them to seek the help of the police in asserting control; by so doing, they helped to establish policewomen as regulatory agents of female sexuality. Parents' willingness in this regard has roots in the traditional social-welfare role of the police. In the Progressive Era, pioneer policewomen strengthened this tradition by proclaiming themselves ready to provide parents with a new social welfare service: help in controlling the sexual rebellion of female youth. Boyles's boast that the "motherly talk of the policewoman has put many a girl right" must have had enormous appeal to many worried parents in Los Angeles. (A detailed discussion of working-class parents' requests for police assistance during the 1910s and 1920s comes later in this chapter.)

Class bias on the part of parents toward the police also shaped the work of pioneer policewomen. In general, the actions of working-class parents show that they had respect for the police as problem-solvers. They may sometimes have approached the police with trepidation, but by going voluntarily to police stations during times of domestic crisis, they demonstrated their regard for the police as a source of expert help in resolving familial tensions. In contrast, the middle class as a whole felt disdain for police officers, viewing them as their social inferiors. The presence of some middle-class women in police work did virtually nothing to change this

Mrs. Alice Stebbins Wells

LOS ANGELES, CALIFORNIA

PIONEER POLICEWOMAN

Lecturer on Social Questions

TOPICS:
The Need of Police Women and Their Work
Modern Reformatory Methods and Institutions
Equal Suffrage from a Policewoman's Standpoint
Vocational Training as a Crime Preventative
The Teaching of Social Hygiene

Cover of promotional pamphlet, 1911. *Courtesy of Raymond Wells.*

Aletha Gilbert,
LAPD assistant jail matron, circa 1900.
*Courtesy of George
and Helene Staininger.*

Alice Stebbins Wells,
LAPD policewoman, circa 1910.
Courtesy of Raymond Wells.

Lucy Uthera Gray,
LAPD jail matron, circa 1890.
*Courtesy of George and
Helene Staininger.*

Alice	Anna	Aletha	Rachel	Elizabeth	Lorel	Loretta	Lillian	Leo
Stebbins	Hamm	Gilbert	Shatto	Feeley	Boyles	McPeek	Toomey	Marden
Wells								

LAPD Juvenile Bureau, 1914.
Courtesy of George and Helene Staininger.

LAPD City Mother's Advisory Board, 1914. City Mother Aletha Gilbert
seated third from right. *Courtesy of George and Helene Staininger.*

Unidentified LAPD officers in the community, circa 1945.
Courtesy of the LAPD Historical Society.

Georgia Ann Robinson, LAPD
policewoman, circa 1920.
*Courtesy of the LAPD Historical
Society.*

sentiment in the early twentieth century, for it lingers still.[20] Consequently, few middle-class parents who felt the need for expert advice during the 1910s and 1920s asked the police for help in controlling their daughter's sexuality. Instead, they took advantage of the growing number of child specialists, such as psychiatrists, psychologists, mental hygienists, and psychiatric social workers. Their antipathy toward the police meant that pioneer policewomen's caseload came predominantly from the working class.[21]

Although important, class bias and generational tensions do not explain all the dynamics of pioneer policewomen's work; gender, race, and culture also played important roles. Accordingly, the discussion now turns to an analysis of how sexual politics in Progressive Era Los Angeles shaped the duties of policewomen in the Juvenile Bureau, and how race, racism, gender, and cultural traditions simultaneously influenced the cases they handled.

On the surface, policewomen's focus on female sexuality indicates a lack of interest in controlling male sexuality and ending the double sexual standard. Many of pioneer policewomen's public remarks support this superficial interpretation. In 1914, LAPD women officers began a joint statement describing their work with the words, "Prevented girls and young women from entering lives of shame."[22] There is no mention of boys and young men. Certainly, pioneer policewomen had their reasons for being preoccupied with adolescent female sexuality; they thought that premarital sex posed more hazards to women than to men and that premarital sex weakened women's collective position with regard to men. But close attention to their statements reveals that pioneer policewomen in Los Angeles repeatedly asserted a zealous interest in controlling "lustful men." In her speeches across the nation in the early 1910s, for example, Alice Stebbins Wells frequently railed against the sexual double standard, lamenting the fact that "from time immemorial," society had always "dragged the woman before the bar of justice" for sexual misconduct, but never the man. "The men must be made to bear their share of the responsibility," she told the members of the City Club of Chicago in 1912.[23] Similarly, in 1914, Anna Hamm of the LAPD urged teenage girls and their parents to report sex crimes, for "it is only by bringing offenders against girls and women to the bar of justice that . . . the practice may be checked."[24]

While Wells and Hamm spoke in generalities about the need to prosecute men for sexual misconduct, Aletha Gilbert discussed specifics. In a lengthy interview she gave in 1913, a year before she became City Mother, she describes Los Angeles policewomen's attempts to regulate male sexuality. Her remarks provide a glimpse into the battles waged over state control of sexuality in Los Angeles during the Progressive Era.

Gilbert's interview with journalist Estelle Lawton Lindsey initially focuses on changes taking place in policewomen's patrol assignments. "From now on,"

Gilbert explains, "we shall have three women patrolling the streets from 3:30 [P.M.] to 11:30 [P.M.]." She lists their patrol duties as follows: to return teenage girls found loitering on street corners to their homes, to lecture the girls' parents about urban sexual dangers and parental duties, and "to report and bring to prosecution" all men who took teenage girls on "joy-rides." In this context, joy-rides were excursions in automobiles that involved illicit sex. Gilbert refers to men who took teenage girls and young women on joy-rides as "automobile mashers." She claims that policewomen frequently found automobile mashers "waiting around places where girls are compelled to work at night and inviting them to take automobile rides as they come out." She portrays these men as criminals whom she and other policewomen were determined to see "investigated and exposed." "At a recent trial in juvenile court," she asserts, "I had six of them up for contributing to the delinquency of one 15 year old girl. The shame of it."

Gilbert freely acknowledges that policewomen's investigations of male sexual misconduct were not universally approved. "Some of the business men here are becoming rather excited about all this, and many have rung me up and protested that the thing was going too far; a few, poor innocent things, complain that the girls are enticing THEM." She then hastens to say that she could not deny that sometimes teenage girls initiated episodes of joy-riding, but she holds the men responsible nevertheless, pointing out that these "mashers" were not teenage boys, but mature men.

> My quarrel with men is that they do not let the kids alone. It is an unfair contest, a mature man against a silly young girl. Suppose she does attempt to entice him? If he is a man, he then has his chance to show her the folly of her conduct; but, since he doesn't, we need policewomen to save him from temptation.

Warming to her theme, she adds, "I will guarantee you that if we follow this work up closely enough we shall find that the father of the girl we rescue from the automobile masher is out somewhere in another machine enticing some other man's child."

Gilbert concludes the interview with the suggestion to clubwomen that they should help awaken men to their social responsibilities. She urges them to "cut from their visiting list" every man found guilty of a morals offense or sex crime. "It will be comparatively easy now to know who such men are, for Mrs. Alice Stebbins Wells, Mrs. Rachel Shatto and Mrs. Nell Tarbell will be watching any little girls who are out on the streets alone in the evenings—no wonder the men think this movement is going too far."[25]

This interview can be interpreted in several ways. Historians of middle-class moral reform might point out that Gilbert revealed her class bias by infantilizing young working-class females. She calls them "little girls" and "kids" who were too "silly" to know what they were doing. By the same token, she granted adult status to the "automobile mashers," referring to them as "mature" and claiming that they were themselves the fathers of teenage daughters. In drawing these age distinctions, Gilbert followed a formula set down in nineteenth-century seduction tales, which nearly always depict a female victim of seduction as significantly younger than her male seducer.[26] What is more important, by exaggerating the youth and immaturity of working-class females, she made policewomen's intervention seem both necessary and desirable.

Other historians might argue that Gilbert's portrayal of automobile mashers as mature businessmen squares with the economics of car ownership in Los Angeles during the early 1910s. In 1913, the year Gilbert gave the interview, the least expensive new car available, the Model T Ford (Tin Lizzie), cost $550, a scant $30 less than the average annual wage of U.S. laborers in manufacturing. Most new cars cost more than twice as much. Moreover, the prices of used cars in Los Angeles did not differ greatly from those of new cars. Classified advertisements in the *Los Angeles Times* of mid-1913 reveal a range in used-car prices from approximately $300 to $3,000; most advertised used cars cost at least $400, a price few working-class teenage boys and young men could afford.[27] Moreover, Gilbert's suggestion to clubwomen that they "cut from their visiting lists" all men convicted of morals offenses and sex crimes makes it clear that she believed that clubwomen and the convicted men socialized with one another.[28]

Alternatively, historians of gender might argue that Gilbert portrayed working-class females as "kids" and automobile mashers as fathers in order to emphasize her point that the men's actions were irresponsible, immoral, and perhaps in a large societal sense, incestuous. In addition, her stress on age difference can be interpreted as an analogy for differences in power between men and women, because the hierarchy of age helps to construct and reinforce other power hierarchies, such as those of gender, class, race, and ethnicity. By suggesting that "if he is a man," the automobile masher will not give in to "temptation," Gilbert implied that true manhood is characterized by sexual self-restraint. This idea formed the nucleus of the Woman's Christian Temperance Union (WCTU) slogan "the white life for two," a call for a single sexual standard for men and women. Gilbert thus cast a slur on the manhood of all men who engaged in sexual relations outside marriage. Finally, the interview reveals that Los Angeles policewomen's investigation of male sexual misconduct posed a serious challenge to male sexual prerogatives.

These interpretations do not so much contradict each other as stress different dynamics. Interpreting pioneer policewomen's role as regulatory agents of adolescent female sexuality requires careful assessment of all these dynamics; it also requires an understanding of policewomen's relative lack of power in police departments. Pioneer policewomen were a tiny, much-despised minority within police work. Even when they had the rare fortune of having a supportive chief, they had to push hard to put any of their ideas into practice. And when their activities threatened male privilege, especially male sexual prerogatives, they invariably encountered heavy opposition.

In Los Angeles, policewomen's opponents initially had to contend with LAPD Chief Charles Sebastian, policewomen's strong ally. Sebastian had warmly endorsed and actively sought the employment of women officers during his tenure as chief in the early 1910s (see Chapter Three). He even advised other chiefs of police to follow his example. In a speech he gave in 1913 to the International Association of Chiefs of Police, he spoke enthusiastically about the movement for women police, linking it approvingly to woman suffrage.[29] Unfortunately for Los Angeles policewomen, Sebastian's successor at the LAPD, Clarence Snively, did not share Sebastian's enthusiasm for policewomen. Shortly after taking office in 1915, Snively began to assign patrolmen to the Juvenile Bureau in numbers roughly equal to those of policewomen, and in so doing, he fundamentally changed the nature of policewomen's patrol work by having male officers accompany female officers on patrol. As in other occupational partnerships between men and women during the early twentieth century, gender hierarchy decreed that policewomen take the role of the junior partner. The male-female patrol partnership was relatively short-lived, however. Sometime between the late 1910s and the mid-1920s, LAPD officials relieved policewomen of all patrol duty; neither their official reasons, nor policewomen's reactions were recorded.[30]

No explanation for Snively's decision to assign patrolmen to the Juvenile Bureau appears in the LAPD *Annual Reports*. It seems likely, however, that some of the men who complained to Gilbert about policewomen also complained to the chief. Any men who complained to Sebastian probably did not get a sympathetic hearing, and those who knew his record of support for policewomen might not have bothered. As we have seen, Sebastian promoted Gilbert from jail matron to policewoman in 1912 in response to her desire to arrest a few "miserable brutes" who were accosting young women on the streets of Los Angeles. After Snively became chief, men's complaints were probably taken more seriously. Did Snively assign patrolmen to the Juvenile Bureau because of men's complaints about policewomen? The question cannot be answered categorically. It is clear, however, that by making such assignments, Snively undermined policewomen's authority on patrol and greatly reduced the degree of interaction between policewomen and male citizens in public. Diminished authority and minimal interaction might well have meant fewer complaints from men.

Regardless of the reasons for Snively's decision, a comparison of adult arrest statistics before and after 1916 reveals that once patrolmen began working in the Juvenile Bureau, they gave men in Los Angeles little cause to complain of overzealousness. LAPD *Annual Reports* for 1913–14 and 1914–15 show sixty and seventy arrests, respectively, for "contributing to the delinquency [or dependency] of a minor." In 1916–17 and 1917–18, the first full two years in which patrolmen worked in the Juvenile Bureau, the number of arrests dropped to twenty-three in each year. Moreover, the number of arrests for the crimes of rape and seduction did not show much change from 1913–14 and 1914–15; had this number risen, it might indicate that juvenile officers charged male suspects with those crimes rather than with "contributing." In the absence of changes in the laws regarding these offenses, the arrest statistics strongly suggest a positive relationship between all-female patrol and the arrest of men for offenses involving juveniles. That is, when policewomen were permitted to patrol the streets of Los Angeles on their own, without male partners, they had a decisive impact on the number of men arrested for the crime of "contributing to the delinquency [or dependency] of a minor." Significantly, "contributing" arrests per capita in Los Angeles stayed below the levels of 1913–14 and 1914–15 during the remainder of the 1910s and 1920s.[31]

Taken together, Gilbert's interview and Snively's actions help to illuminate the constraints under which policewomen worked. In Los Angeles, as in most cities across the nation, the sexual division of labor within police departments restricted women officers to investigations of women, girls, and prepubescent boys. Furthermore, policewomen helped to foster the sexual division of labor with their claim that they could handle the cases of women and children better than policemen handled them. Yet when policewomen made this claim, they did not mean to exclude investigations and arrests of men suspected of crimes against women and children, especially sex crimes. "Arrest people?" Wells asked in a speech she gave in New York City in 1913, "Of course I do, men and women, for my work is not confined to women alone."[32] After the sexual division of labor hardened in the late 1910s, neither she nor the other women officers of the LAPD could make a similar claim.

"Girls' Department"

The assignment of male officers to juvenile detail gradually split the Juvenile Bureau into two units, known formally in the late 1920s as the "Girls' Department" and the "Boys' Department."[33] In theory, the "Girls' Department," staffed by policewomen, handled all cases (including all arrests) of female juveniles, most dependency cases, and all cases of boys under the age of eight. In practice, policemen on patrol and investigation sometimes arrested female juveniles, although after making the arrest they were supposed to turn the case over promptly to a policewoman. The "Boys' Department," staffed by policemen, handled the cases of boys over eight years old and the investigations of men suspected of crimes against juveniles.[34]

Because the LAPD has destroyed virtually all its internal records from the pre-1950 era, scant information exists about the day-to-day operations of the Juvenile Bureau during the early twentieth century.[35] Nevertheless, in its *Annual Reports*, the LAPD consistently published statistical information about juvenile cases. During the 1910s and early 1920s, the statistics covered little more than the number of male and female juveniles whom the police investigated or arrested during the previous fiscal year (July 1 to June 30). In the mid-1920s, the LAPD began to collect more detailed information about the youths under arrest or investigation, such as race and nativity.[36] Although the kind of information the LAPD published varied from year to year, overall, the statistics throw considerable light on policewomen's work in the Juvenile Bureau in Los Angeles.

At first glance, the early statistics suggest that, compared to policemen, policewomen had very few cases, because male youths came to the formal attention of the police in far greater numbers than female youths did. For example, in July 1918, Marden reported that in the previous year, the Juvenile Bureau handled the cases of 1,970 boys but only 297 girls.[37] These statistics, however, do not include the number of girls whom policewomen investigated but did not arrest and whose names were purposely kept off police records. According to policewomen, "off-the-record" cases constituted a major part of their work. In 1928, the female supervisor of the "Girls' Department" claimed that policewomen handled thousands of cases every year through "understanding and motherly sympathy" rather than through official "prosecution" and arrest. "Our province," she explained, "is to adjust the child and the domestic problem in the home and not in the courts or jails."[38]

These thousands of cases probably included instances in which a policewoman made an official record of her investigation into a complaint about an individual girl or young woman, perhaps even placed her under arrest, but did not file formal charges. Pioneer policewomen generally referred to these cases as their "social adjustment" cases. In handling social adjustment cases, pioneer policewomen usually advised adolescent girls about sexual hygiene, tried to interest them in "wholesome" organized recreation, found them "respectable" employment, talked with their parents and teachers, and made referrals to social welfare agencies. Sometimes policewomen placed female youths on police probation, an official alternative to juvenile court that required regular meetings with a policewoman. In 1930, LAPD Officer Marguerite Curley asserted that social adjustment cases formed the core of female officers' daily work: "Every one of us, every day, does the same kind of work . . . adjusting cases out of Court, advising, counselling, cheering, scolding and working in harmony with every agency that is interested in child-welfare work, including all the schools."[39]

Statistics from the LAPD *Annual Report* of 1926–27 support Curley's claim. That year, the LAPD published detailed information about the total number of female and male juveniles whom officers investigated or arrested. (In earlier years, the LAPD did not clearly distinguish between the number of juveniles arrested and the number investigated but not arrested; in subsequent years, it published information only about juveniles placed under arrest.) According to the report, the Juvenile Bureau handled the cases of 7,021 boys and 1,679 girls between July 1, 1926, and June 30, 1927. Of the 1,679 girls under investigation, policewomen arrested 945 (56 percent) on delinquency or dependency charges.[40] According to information furnished by the Juvenile Bureau on 652 of the 945 arrests (the LAPD did not keep track of the other 293 arrests), policewomen referred 171 girls to juvenile court (26 percent) but simply released 363 (56 percent) of the girls without filing any charges against them.[41] The 289 girls against whom charges were not dropped were put on police probation or were sent to a public or private institution, such as a home for unwed mothers, or were released to their homes in other cities.[42]

Unfortunately for the researcher, the LAPD failed after 1927 to publish exact figures on the number of girls whom policewomen investigated but did not arrest.[43] Instead, the *Annual Reports* occasionally mentioned in passing the approximate number of all cases handled by the Girls' Department. For example, in July 1935, Captain Edward M. Slaughter, Marden's successor as head of the Juvenile Bureau, reported that in the previous fiscal year "approximately 2500 cases involving girls under eighteen years of age, as well as small boys, were investigated by this detail." (By 1935, the Juvenile Bureau generally did not handle the cases of young women between the ages of eighteen and twenty-one.) Slaughter then pointed out that "by a careful study of the social problems, background and the environmental elements of the individual cases" policewomen were able to handle over half the cases as social adjustment cases. "It is interesting to note," he concluded, "that less than 15% of the children were filed on in Juvenile Court, successful adjustments being made without resorting to drastic measures."[44]

Decisions regarding how to handle a case rested with the individual policewoman. Analyzing these decisions is difficult, particularly in cases where no arrests were made, because of a lack of documentation. Luckily, the story of one case in which a policewoman refused to make an arrest reached Los Angeles newspapers in August 1912. It provides several clues to understanding the class, gender, family, and generational dynamics in pioneer policewomen's work.[45]

Parents, the Police, and Disobedient Daughters

Seventeen-year-old Cora Weaver, her parents, and her eight siblings moved to Los Angeles in March 1912 from Brooklyn, New York. Although Cora wanted to attend high school in Los Angeles, her father, Wilson Weaver, insisted that she go to work and turn over all her wages to the family. This was by no means a new demand, for three years earlier, he had forced Cora to drop out of school in Brooklyn. As she explained, "Before my first year [of high school] was finished, my fourteenth birthday came, and the next day I was taken from school, as in New York children over 14 may work. A job was found for me and my wages taken by my parents."

Once in Los Angeles, Cora found employment as a stenographer. Her desire to continue her education remained strong, however, and she decided to study on her own at night. She soon fell into the habit of studying after she came home from work. The hours she spent with her books greatly annoyed her father because he wanted her to spend her evenings doing housework. He demanded that she give up her studies, and when she refused, he beat her. Shortly thereafter, she packed her belongings and left home. Her independence so enraged her father that he went to the LAPD Juvenile Bureau and demanded that someone arrest his daughter for disobedience. A policewoman who talked with both Cora and her father refused to make the arrest. Undeterred, Cora's father filed a delinquency petition in juvenile court.

At the court hearing, Wilson Weaver made his position plain: "I have nothing to say against Cora except that she has a will that I am going to break. She is smart and I'm proud of her, but I intend to make her do just as I tell her. I have beaten her and threatened her. I did it to show her that I was to be minded in every event." When Cora's turn to testify came, she explained that she was trying to educate herself because she wanted to be "nearer the plane of the good man who wishes to marry me." She identified her fiancé as C. W. Jean, her former employer in New York, a well-educated, "wealthy young man." She also pointed out that although she had left home, she continued to give some of her salary to her parents to pay for her sister's music lessons. At some point during her testimony, her father jumped up and screamed, "She lies!" The judge, Curtis D. Wilbur, immediately found Weaver in contempt of court and gave him the option of paying a ten-dollar fine or spending five days in jail. Weaver did not have the money to pay. As the bailiff led Weaver away, Wilbur ruled in Cora's favor, declaring that in his opinion she was not "willful, headstrong, incorrigible, or a dependent." Nevertheless, because she was a minor, Wilbur placed her in the temporary custody of Aletha Gilbert, then a member of the Juvenile Bureau, until a foster home could be found. Gilbert probably took Cora home with her, as she had done with other female youths placed in her temporary custody by the judge.[46]

Like many other cases of female delinquency in early twentieth-century juvenile courts, Cora's case centered on the battle between a working-class parent and daughter over the daughter's use of leisure time. As historians of women have discovered, this battle took place within countless working-class families across the United States during the late nineteenth and early twentieth centuries, as daughters entered the paid labor force, gained a sense of autonomy and power, then chafed under parental constraints. Wages and housework were common areas of familial conflict. As in Cora's case, many parents demanded that their daughters turn over all wages to them and come straight home after work to do household chores. In essence, parents expected their daughters to fulfill a traditionally masculine role, that of contributing to the family income, while also continuing to fulfill a traditionally feminine role, that of doing housework. Pioneer policewomen's sympathy often lay with the daughters, perhaps because they were working women themselves. As New York pioneer policewoman Mary Sullivan observed,

> A girl is expected to bring home every cent of her earnings and spend her evenings doing housework, without an hour of time for herself. If she rebels, the family wants to wash its hands of her and have her put in a corrective institution. They often have no sympathy for a girl's desire to better herself.[47]

As Sullivan's remarks show, neither Cora's ambition "to better herself" nor her father's reaction was unusual. In going first to the police, and then to the juvenile court, Cora's father followed the example set by countless other parents who looked to the state to enforce their flagging authority over their rebellious children. According to one study, family members initiated nearly half (47 percent) of the petitions for delinquency filed in 1920 on behalf of female youths in the Los Angeles County Juvenile Court. Most of the family members were parents.[48] Prior to filing a petition in juvenile court themselves, or asking the police to do so, many parents in Los Angeles brought their daughters into police stations or the City Mother's Bureau to be questioned or lectured.

Cora's case differs from the typical juvenile court case of female delinquency in one important respect: the absence of any allegations of immorality. In 1920, 81 percent of the 218 delinquency petitions filed on behalf of female youths in Los Angeles involved charges of "intercourse or suspected intercourse" or "morally suspect behavior."[49] Both the public and the authorities labeled these girls and young women "sex delinquents." In fact, insofar as the general public was concerned, all adolescent girls and young women who appeared before the juvenile court were sex delinquents. Indeed, during the early twentieth century, the association of female delinquency with sex delinquency was so strong that the female activist community in Los Angeles took steps in the mid-1910s to safeguard the reputations of girls and young women in court. Specifically, women activists decided that since the public stigmatized all girls and young women who appeared before the court as immoral, female juvenile cases should be heard in a hearing room far from the public eye, so that only the people directly involved with a particular case would see a girl or young woman enter or leave the hearing room. Women activists therefore advocated the establishment of a separate, isolated hearing room for female juveniles.

Court authorities agreed with their reasoning, and by 1920, all hearings in female juvenile cases took place in the juvenile detention home, located a short distance from downtown. The cases of teenage boys continued to be heard in the downtown Hall of Justice.[50]

The lack of any accusations of sexual misconduct in Cora's case explains why the policewoman refused to arrest her. This refusal, together with the judge's decision, signifies approval of Cora's goal of upward social mobility and her method of achieving it. The image of Cora poring over books at night after a long day at work resembled a scene from a Horatio Alger rags-to-riches story, an image rich in positive connotations for many middle-class Americans. Because of Cora's sex, however, a standard variation of the story applied: upward social mobility through marriage, rather than through business enterprise. Yet even if Cora had had no immediate plans for marriage, the fact remained that she spent her leisure time studying, and that is what largely determined the outcome of her case. This use of leisure time greatly appealed to the middle-class sensibilities of the policewoman and judge because it showed that she had internalized middle-class values. Nevertheless, Cora's father saw only that she was being disobedient. Her actions made it clear to him that she rejected his claim to patriarchal authority.

Wilson Weaver undoubtedly felt betrayed by the criminal justice system: by the policewoman who refused to arrest his daughter, and by the judge who sent him to jail for contempt of court, then ruled in his daughter's favor. Weaver must have thought the world had gone out of whack. But Weaver's inability to bend the police and the juvenile court to his desires and point of view typified the experiences of many people who sought the help of public or private agencies in resolving domestic problems. Parents who asked the Los Angeles City Mother's Bureau for help with their daughters, for example, did not always get the kind of help they wanted.[51]

Culture, Class, Race, and Family in Female Sex Delinquency Cases

Many parents initially went to the LAPD Juvenile Bureau because they wanted the police to reinforce parental authority over daughters' social lives and sexual activities. Not seeking an arrest, these parents often took advantage of the policy of police probation. Several cases illustrate, however, that neither police probation nor policewomen's "motherly talks" changed the behavior of some disobedient, sexually adventurous teenage girls. These cases, drawn from the files of the Los Angeles County Juvenile Court, speak to the power struggles and negotiations underlying pioneer policewomen's daily work: struggles and negotiations between teenage girls and their parents or stepparents, between teenage girls and policewomen, between parents and policewomen, and between parents and court officials. These cases also support the hypothesis that a disproportionately large share of teenage girls and young women who faced charges of sex delinquency in the early twentieth century came from single-parent families.[52]

Juvenile court records offer an extraordinarily valuable window into pioneer policewomen's work and the state regulation of adolescent female sexuality. By their very nature, however, court records give a skewed picture because they portray only the most coercive aspects of pioneer policewomen's work—the detention, arrest, and incarceration of teenage girls. Court records are also almost completely silent about pioneer policewomen's "social adjustment" cases. From the point of view of Los Angeles policewomen, the cases discussed below constitute distressing evidence that policewomen's much-vaunted social work methods did not always work or did not always seem appropriate. Nonetheless, in the absence of LAPD case records of girls and young women whom policewomen treated as "social adjustment" cases, juvenile court cases offer the closest look possible at policewomen's work in the LAPD Juvenile Bureau.

In September 1915, Carl Chapman, a white Euro-American carpenter, brought his fifteen-year-old daughter, Eleanor, to the Juvenile Bureau for questioning because he suspected her of slipping out of the house at night to meet boys. As he later testified in court, "She was getting beyond my control; she would go out at night, and she would not stay in, so I took her . . . [to the police station] and they questioned her down there." During the following six months, he brought her back to the Juvenile Bureau several times, perhaps as many as six; Eleanor could not remember exactly. Eleanor's stepmother did not accompany them on these visits (Eleanor's mother was dead). At one point Chapman asked a policewoman to arrange for Eleanor to have a pelvic examination at Juvenile Hall, a detention facility that employed a woman physician to perform pelvic examinations on girls and young women charged with morals offenses. Los Angeles policewomen, including City Mother Aletha Gilbert, sometimes referred parents who wanted their daughters to have a pelvic examination to this physician.[53]

Chapman's suspicions were not unfounded; according to Eleanor's testimony of June 1916, she had been having sexual relations with two boyfriends every week beginning the previous February, when she was fourteen. Occasionally during this time, she also had sexual relations with other teenage boys. She testified that policewomen at the Juvenile Bureau had told her that premarital sex "was not the right thing to do," but she had ignored their advice and continued to sneak out of the house at night. Her father said that on one of his visits to the Juvenile Bureau he had been told to expect a home visit soon from the police, but no officer ever came. He added that he had heard that a police officer had visited one of Eleanor's sex partners, but by then, he remarked, it was too late—Eleanor's "boys" just kept coming to the house. Chapman offered his opinion that the Juvenile Bureau had not sent out an officer as promised because the police simply had "too much ground to cover."

By June 1916, Eleanor was pregnant. With the help of one boyfriend, she took an abortifacient. It made her ill, and in a panic, she confessed everything to her grandmother. An unidentified family member informed the Juvenile Bureau about Eleanor's predicament. Policewoman Rachel Shatto took the case and promptly arrested Eleanor for sex delinquency. Three of Eleanor's sex partners were also placed under arrest.[54]

In Shatto's report of Eleanor's case, she emphasized that Eleanor usually arranged to meet her two boyfriends away from home on the same night and had sexual relations with each of them in turn, "in the presence of the other."[55] This fact, more than any other, probably led to Shatto's decision to file a petition in juvenile court because it indicated a complete disregard of middle-class moral standards. Moreover, Eleanor had amply proven that policewomen's lectures on morality were insufficient to change her behavior. In Shatto's eyes, Eleanor needed the strong hand of the juvenile court. The court placed Eleanor in the Truelove Home for unwed mothers, then, after she had given birth, it granted her permission to live with her aunt in Kansas. Eleanor's stepmother did not want Eleanor to come back home; she claimed that Eleanor was a bad influence on her younger sister. Because paternity of Eleanor's baby could not be established, the court ordered each of the three teenage boys under arrest to contribute five dollars each month to help support Eleanor and the baby.[56]

Carl Chapman spoke deferentially in court about the police but he probably felt shortchanged. He had brought Eleanor to the Juvenile Bureau several times in the expectation that the police could stop her from sneaking out of the house to have sex with boys, but Eleanor did not pay any more attention to the police than she had to him. Not until Eleanor became sick from a failed attempt at abortion did a policewoman become actively involved in Eleanor's life. Although Chapman excused policewomen's early failure to visit his home as promised, he had ample grounds for complaint. Did he ever ask the police outright to arrest his daughter, or to file a petition in juvenile court? The case record is silent on these points. Chapman could have filed a petition in juvenile court himself, as many other working-class parents in Los Angeles did every year during the 1910s, but he chose instead to bring his daughter repeatedly to the Juvenile Bureau. This action suggests either a stubborn faith that policewomen would one day prevail upon his daughter to change her behavior or a simple reluctance to hand over his daughter directly to the Juvenile Court himself, or both. His hope that policewomen could help him corresponded with, and may have even arisen from, policewomen's public boasts that they "saved girls from lives of shame" through "motherly talks." Perhaps Chapman felt that since Eleanor's own mother was dead, a policewoman could guide her better than a stepmother, who obviously had not controlled Eleanor's behavior. Whatever his reasons, Chapman placed his trust repeatedly in the policewomen of the Juvenile Bureau, who treated

Eleanor as a "social adjustment" case until she attempted abortion. At that point, the policewomen and Carl Chapman were forced to recognize that motherly talks had failed.

In another case the same year (1916), policewoman Rachel Shatto placed fourteen-year-old Mamie O'Rourke, a white Euro-American, on police probation without first arresting her. Mamie's unemployed father, William O'Rourke, had brought his daughter to the LAPD Juvenile Bureau; Mamie's mother, a "semi-invalid" did not accompany them. According to O'Rourke, Mamie had developed the habit of staying out late at night and going to dance halls. Although the case record does not say so, Shatto probably lectured Mamie on the dangers of dance halls before placing her on police probation. According to the terms of probation, Mamie had to call or visit Shatto once a week. Additionally, Shatto instructed Mamie's father to inform her immediately if Mamie broke her promise to obey.

For the next several weeks, Mamie dutifully made the weekly telephone calls and told Shatto that everything was "lovely" between her and her parents. Shatto heard nothing from Mamie's father and assumed that everything was indeed going well. Then, in mid-July, Mamie's father contacted Shatto because Mamie had stayed out all night. Upon questioning Mamie, Shatto learned that she had continued to sneak out of the house at night to go to the Silver Swan Dance Hall and she had exchanged sexual favors for cash. According to Shatto's report, Mamie said that she and two other teenage girls received from one to three dollars from a married man each time they had sex with him in his office. Mamie also claimed that the married man took her and her two friends in his car every Saturday to the beach, where they stayed for hours. When Shatto heard this admission, she arrested Mamie and filed a petition in juvenile court on her behalf. Shatto also arranged for the arrest of the married man.

While awaiting her hearing in Juvenile Hall, Mamie changed her story. She told her probation officer that although the married man tried to have sexual intercourse with her, she did not let him. She claimed that the money she received from him was only a bribe to keep her quiet about his sexual relations with the two other girls.[57]

Mamie's case is unusual because of the issue of prostitution. As juvenile court records show, relatively few female youths arrested for sex delinquency in the early twentieth century accepted money (or admitted to having accepted money) in exchange for sexual intercourse. Instead, some of them traded sexual intimacies for "treats," such as theater tickets, rides in amusement parks, boat excursions, and similar outings. The system of treating had emerged in the late nineteenth century, giving working-class teenage girls and young women a chance to partake of commercial amusements far more freely than they could have otherwise afforded on their meager incomes.[58]

Mamie's parents must have felt shocked by her confession. According to the probation officer's report, both parents had always tried to give Mamie "all the pleasures they can afford, which would be to attend a picture show once or twice a week." All Mamie's parents asked in return was for Mamie "to come in when she promises to do so." Until recently, she had always obeyed. Clearly worried about her stay in Juvenile Hall and the verdict of the court, Mamie's parents asked the probation officer to release Mamie to them immediately. They missed her and wanted her safe at home. This request suggests that Mamie's father had not asked Rachel Shatto to arrest Mamie when he first brought her into the police station. Like many other parents, he probably just wanted the police to bolster his authority over his daughter. According to pioneer policewomen, police probation often accomplished this goal, but in Mamie's case, it failed.

In an attempt to persuade the court to release their daughter early, the O'Rourkes promised the probation officer that they would be responsible for finding Mamie a "suitable" job to fill her leisure time. Presumably they meant a temporary summer job, or a permanent part-time job, because California law required children under the age of sixteen to attend school. The court did not grant their wish; instead, it required Mamie to live a month at Juvenile Hall, pending further investigation of her case. Although she and her parents must have felt disappointed, Mamie was luckier than many other girls in juvenile court because her parents wanted her back, despite her repeated deceptions. As Eleanor Chapman's case illustrates, some teenage girls charged with sex delinquency had families less forgiving.

White Euro-Americans such as Eleanor Chapman and Mamie O'Rourke typified the female youths whom Los Angeles policewomen arrested. According to LAPD juvenile arrest statistics, just under three-quarters of all female juveniles arrested between 1926 and 1940 were white (see Table 4). The percentage of white female juveniles arrested would have been much higher, however, if it had matched the percentage of whites in the population of Los Angeles as a whole during the first half of the twentieth century. But LAPD women officers, like their male counterparts, arrested proportionately fewer whites than people of color. For example, between 1926 and 1940, arrests of African American girls and young women averaged 8 percent of all female juvenile arrests, approximately double the percentage of African Americans in the Los Angeles population.[59] Similarly, arrests of young Latinas during the same period averaged 17 percent of all female juvenile arrests, a figure higher than most estimates of the Latino population in the city. (In this context, "Latino" and "Latina" refer to people who either immigrated to the United States from Latin America, or whose ancestors came from Latin America. The most common country of origin was Mexico.)[60] Relatively few girls and young women of Asian descent and Native American descent attracted the attention of the police. Together, they composed less than 2 percent of all arrests of female juveniles between 1926 and 1940.

TABLE 4. LAPD RACE CLASSIFICATION OF FEMALE JUVENILE ARRESTS

Year	Red (%)	Black (%)	White (%)
1926–27	15.0	7.8	77.0
1927–28	15.8	7.4	75.1
1928–29	19.3	7.6	66.7
1929–30	17.5	7.8	73.5
1930–31	16.6	7.6	74.4
1931–32	13.0	8.2	78.1
1932–33	14.0	9.2	75.9
1933–34	15.3	9.1	74.6
1934–35	16.7	5.4	77.5
1935–36	17.5	11.8	70.2
1936–37	21.2	5.8	72.5
1937–38	16.9	10.3	71.8
1939	19.5	7.3	72.3
1940	23.0	8.6	67

Source: LAPD, *Annual Report,* fiscal years 1926–27 through 1940.
Note: The LAPD classified juveniles by color. "Red" denoted Native Americans and Latinas; however, police arrested relatively few Native American girls and young women, so "Red" primarily denoted Latinas. "Brown" denoted Filipinas and "Yellow" denoted Asians and Asian Americans. Statistics for "Brown" and "Yellow" are not included in Table 4 because between 1926 and 1940, the LAPD classified less than 1 percent of female juvenile arrests under "Brown" and "Yellow," respectively. (Percentages may not total 100 because of rounding.)

Why did Los Angeles policewomen arrest a disproportionately high percentage of Latin American and African American female youth? Racism provides a large part of the answer. Throughout the nineteenth and early twentieth centuries, racist myths about women of color influenced criminal justice policies. According to these myths, women of color were inherently more "primitive," sensual, and sexually promiscuous than white women. In the South, whites long excused white men's rape of black women on the spurious grounds that black women were always willing to have sexual intercourse.[61]

The power of racist stereotypes notwithstanding, race dynamics in female sex delinquency cases operated in more complex ways than is suggested in the simplistic formulation of racist white LAPD officer versus teenage girl or young woman of color. In some instances, people of color voluntarily turned to criminal justice agencies for help in resolving familial tensions. According to one study, nearly 23 percent of the people who sought the City Mother's help in 1933 and 1934, respectively, were Mexican American; this percentage rose to 35 in 1938.[62] According to another study, Latin American immigrants composed 21 percent of all parents who filed petitions on their daughters in the Los Angeles County Juvenile Court in 1920.[63] This figure is roughly twice that of the percentage of Latinos in the county as a whole.

Before one assumes that Latino parents were extraordinarily willing to bring their daughters to the police or juvenile court, two mitigating facts should be taken into account: the working-class orientation of the juvenile court and the working-class identity of most Latinos. Eighty percent of the girls and young women who appeared before the juvenile court in 1920 came from working-class families, and nearly all Latinos were working-class. It is possible that one in five working-class families in Los Angeles County in 1920 were Latino. Therefore, the fact that 21 percent of all parents who filed petitions on their daughters in 1920 were Latino may correspond with Latinos' representation in the working class of Los Angeles County as a whole.[64]

Both sets of statistics regarding Latinos support the findings of a team of researchers in the late 1970s who investigated the distinctive culture of Los Angeles barrios. According to their research, antipolice attitudes did not prevail within the Mexican American community prior to U.S. entry into World War II.[65] Available statistics paint a far different picture, however, of the black community in Los Angeles. In 1938, approximately 4 percent of the clients of the City Mother's Bureau were African Americans. Similarly, in 1920, only 6 percent of all parental referrals of female juveniles to the Los Angeles County Juvenile Court were from African Americans.[66] Socioeconomic status cannot explain these low percentages, because nearly all African Americans in Los Angeles were working class.

These statistics are extremely fragmentary, but they point to a sharp difference in the willingness of blacks and Latinos in Los Angeles to use criminal justice agencies to solve domestic problems, a difference arising in part from cultural factors. By the 1910s, African Americans had built a variety of voluntary organizations to solve problems and address social injustices. Many of these organizations in the early twentieth century owed their existence to black women's extraordinarily high level of public activism. Beginning in the late nineteenth century, black women activists in cities across the nation bent their efforts to protecting the female youth of their communities from moral dangers and male sexual license. Sometimes they turned to the state for help in this regard, but racism ensured that they met with only mixed success. They therefore continued to build and work in private organizations. One such organization in Los Angeles, the Sojourner Truth Industrial Club, tried to steer African American female youth away from moral dangers.[67]

No statistics exist on the number of people of color who asked the LAPD for help in controlling their daughters in the early twentieth century. But beginning in the mid-1910s, African Americans who went to the Juvenile Bureau usually had an opportunity to talk to an African American policewoman. In 1916, the LAPD hired Georgia Ann Robinson, the first black policewoman in the United States. A year later the LAPD hired Mary del Valle, a Chicana who worked as a police officer through the 1920s, specializing in cases involving young Latinas. Other women of color who became pioneer policewomen include Lucille Shelton, an African American who spent most of her career from 1925 through the mid-1930s in the Juvenile Bureau, and Ella Aguilar, a Chicana whose exact employment dates are unknown but who worked in the Juvenile Bureau during the mid-1920s. Robinson and Shelton handled the cases of African American female youth exclusively, but del Valle and Aguilar handled cases of girls from every ethnic and racial background. Similarly, white Euro-American women officers often handled the cases of young Latinas, but they usually did not work with black women and girls. No officers of Asian descent, male or female, worked for the LAPD during the early twentieth century.[68]

The social activism of African American clubwomen in Los Angeles played a central role in the hiring of Georgia Ann Robinson. The circumstances surrounding Robinson's appointment deserve consideration because they illuminate some of the race dynamics underlying the issues of female sexuality and the perceived moral hazards of the city. These issues held a somewhat different meaning for black women activists than for white women activists.

In October 1915, a delegation of African American women formally asked Mayor Charles Sebastian and Chief of Police Clarence Snively to appoint black women officers and to create a black City Mother's Bureau to serve the black community.[69] When they made their request, they knew very well that no police department in the country employed black women officers. Indeed, they knew that few police agencies in the world employed white women officers. These circumstances did not deter them. Five years earlier, they had observed the leading role white women in Los Angeles played in the birth of the movement for women police; a year earlier, they had watched the establishment of the LAPD City Mother's Bureau. Although they must have approved of these reforms in principle, they must also have thought that white women officers could not, or would not, adequately serve the needs of African American women and children in Los Angeles.

Black women's request for black policewomen reflected some of the same concerns that spurred and shaped the movement for women police nationwide. Like white women activists, black women activists wanted to protect female youth from the moral hazards of the city and from sexual exploitation. For black women, however, the prevalence of racist myths regarding black female sexuality gave the issue of sexual exploitation a special urgency. Racist stereotypes of black women's sexuality undoubtedly contributed significantly to the sexual exploitation of black women and girls by men and boys of all races. At the turn of the century, black women activists throughout the United States began to organize to combat the myth of their promiscuity and the sexual exploitation it helped to cause. By the thousands, they joined the National Association of Colored Women (NACW), an umbrella organization founded in 1896 with the primary aim of eradicating negative images of black women's sexuality and replacing them with positive images. By 1914, the NACW had fifty thousand members.[70]

In Los Angeles, the request for African American policewomen and an African American City Mother's Bureau came from women who belonged to local affiliates of the NACW, such as the Sojourner Truth Industrial Club, founded in 1904 by twenty-three members of the First African Methodist Episcopal Church.[71] NACW members' concern over racist stereotypes and sexual exploitation helps to put into historical context black women's request for black policewomen because the issues of female sexual vulnerability and female sexual exploitation underlay the daily work of pioneer policewomen, white and black.

At first, Mayor Sebastian appeared to assent to black women activists' request. The day following his meeting with them, Sebastian announced to the press his intention of establishing a "Negro City Mother's Bureau" forthwith.[72] Although the promised bureau never materialized, city officials did not entirely ignore the clubwomen's concerns. In early 1916, a LAPD recruiter approached Georgia Ann Robinson, a well-known member of local African American women's clubs and civic organizations. (Although no evidence survives to confirm it, Robinson may well have been a member of the women's delegation to the mayor and police chief the preceding October.) The recruiter asked Robinson if she would consider joining the LAPD, where her duties would involve handling all cases of African American women and children. Robinson agreed, and on July 25, 1916, she began her thirteen-year career as an officer with the LAPD, working primarily in the Juvenile Bureau and the Women's Jail.[73]

The case of Angela Thompson, a seventeen-year-old African American, provides an excellent example of the kinds of juvenile cases Robinson handled. Angela first officially came to Robinson's attention in January 1920, when Loretta Thompson, Angela's mother, asked the LAPD for help. Thompson, who had long been separated from Angela's father, telephoned the police because she suspected that Angela was lying to her about how she spent her evenings. Angela had told her mother that she spent her evenings at her employer's house, where she worked as a domestic. In reality, Angela went out to public dances and on automobile rides with men. Thompson found out the truth from Angela's employer, who told her that "Angela was too nice a girl to be going the gate [gait] she was going, men and girls calling her up." Additionally, Angela had stayed out all night three times, on Thanksgiving night, Christmas night, and New Year's Eve 1919.

Thompson at first tried to correct her daughter's behavior without involving the police. She "talked and explained and argued to no avail" to persuade Angela to change her ways, but Angela kept "running out nights and being intimate with boys." Finally, terribly distraught, Thompson called the LAPD and explained the problem to Robinson. When Robinson went to question Angela, she recognized the teenager as someone she had seen frequently in dance halls. Under questioning, Angela admitted she was no longer a virgin. Robinson arrested her and filed a petition in court for sex delinquency. While in Juvenile Hall, Angela tested positive for gonorrhea, for which she received treatment while awaiting her court hearing.[74]

During Angela's stay in Juvenile Hall, Loretta Thompson told Angela's probation officer that she would like the court to send Angela to stay with family members in Phoenix, Arizona. At Angela's hearing, the court readily complied with this request. Angela's stay in Phoenix was brief, however. After only three months, she returned to Los Angeles because her family in Phoenix had decided to move elsewhere. As soon as Angela returned to Los Angeles, her mother placed her in the Sojourner Truth Home, a residential institution for young black women built and operated by the Sojourner Truth Industrial Club with an eye toward keeping the residents on the straight and narrow path. The court approved of the Sojourner Truth Home as an appropriate placement for Angela.[75] Once in the home, Angela began work in a "respectable" cafe. Angela's mother was happy with the arrangement, but Angela chafed under the strict regime of the home, and she ran away a few months later, in autumn 1920. At that point, the court permanently lost all contact with her.[76]

Court records do not indicate what Angela's mother wanted from the police when she first called the LAPD in January 1920. Perhaps she simply wanted Robinson to have a stern talk with Angela. She probably knew that Robinson would be assigned to the case because the African American community in Los Angeles was neither large nor scattered, and Robinson stood out as a prominent member. Nor do court records indicate whether Angela's mother was pleased or upset over how swiftly Robinson arrested Angela and filed a petition in juvenile court. In placing Angela in the Sojourner Truth Home a few months later, however, Angela's mother took a course of action that suggests she did not harbor a grudge against Robinson, because Robinson helped to direct policy at the home and served from time to time as its president.[77] In fact, placing Angela in the Sojourner Truth Home was virtually the same as placing her directly under Robinson's care. Angela may have felt the same way; that is, she may have felt that living in the Sojourner Truth Home was akin to living in jail. Running away from the home in the autumn of 1920 won her independence from the watchful eyes of Robinson, the juvenile court, and probably to some extent, her mother.

The case of Angela Thompson strongly suggests that African Americans who sought help from the LAPD did so for much the same reason as white Euro-Americans: to gain better control over the social and sexual lives of their teenage daughters. At seventeen, Angela was slightly older than the average teenage girl who appeared before the Los Angeles County Juvenile Court; by the time she ran away from the Sojourner Truth Home, she was either eighteen years old, or only a few weeks shy of eighteen (her birthday was in November). Because she was older, she may have been less willing than younger girls to submit to the terms of her probation.[78]

The case of thirteen-year-old Carolyn Yamamoto, who was adopted when she was three, provides a sharp contrast to all the cases discussed in this chapter because her father, Ota Yamamoto, demanded that she be sent to an institution. Bringing his daughter into the LAPD Juvenile Bureau on Sunday, October 28, 1927, Yamamoto immediately asked the policewoman on duty, Estelle Wallen, to hold Carolyn for interrogation and to arrange for a gynecological examination. His fury toward his daughter plainly shows in the juvenile court case records. According to him, Carolyn had been behaving badly for a long time, and her most recent act of defiance had just occurred: She had stayed out all Saturday night without his permission. Then, when she came home in the morning, she steadfastly refused to tell him or her mother where she had been. Her father suspected that she had had sexual relations with a man.

When Wallen questioned Carolyn, Carolyn admitted that she had willingly spent the night with a sailor named George, whom she had first met at a downtown movie theater two weeks earlier. George had taken her to his hotel room, where they had sexual relations in the presence of two, or possibly three other people, one or two men (or teenage boys) and a woman. As soon as Yamamoto heard about his daughter's sexual activities, he asked Wallen to arrest his daughter and file a petition in juvenile court. He also informed Wallen that he and his wife were Roman Catholic and that he wanted Carolyn to be placed in the Convent of the Good Shepherd, where she would receive "correctional care." Wallen agreed to the arrest and the petition.[79]

According to Wallen's report, Yamamoto "felt very keenly the affront to the family honor" when he learned of his daughter's sexual adventures. Wallen's subsequent investigation in the case probably fed Yamamoto's sense of outrage because Wallen discovered that Carolyn had a reputation at school as a "sailor's girl." When Wallen asked Carolyn about this matter, Carolyn explained that she began having sex with sailors the preceding May, after she had heard "American" girls boast about their sexual conquests with men from the U.S. Navy. Carolyn said that she had had sex with sailors on nearly every ship in the navy. Wallen concluded that Carolyn "seems to have made friend[s] with the most undesirable class of American girls and . . . seems to be ashamed of Japanese customs, etc."[80]

In a poignant interview with a probation officer, Carolyn said she liked living in Juvenile Hall better than living at home. She was especially glad to escape her mother, who she said beat her severely for misbehaving. But she was sad that her father no longer wanted her living at home, and she hated the thought of living in an institution. Nonetheless, she lived at the Convent of the Good Shepherd for over a year, possibly as long as two years, before returning to her family. Once she was home again, she told the court that aside from going to school and helping her father in his nursery business, she went out only in her mother's company.

Her probation officer recommended that her case be dismissed on the basis of "ward having made good." The court agreed to allow Carolyn to live at home, albeit "under the friendly supervision of the Catholic Big Sisters."[81]

Carolyn's case illustrates a theme commonly associated with juvenile court cases involving teenage girls of Asian or Latin American descent: the belief that a daughter's premarital sexual activity is an affront to patriarchal authority and the family's honor. According to Mary E. Odem, Mexican and Mexican American fathers in Los Angeles often viewed their daughters' sexual behavior in this light.[82] But the case of Linda Lopez provides an example of a Mexican-born father who sought the help of the police, not simply or even necessarily because he wanted to assert patriarchal authority over his daughter, but because he wanted to assert authority over his daughter's lovers.

Roberto Lopez found out that his thirteen-year-old daughter, Linda, was pregnant in 1915. According to court records, Linda had been having sexual relations since she was twelve with Frank Pulido, a married man in his late twenties. When Lopez learned of his daughter's sexual activities and her pregnancy, he sent her to live with her aunt (Linda's mother was dead). While at her aunt's house, Linda gave birth to a son. Ten months later, Frank Pulido visited her, telling her that he was going to Mexico. Upon hearing of Pulido's visit, Linda's father immediately telephoned the police and named Pulido as the father of his daughter's baby. Lopez did not speak English well, if at all, so he probably had an interpreter make the call for him. A policeman charged Pulido with contributing to the delinquency of a minor. Meanwhile, policewoman Lillian Toomey of the LAPD Juvenile Bureau filed a petition in juvenile court charging Linda with dependency. Toomey did not arrest Linda but returned her to her aunt's home pending the probation department's investigation of the case.

Undoubtedly to Lopez's disgust, the district attorney refused to prosecute Pulido. According to Toomey, the district attorney dropped the charge against Pulido because he regarded Linda as having a "low mentality." By using this excuse, the district attorney was in effect sanctioning sex crimes against developmentally disabled people. In addition, his excuse corresponds to the common belief among white Euro-Americans that most Latinos were stupid. As George J. Sánchez has noted, Los Angeles city school board officials segregated Mexican and Mexican American children from white Euro-American children during the 1910s, 1920s, and 1930s on the basis of their belief that Latino children were "slow."[83]

The court allowed Linda to live with her father and her baby. This arrangement worked well for approximately a year, then, in September 1929, Linda ran away from home for a few days with Eduardo Moran, who was in his early thirties. They went to Oxnard, a city north of Los Angeles, where they applied for a marriage license but were refused (Linda probably looked too young to marry legally). Someone from Linda's school notified the police of Linda's absence; when she returned home, her father notified the authorities. A policeman arrested and jailed Moran on a "contributing" charge. This time the district attorney did not refuse to prosecute. Police investigated Moran's background and found a woman who claimed to be his wife. Moran denied he was married, but he pleaded guilty to the charge of contributing to the delinquency of a minor. Meanwhile, Linda's probation officer, Anita Aguerre, placed Linda in Juvenile Hall, pending the outcome of Moran's trial, at which Linda served as a witness. While in Juvenile Hall, court officials, probably Aguerre, asked Linda's father to sign a petition requesting the court to commit Linda to Pacific Colony, an institution for the "feeble-minded." At the hearing, her father agreed through an interpreter to have her committed.[84]

Although he could not speak English well, Roberto Lopez used the criminal justice system aggressively. His determination to see his daughter's lovers arrested indicates that he felt outrage at their behavior. His attitude toward his daughter is difficult to assess because the court records do not feature his perspective. His agreeing to Linda's institutionalization does not necessarily indicate that he wanted nothing more to do with her; perhaps he was at his wits' end regarding how to control her or protect her from men, or perhaps no one explained to him the kind of life his daughter would lead as an inmate of a mental institution. Given the strength of familial ties in most Mexican and Chicano families, he probably found her institutionalization hard to bear.

Policewomen on Criminal Investigation and Patrol

Of course, not all arrests of female juveniles resulted from the complaints of parents or other family members; policewomen made some arrests during criminal investigations, and until the LAPD relieved women officers of patrol duty sometime between the late 1910s and mid-1920s, they made some arrests while on patrol. Because no case records from the Juvenile Bureau have survived, the ratio of arrests originating with the family to those resulting from policewomen's investigative-patrol work remains unknown. According to one study of the Los Angeles County Juvenile Court, however, law enforcement agencies in Los Angeles County initiated only 27 percent of all court cases of female juvenile delinquency in 1920 (approximately 57 of 209 cases).[85] This is a small percentage, given the number of law enforcement agencies in the county in 1920. In addition to the LAPD, the county had a sheriff's department and several small city police departments, such as the Long Beach and Pasadena Police Departments.

Typically, policewomen arrested teenage girls whom they or a policeman found engaging in sexual intimacies, acting in ways policewomen deemed sexually provocative, or entering a disreputable hotel or rooming house with a man.

On the morning of April 1, 1920, Mary del Valle arrested Florence Strasbourg at San Pedro dockyards when she saw a sailor fondling Florence's breasts. (Del Valle had been called to the scene by a policeman, so her presence on the street is not proof that Los Angeles policewomen still had patrol assignments in 1920.) Upon questioning, Florence admitted that since her fourteenth birthday exactly two months before, she had had sexual intercourse with five men. She also admitted that LAPD Officer Elizabeth Feeley had arrested her four weeks earlier but had released her without pressing charges. The lack of charges means that Feeley had treated Florence as a social adjustment case; Feeley had perhaps even given Florence a "motherly talk" before releasing her. Del Valle sent Florence to Juvenile Hall, where she tested positive for gonorrhea. Shortly thereafter, del Valle filed a petition for sex delinquency; the sailor faced "contributing" charges.[86]

Similarly, policewoman Bertha Arenburgh arrested fifteen-year-old Yolanda Grijalva for sex delinquency one morning when she came across her and twenty-year-old George Lujan immediately after they had had sexual intercourse in Lincoln Park. Yolanda told Arenburgh that she had met Lujan and three other young adult men the night before on a street outside a movie theater. Yolanda and her eleven-year-old friend, Marta Martinez, spent the night with the four men, "petting" and riding around in an automobile. Under questioning, Yolanda confessed that Lujan was not her first sex partner. Arenburgh noted in her report that she had secured a rape complaint against Lujan but that she had not succeeded in obtaining "contributing" complaints against the other three men.[87]

Policewomen arrested some girls and young women as part of their investigations into complaints about men. Occasionally, these investigations were initiated by complaints filed in the Juvenile Bureau by angry and scared girls and women. For example, in 1916, Rachel Shatto arrested fifteen-year-old Alice Lake during the course of an investigation into certain allegations made by several teenage girls about Howard Watkins. Alice's case deserves close attention because it illustrates pioneer policewomen's faith in the state and in themselves as protectors of female youth. It also shows the working relationship between pioneer policewomen and other pioneer women workers in the criminal justice system.

Policewoman Rachel Shatto and an unidentified policeman began to investigate the private life of Howard Watkins after several teenage girls complained to the Juvenile Bureau that Watkins frequently made unwelcome sexual advances to them. Watkins, who was sixty-four, worked as an elevator operator in the Tajo Building in downtown Los Angeles; the teenage girls who complained about him worked in the same building. During the investigation, Shatto and her partner found Alice Lake with Watkins in compromising circumstances in the Estelle Rooming House, across the street from the Tajo Building. They arrested Alice and Watkins on the spot.

Shortly after her arrest, Alice, who was married, made a full confession to

Shatto. She admitted that she had engaged in sexual relations with Watkins approximately once a week for the preceding six weeks in exchange for cash. (Watkins paid her two dollars each time.) She further admitted that she had recently had intercourse with a friend of Watkins's, who had also paid her. She then offered an unusual explanation for her crime, which Shatto and all the court officials involved in the case seemed to accept at face value. According to Alice, she engaged in prostitution because she needed money to send to her ailing parents in Utah. She maintained that she had not told her husband about her parents' financial need because she did not want him to know the extent of her family's poverty.

Two days after her arrest, Alice appeared before Orfa Jean Shontz, the Girls' Referee of the Los Angeles County Juvenile Court. Also present at the hearing were Alice's husband, her older sister (her only relative in Los Angeles), Shatto, and a woman probation officer named Louise Marlow. Watkins waited outside in the hallway under guard. In a separate interview with Shontz, Alice's sister corroborated Alice's story about their parents' illness and poverty. She acknowledged that she had urged Alice to send money to their mother, and that over the preceding few weeks, Alice had given her a few dollars for that purpose. She also confessed that she had introduced Alice to Watkins, even though she knew "what kind of man" Watkins was. She then conceded that Watkins had once made improper advances to her but that she had purposely kept this information from Alice. Shontz found the sister's behavior appalling and ordered her to keep away from Alice and not to communicate with her.

Twice during the hearing, Shontz sought Shatto's opinion of whether Alice should be declared a ward of the juvenile court or "let go" and the case dismissed. The first time Shontz asked her, Shatto replied that she thought Alice's case was one of the few in which it would be safe simply to let her go. Shontz next asked Alice's husband his opinion of the situation. He answered that he did not intend to take Alice back. This statement contradicted Alice's assurances, made prior to her husband's entry into the hearing room, that he would definitely take her back. Shontz asked the husband a few questions, then told him she thought he should "forget all this" and give Alice another chance. Shontz then sent Alice and her husband into the next room to talk things over. When they returned, the husband announced that he was willing to resume married life if Alice agreed never to see her sister again, and if by taking her back, he was not jeopardizing his chances of obtaining a divorce in the future. Shontz admonished him to "take her back with no thought of divorce. Take her back with the thought that there is not to be any cause." Shontz then once again asked Shatto her opinion. This time, Shatto replied that she thought Alice might benefit greatly from the supervision of the probation officer, Louise Marlow: "I feel that Miss Marlow might be a big help to the girl when little perplexities came up between her and her husband." Shontz agreed, placed Alice on probation for four weeks, and released her to the custody of her husband.[88]

Although Alice admitted to being a prostitute, Shontz and Shatto viewed her as more a victim than a criminal and treated her accordingly. Had Alice's husband never mentioned his intention to leave Alice, Shontz might well have dismissed the case. But once he gave voice to his feelings, he killed the chances of dismissal. A divorce would mean that Alice would be left on her own, far from her parents, with her sister as the only family member to whom she could turn for help. In the eyes of the authorities, Alice's sister had proven herself unworthy of looking after Alice's best interests. Equally important, Alice had amply demonstrated that, if the circumstances appeared to demand it, she would prostitute herself.

Shatto's recommendations imply a distrust of Alice's judgment and a desire to see that an authority figure—preferably Alice's husband, but in lieu of him, a probation officer—be an active presence in Alice's life. When Shatto thought that Alice's marriage was solidly intact, she recommended dismissal of the case; after she learned of the possibility of divorce, she recommended probation. Her original recommendation of dismissal undermines the notion that pioneer policewomen were interested only in extending state supervision over female sex offenders.

Shatto couched her revised opinion in language that reflected her maternalist view of the state. According to her, the state, through the person of probation officer Louise Marlow, would provide Alice with the wise and kindly assistance she needed in the days ahead. In effect, Marlow would act as a substitute mother, giving advice to help resolve the "little perplexities" of married life. And although Shatto did not say so, she implied that if the marriage fell apart, Marlow would be there to try to keep Alice from turning once again to prostitution as a source of income.

In March 1917, eight months after her arrest, Alice asked Marlow if her case could be dismissed. According to Marlow, Alice claimed that she and her husband were very happy together, and that they were "more comfortably fixed financially than at any time since their marriage." In fact, Alice's husband had joined the LAPD as a patrolman two months before, at a salary nearly double his former wage of approximately fifty dollars a month. Alice added that she and her husband "would both be glad to feel that they can do without the assistance of the court." Based on these statements and on Marlow's recommendation, Shontz dismissed the case.[89]

Preventive and Protective Officers

The case of Alice Lake points up the themes of discipline and protection that pioneer policewomen attempted to weave together in the crime prevention model of police work and in their own working lives. But Alice's case, like the other cases discussed, does not illuminate the literal interpretation some pioneer policewomen in Los Angeles gave their role as preventive and protective officers.

Throughout the 1910s, 1920s, and 1930s, some LAPD women officers personally provided food, clothing, or temporary room and board to destitute women and girls. Georgia Robinson and Minnie Barton, for example, opened their homes to indigent women and girls. Robinson, whose career with the LAPD spanned thirteen years (1916–29), brought home so many women and girls that her husband, Morgan, claimed that he never knew how many people would be at his dinner table each night when he came home from work. Additionally, during the late 1910s and 1920s, Robinson devoted much of her off-duty time to drumming up support for the Sojourner Truth Home. This institution supervised black female youth who, like Angela Thompson, were wards of the juvenile court. It also provided homeless black women and girls a place to stay until they found something better. Robinson remained an active volunteer with the Sojourner Truth Home even after she lost her eyesight and had to retire from the LAPD in 1929. She also served for decades as a leading member of the Los Angeles chapter of the National Association for the Advancement of Colored People.[90]

Minnie Barton, who joined the LAPD in February 1917 and retired in the early 1940s, took home destitute women, most of them convicted prostitutes on probation from the Los Angeles County Women's Court. At first, she simply gave them food and shelter until they had steady, lawful employment. She soon had so many applicants that she made a formal arrangement with Judge Georgia Bullock of the Women's Court to run a residential, vocational training home for women on probation. Barton advocated vocational training because, like many other women reformers, she thought that most prostitutes lacked the necessary skills to earn sufficient money in lawful ways. By the end of 1917, she had founded the Minnie Barton Training Home, later known simply as the Barton Home. It was still going strong in 1935. By that time, Los Angeles judges released some female offenders to the Barton Home in lieu of a jail sentence. Soon after establishing the Barton Home, Barton channeled her abundant energy toward helping the many destitute women and girls who were not on probation but who nevertheless applied to the Barton Home for aid. To meet their needs, she founded the Big Sister League of Los Angeles. Within a short time, the Big Sister League opened the Bide-a-Wee Home for unwed mothers and homeless women and their children. Barton served as the superintendent of both the Barton Home and the Bide-a-Wee Home throughout the 1920s and most of the 1930s. In addition, she frequently talked to women's clubs on the topic of crime. She told the Women's City Club of Los Angeles that "wife desertion should be made a felony the same as forgery. . . . This is a matter that the women of this club should attend to and lend their aid to pass laws at the next session of the State Legislature." Amazingly, she undertook all these projects—the founding and superintendency of the Barton Home and the Bide-a-Wee Home, the establishment of the Big Sister League, and an active speaking schedule—while working full time as the officer in charge of the LAPD Women's Probation Bureau.[91]

Hamm, Robinson, and Barton were not the first women of the LAPD to extend a helping hand to destitute women; while a jail matron, Aletha Gilbert gave small sums of her own money to some women inmates upon their release from jail. The letters of gratitude she received from these women acknowledged the money as well as her "many kindnesses" during their incarceration. According to family lore, Gilbert's mother, Chief Matron Lucy Uthera Gray, also befriended women inmates and gave them small gifts of clothing.[92]

It is important to note that Robinson and Barton saw their off-duty work on behalf of women and girls as a natural extension of their work as policewomen. To them, and to pioneer policewomen as a whole, the goal of preventing crime and protecting girls and young women from "lives of shame" could be attained through the exercise of police power, as well as through the less coercive methods of social work. This point of view reflects pioneer policewomen's enormous confidence in themselves and in the moral rightness of their cause. Yet despite their boast that they saved countless girls and women from male sexual license and the moral hazards of the city, they did not wield sufficient power to regulate male sexuality and thus were unable to provide all the protection to girls and women they promised. Here was their dilemma: They opposed the double standard of morality, but they were barred from enforcing the single (feminine) standard. Moreover, they shrank from the prospect of women adopting the male sexual ethos. They were convinced that the male sexual ethos imposed much greater moral, physical, and economic hardships on women than on men, and, more important, that civilization itself required women's values to prevail. By clinging to the view that premarital sex was exploitation, they were able to define themselves as preventive and protective officers even as they placed girls and young women under arrest.

Lacking the power to regulate male sexuality, pioneer policewomen bent their efforts to regulating the sexuality of young women and girls. As the case files of the Los Angeles County Juvenile Court attest, policewomen received a lot of help in this task from working-class parents, including some parents from racial and ethnic minorities. Policewomen's work among female youth was shaped by generational conflicts within families and parents' attitudes toward the police, as well as by policewomen's class-based moralism and gender ideology.[93]

After 1930, a new generation of women began to enter police work. At the same time, the social and economic crises of the Great Depression began to change public discourse over crime, causing police administrators to revise personnel policies and place even more constraints on policewomen's work. These constraints forced the second generation of policewomen to try, consciously and subconsciously, to resolve the underlying dilemma of policewomen's double lives, the tensions between discipline and protection, police work and social work, masculinity and femininity. Through these attempts, the second generation unwittingly helped to doom the crime prevention model of police work.

CHAPTER FIVE

From City Mother to "Sgt. Tits": The Death of the Crime Prevention Model

In 1925, the Los Angeles City Council considered a proposal to reclassify the women officers of the city police force as civilian employees. If enacted, the proposal would have lowered policewomen's status in the department and stripped them of their pension rights. This prospect so alarmed policewomen that they organized the Los Angeles Policewomen's Association to protect their interests. Under the forceful leadership of Marguerite Curley, a five-year veteran of the San Pedro Division, the new association lobbied hard against the proposal and won. Three years later, Los Angeles policewomen had another battle on their hands: a measure to create a new, lower-paid category of women officers who would handle juvenile cases exclusively and be known officially as "juvenile officers–female" rather than "policewomen." (Although the name of the proposed category implies the existence of "juvenile officers–male," no such category was suggested or created.) Policewomen lost this battle. Between November 1928 and July 1929, the Los Angeles Police Department (LAPD) hired nine women as juvenile officers–female. Instead of the starting wage of $170 a month, which the rank and file of policewomen and policemen received, the newly hired juvenile officers–female earned only $140 a month.[1]

The failure of the Los Angeles Policewomen's Association to win the second battle proved an omen for the next decade. During the 1930s, the movement for women police collapsed nationwide and the female-gendered crime prevention model of police work disappeared. What went wrong? The answer lies in four key developments of the late 1920s, 1930s, and early 1940s: the increasing politicization of crime prevention, the waning of middle-class women's social activism, the fading sense of urgency over the regulation of adolescent female sexuality, and the rise of the crime control model of police work. To explore how these developments adversely affected the movement for women police and the crime prevention model, this chapter traces the evolution of policewomen's work in Los Angeles during the Great Depression and World War II.

The chapter first places events in Los Angeles in a national context by discussing the politics of crime prevention during the 1930s. It focuses on the emergence of two crime prevention programs that ignored policewomen's role as preventive and protective officers: the Los Angeles County Coordinating Councils and the LAPD Predelinquent Detail. The chapter next examines how urban politics in the early 1930s led to a permanent rupture between the City Mother's Bureau and local women's organizations and why the sex-crime panic of the late 1930s did not revitalize the movement for women police. Finally, the chapter takes a close look at the circumstances surrounding the retreat of second-generation Los Angeles policewomen from the ideals of the pioneering generation. Their retreat coincided in the late 1930s and early 1940s with the LAPD's adoption of a new, male-gendered model of police work known as the crime control model. This model minimized almost to the point of extinction the place of women in policing.

The Politics of Crime Prevention

Crime and its control became increasingly hot political issues during the late 1920s and 1930s. Everywhere Americans turned, they heard judges, politicians, and law enforcement officials warn them that the United States was undergoing the worst "crime wave" in its history. In 1932 Judge Samuel R. Blake of the Los Angeles County Juvenile Court publicly proclaimed that the country was "soaked with crime." Other speakers, equally inspired by the term "crime wave," described U.S. cities as "awash," "flooded," and "drowning" in crime. Like other commentators, Blake blamed much of the alleged increase in lawlessness on the young. "Crime has become a glittering thing to youth," he lamented. "Judges throughout the nation will testify that one short decade ago there was a constant parade of the 'hardened face' before the bar of justice. Today there is apparently an endless march of the 'unshaven face' before the same tribunals."[2] At politicians' urging, Americans demanded new crime legislation, and Congress quickly responded; in 1934 alone, it passed the Interstate Theft Act, the Fugitive Felon Act, and the National Firearms Act.[3]

Did a crime wave really exist? Some criminologists in the 1930s discounted the idea, attributing most of the rise in the crime rate to the sharp increase in the number of traffic violations over the previous two decades. Although this explanation was sound, it did not reassure a badly frightened public, and a sense of national emergency gripped the nation. Looking for an explanation for the soaring crime rate, some Americans in the 1930s blamed Prohibition. According to a survey in 1933, four hundred leading businessmen and public officials believed that Prohibition had created widespread contempt and defiance of the law.[4] Other Americans sought to understand the causes of the crime-wave panic. In 1939, Frederick Lewis Allen theorized that a few highly publicized criminal acts, such as the gangland murders in Chicago during the 1920s and the Lindbergh baby kidnapping of 1932, had significantly raised public awareness of crime. More recently, Samuel Walker has argued that the real force behind the crime-wave panic was Federal Bureau of Investigation (FBI) Director J. Edgar Hoover. Walker believes that Hoover was so eager to expand the FBI that he released to the news media a series of alarming crime reports designed to persuade the public that criminals were taking over control of the country. The reports formed part of Hoover's public relations campaign to portray the FBI as a bulwark of law and order in a dangerous and crazy world. The campaign succeeded. Hoover received increased political support and funding for his agency, and he and his agents (popularly known as "G-men") gained a national reputation as heroes.[5]

Social dislocations caused by the economic catastrophes of the Great Depression and the Dust Bowl in the 1930s also heightened Americans' fear of crime. As Estelle B. Freedman has observed, the specter of anarchy loomed just over the horizon during that decade, when record numbers of men lost their jobs and took to the road as drifters. Their presence in nearly every town provoked feelings of unease because their lives appeared unbound by social, legal, and sexual conventions.[6] How long, many Americans must have wondered, would hungry and demoralized men remain law-abiding? In addition, contemporary accounts of crime, such as newspaper photographs of murdered gangsters and newsreels of bullet-ridden "getaway cars," depicted a bleak picture of American life, filled with images of reckless men committing crimes without hesitation or remorse. For many Americans who had once felt safe and secure in their jobs, their homes, and their beliefs, the crime wave and other crises of the Great Depression came as a terrible shock. No wonder Hoover's carefully cultivated image of a strong and vigilant FBI exerted such extraordinary appeal.

Public anxiety over crime helped to make crime prevention a top priority among two powerful groups, both dominated by men. Professionals in sociology, psychology, criminology, and psychiatry comprised one group, and public officials and administrators in the fields of criminal justice, education, and social welfare comprised the other.[7] In general, the professional group developed theories about the causes of crime, while the bureaucratic group established practical crime-prevention programs. As both groups gained prominence during the late 1920s and 1930s, policewomen saw their role in crime prevention pushed aside and ignored.

Professionals' interest in crime prevention sprang from their fervent desire to raise their status, expand the area of their expertise, and demonstrate their usefulness in solving social problems. According to Margo Horn, professional groups competed fiercely during the early and mid-1930s to stake out crime prevention as part of their disciplinary turf.[8] Not surprisingly, each profession devised its own theories about the etiology of crime. Sociologists argued that crime arose from the collapse of social networks in urban "delinquency areas," psychologists claimed that criminal behavior was learned, and psychiatrists said that crime was a disease whose cure lay in a one-on-one relationship between the "patient" and a physician using psychotherapeutic treatment. These differences in opinion were genuine, but they did not run deep. As Horn has pointed out, most professionals agreed that "antisocial" behavior in children predicted criminal behavior in adults. In the words of Sheldon and Eleanor Glueck, criminologists famous in the 1930s for their work on juvenile delinquency, "Most criminals show definite antisocial tendencies of attitude and behavior early in childhood."[9] Charles S. Thompson, a sociologist, was more graphic. Referring to children living in a "delinquency area" in Los Angeles, Thompson claimed that he knew "boys ten, twelve, fourteen years of age, who were literally marching toward the gates of San Quentin Prison."[10]

By the late 1930s psychiatrists had established themselves as the professional experts in the field of crime prevention.[11] Horn attributes the ascendancy of psychiatric theories to psychiatrists' status as medical doctors: This status "gave them powerful authority and leverage when compared with sociologists working on crime, or with educators or social workers."[12] Or, Horn might have added, with policewomen. To paraphrase and add a gender dimension to her conclusion, the fact that nearly all psychiatrists were professional men gave them powerful authority and leverage when compared with women police and social workers.

The triumph of the psychiatric approach to crime prevention reflected ongoing trends in social work and criminology that eventually culminated in public policies rejecting broad-based reform and state intervention in favor of psychiatric understanding and treatment of an individual offender's mental processes.[13] In the field of criminology, for example, Freudian concepts of psychosexual development began to gain widespread acceptance in the 1920s and 1930s.[14] Freudian concepts found the causes of crime in individual personalities, rather than in the social environment. As a result, the environmental theories of crime that women social scientists had helped to develop at the turn of the century as part of their commitment to social reform and social justice lost popularity.[15]

The medicalization of crime and delinquency undermined policewomen's crime prevention model of police work because it made their short-term social casework with juveniles, especially their "motherly talks," appear both amateur and useless. By the early 1940s, news reporters who wanted to talk to an "expert" on preventing crime usually turned to a psychiatrist rather than a policewoman. During the early and mid-1930s, however, the immediate challenge to policewomen came from local public administrators and officials, such as probation department heads, juvenile court judges, school principals, police chiefs, and social-work administrators. Between 1932 and 1940, this group, which was composed almost entirely of men, established hundreds of programs throughout the country designed to prevent juvenile delinquency through interventions with school-age children. In most instances, the programs differed little from what pioneer policewomen had been doing and saying for years; nevertheless, the founders of the programs neither recognized nor used policewomen as crime prevention specialists.[16] The Los Angeles County Coordinating Council (LACCC), organized by Chief Probation Officer Kenyon Scudder in 1932, provides an instructive example.

Scudder laid the groundwork for the LACCC in autumn 1931 at a one-day local conference on juvenile delinquency. He called the conference because he wanted to put into practice his ideas about preventing crime that he had developed two years before, when he was member of the California Commission for the Study of Problem Children. While on a fact-finding tour for the commission, he went to Berkeley, where he studied the operations of the Coordinating Council, a delinquency prevention program established by Chief of Police August Vollmer. Under Vollmer's direction, representatives from schools and the police department met weekly to discuss individual children and teenagers with suspected or documented "antisocial tendencies." Some of the youths under discussion had arrest records, while others were simply known for misbehaving at school. Scudder liked what he saw in Berkeley, and after he became chief probation officer in Los Angeles in 1930, he thought that a similar program could work there on a much larger and more elaborate scale. He therefore organized the one-day conference on juvenile crime, calling together dozens of representatives from local law enforcement agencies, social work agencies, community service organizations, and schools. No record survives documenting whether any policewomen attended the conference, which was held on a Saturday.

Scudder opened the conference by describing the work of the Berkeley Co-ordinating Council. He then asked his listeners if they would be willing to help him establish a coordinating council in every high school district in Los Angeles County.[17] He explained that membership on Los Angeles coordinating councils would not be limited to police officers and school teachers and administrators, as it was in Berkeley. Instead, social and settlement house workers, probation officers, city recreation directors, and members of civic and fraternal organizations, such as the Elks Club, would be invited to join. The more varied the backgrounds and interests of volunteers, Scudder believed, the better.

Scudder proposed that members of coordinating councils meet weekly for several hours to talk about how to handle individual cases of "problem" boys and girls and how to eliminate the immediate causes of juvenile delinquency in the district. In theory, council members would learn of individual cases of troublesome youths from the police or another participating agency, such as a school. Regardless of the source of referral, all participating agencies would share their records on individual youths with other participating agencies. Scudder made it clear from the start that at no time were the children or teenagers under discussion, or their parents, to appear before the council. The councils were not a juvenile court or a social work agency. Instead, council members were supposed to decide which member agency should intervene in the young person's life and steer him or her away from crime. For example, council members might decide to handle one case by enrolling a teenager in an organized recreation program. In another case, council members might decide to file a petition in juvenile court.[18]

Scudder's plan drew an enthusiastic response from his audience. Several people, including Scudder, LAPD Chief Roy E. Steckel, and Judge Samuel Blake of the Juvenile Court, formed an Executive Board on the spot to oversee planning and all operations; this board did not include any policewomen. The board swiftly decided to divide every coordinating council into three committees: character-building, environment, and adjustment. Together, these committees performed all the work of the individual coordinating councils.

Los Angeles policewomen must have had mixed feelings when they learned that the functions of the three committees paralleled different aspects of their work. Specifically, the character-building committee encouraged the growth of "wholesome" organized recreation for teenagers, such as community dances; the environment committee uncovered "demoralizing" conditions in a given high school district, such as stores that sold liquor to minors; and the adjustment committee decided which course of action to take regarding individual youths, both boys and girls, who were referred to it by the police or another member agency.[19] Pioneer policewomen first undertook all these activities in the early 1910s.

Shortly after the initial meeting of the executive board, Scudder and an assistant, Probation Officer Kenneth S. Beam, organized the first sixteen councils; by July 1934, they had organized forty-eight in southern California.[20] Scudder was proud of the councils and eager to advertise them, so he welcomed the interest of Martin H. Neumeyer, a sociologist from the University of Southern California, and Norman Fenton, a psychologist from the California Bureau of Juvenile Re search. In 1936, these men published separate, glowing accounts of the Los Angeles councils in professional journals. Other academics and professionals in social work soon became intrigued by the "coordinating council idea," as Lawrence Riggs of Johns Hopkins University called it.[21] Coordinating councils began to spring up first in central California and then throughout the nation. Some cities sent representatives to Los Angeles to learn about the councils, but other cities simply asked Scudder to mail information. Kenneth Beam, Scudder's assistant, went to conferences around the country to discuss the wonders of the LACCC. By autumn 1936, over 250 coordinating councils had formed in 146 municipalities throughout twenty states. As in Los Angeles, local government agencies (usually the probation department or juvenile court) sponsored the councils.[22] Some people enthusiastically, if mistakenly, compared the councils to New England town meetings or claimed that the councils strengthened American democracy. "The coordinating council idea," Riggs declared in 1940, "provides opportunity for the kind of democratic participation in community affairs that is needed in America today."[23]

None of the scholars or journalists who praised the LACCC knew or mentioned that the individual councils did not operate according to plan. Although schools and social work agencies in Los Angeles referred hundreds of youngsters to the councils, arrest statistics provide unmistakable evidence that the LAPD stoutly resisted full participation. From mid-1932 to mid-1934, LAPD officers did not make any referrals of juveniles they had arrested; from mid-1934 through mid-1935, they referred only 16 of the 2,603 male youths they arrested, and none of the 737 female youths. After mid-1935, the category "Coordinating Council" disappears from the "Disposition of Juvenile Arrest" tables in the *Annual Reports*. Its disappearance strongly suggests that after mid-1935, LAPD officers referred no young people under arrest to the councils, because the LAPD routinely added categories to its juvenile arrest tables as needed, even if only one juvenile arrest fell into the new category. In some years, for example, the tables include the category "Died" or "Escaped" to show what happened to a young person under arrest prior to the processing of his or her case.[24]

It is important to understand that LAPD officers may have referred children and teenagers whom they did not arrest to the councils, but no records of these referrals exist. If LAPD officers did make such referrals, however, they probably made them prior to autumn 1935, because the LAPD in late 1935 duplicated some of the functions of coordinating councils through the newly created Predelinquent Detail (discussed below). Despite the low number of police referrals in the 1930s, coordinating councils in Los Angeles County continued to thrive during the 1940s and 1950s. They were still in existence in the mid-1980s.

The reluctance of the police to refer cases to the councils probably stemmed from occupational territorialism.[25] In all likelihood, officers resented the idea that they were no longer supposed to decide how to handle some of their cases themselves but instead were supposed to turn them over to an outside agency whose members were not necessarily familiar with police procedures or laws regarding juveniles. Moreover, referrals to coordinating councils posed a risk to the police because referrals increased the chances that an officer would be charged with misconduct. Once council members learned of the circumstances surrounding the arrest of an individual boy or girl, council members might question the legality or appropriateness of the arresting officer's actions.[26]

The fact that LAPD officers did not refer any teenage girls whom they arrested to the councils suggests that policewomen in the 1930s still believed that girls' cases—especially those involving the charge of sex delinquency—should be handled with confidentiality. Two decades earlier, Aletha Gilbert had insisted on locating the City Mother's Bureau outside a police station, claiming that "wayward girls" and their families needed more privacy to discuss their problems than a police station could provide. Privacy and confidentiality were also major issues in the early debate over whether policewomen should wear uniforms. In the

1910s, policewomen had argued against uniforms on the grounds that they wished to draw as little attention as possible to their interactions in public with girls and young women. Policewomen knew that if word got out that they had questioned an individual teenage girl, the girl might well be stigmatized as immoral simply on the basis that the police had shown an interest in her. Policewomen feared that for some teenage girls and young women, the stigma would become self-fulfilling. Referrals of teenage girls to coordinating council therefore had the potential of bringing about the very outcome that policewomen wished to avoid.

Veteran policewomen may also have resented that they were no longer recognized as the chief agents of crime prevention in Los Angeles. All the positive publicity once given to Alice Stebbins Wells and the City Mother's Bureau now focused on Kenyon Scudder and the probation department. Moreover, neither Scudder nor other key figures in the coordinating council movement (all of whom were men) acknowledged their debt to pioneer policewomen's crime prevention model of police work. Significantly, no policewomen appear on lists of people who served on the Executive Board of the LACCC. Perhaps worse from the standpoint of pioneer policewomen, their role in the councils did not differ significantly from that of policemen. Both policemen and policewomen were simply police officers, not "detecting-arresting" policemen and "preventing-protecting" policewomen. Policewomen's unique occupational identity, which they had struggled for years to establish, went entirely unnoticed. This was bitter medicine, particularly because, in many respects, coordinating councils duplicated pioneer policewomen's work and ideals.

No public record survives that indicates how policewomen felt about the coordinating councils or many of the changes in police practices that affected their work and work identity in the 1930s and 1940s. Of course, with respect to the coordinating councils, newspaper reporters did not seek policewomen's opinion because policewomen had no role in creating the councils or directing policy. Yet even if reporters had asked policewomen's opinion, they may not have received much of an answer; by the mid-1930s, most policewomen had learned to be extremely circumspect around journalists. They were wary of saying anything that might displease their male superiors or politicians.

The apparent ease with which the male leadership of the LACCC ignored policewomen has some roots in pioneer policewomen's focus on adolescent female sexuality. Throughout the 1910s and 1920s, pioneer policewomen had insisted that protecting female youth from moral dangers was the core of their work. But their preoccupation with "saving girls from lives of shame," as they phrased it, eventually facilitated their exclusion from crime prevention programs that dealt with nonsexual juvenile delinquency, such as property crimes committed by teenage boys. Indeed, in the late 1920s and 1930s, male juvenile delinquency received much more public attention than adolescent female sexuality; the "girl problem" had disappeared as a social crisis. For policewomen, the disappearance of the girl problem meant a lowered public profile. Women's clubs, for example, stopped pressing for the appointment of women to the police force, and newspapers stopped carrying stories about policewomen's work. In Los Angeles, the fact that women served on the city police force no longer excited interest because policewomen were no longer a novelty. Press coverage of LAPD women officers in the 1930s therefore dwindled. Without an urgent social crisis for policewomen to discuss, without women's clubs advocating the appointment of women officers, and without a strong visible presence on the LAPD, policewomen were easy for LACCC officials to ignore.

In December 1935, policewomen in Los Angeles received further, incontrovertible proof of their eclipse in crime prevention. That month, Chief James E. Davis organized a new unit, the Predelinquent Detail. According to the LAPD *Annual Report* for 1935–36, the Predelinquent Detail had a twofold purpose: "to discover children who are in danger of becoming delinquent, and to find and eliminate all moral hazards affecting the youth of the community." Davis assigned thirty-two men to the detail but not a single woman.[27] Thus, a quarter-century after Alice Stebbins Wells staked out a special place for women in the LAPD, she and other women officers watched Chief Davis usurp their territory.

Policemen assigned to the Predelinquent Detail worked only at night; hence, they were sometimes called the Special Juvenile Night Patrol. They spent most of their time looking for young people in public places after curfew. (The hour of curfew changed periodically.) Like pioneer policewomen of the 1910s, officers routinely patrolled parks, dance halls, pool halls, train stations, movie theaters, and other places where young people gathered. Unlike pioneer policewomen, they also cruised the streets in unmarked cars and each night conducted over one hundred "street interviews" of young people of both sexes. As the name implies, a street interview was an on-the-spot interrogation; these interrogations sometimes resulted in arrests. During the first six months of 1936, the Predelinquent Detail conducted street interviews of 21,667 youths "found unsupervised on the streets at night." Officers arrested 4 percent (881), of whom an undisclosed number were girls.[28] Officers routinely turned over girls' cases to policewomen the morning after the arrest.

In some respects the Predelinquent Detail worked like the character-building committees of coordinating councils. Between January and June 1936, officers referred 1,218 boys and girls whom they "interviewed" to organized recreation activities co-sponsored by the LAPD and the City Playground and Recreation Department. The activities included scout troops, softball teams, and overnight camping trips.[29] According to the LAPD, these referrals were suggestions, not commands.

> *If the parents want their children to take advantage of any available*
> *programs, cards of introduction are given the children to be presented*
> *to the directors of the activities recommended. However, at no time is*
> *there an attempt to force the issue, the action being left entirely to the*
> *discretion of the parents.*[30]

It seems doubtful, however, that all parents would have agreed with the LAPD that they felt no pressure from the officers to enroll their children in programs.

In appointing thirty-two men but not a single woman to the Predelinquent Detail, Chief Davis continued the policy, established sometime between the late 1910s and mid-1920s, of refusing to assign women to patrol work. In this respect the Predelinquent Detail broke no new ground. But by assigning only male officers to the unit, Davis demonstrated his rejection of policewomen's gender-based arguments for the employment of women in police work. Specifically, he denied policewomen's claim that they were inherently better-suited than men to be crime prevention officers.

Davis's failure to assign women to the Predelinquent Detail is typical of other actions he took during his two stints as LAPD chief (April 1926 through December 1929 and August 1933 through November 1938). In 1934, for example, he broke with tradition by ordering policewomen to wear uniforms. Although no evidence survives to indicate why he wanted policewomen in uniform—in fact, he had argued against it a few years earlier—he may have wanted to quash the symbolic independence conferred by policewomen's plainclothes status.[31] According to Stephen Leinen, a police uniform imposes strong psychological pressure to conform to certain behavioral stereotypes because it designates anyone who wears it as an official representative of the law. Once in uniform, Leinen argues, police officers adopt an aggressive, "conflict" style of behavior. Similarly, the civilian clothing of plainclothes officers frees them from the need to conform to any particular style of behavior.[32] Leinen's analysis suggests that by ordering policewomen to wear uniforms, Davis seriously weakened their psychological autonomy. Davis may have also wanted to eliminate any suggestion created by policewomen's plainclothes status that their rank was superior to that of uniformed policemen.

In 1937, Davis struck another blow at policewomen's independence by ordering the relocation of the City Mother's Bureau from the City Hall to Georgia Street Division, a police substation. He had tried once before, in 1929, to relocate the bureau and its records to a police station, but women activists stopped him. (See Chapter Three.) For reasons discussed below, women activists remained silent in 1937. Without the support of women outside the LAPD, City Mother Elizabeth Fiske could not effectively protest the order. In December she and her assistants moved to Georgia Street Division. Within a few weeks of the move, the number of people seeking her advice began to fall steadily.[33]

The decline in the number of people who went to the City Mother's Bureau for help proved that the bureau's location outside the police station had been critical to its success, just as Aletha Gilbert had predicted in 1914, when she first argued that many women would hesitate to go to a police station for advice on highly confidential matters. Gilbert may have also foreseen that as long as the bureau remained physically separate from the police station, only the City Mother and her staff would have easy access to, and control over, case records. Sometime after Fiske moved into Georgia Street Division, Davis ordered her to file two copies of each case record with the captain of the Crime Prevention Division.[34] (Beginning in 1925, the Juvenile Bureau, the Probation Bureaus, and the City Mother's Bureau were known collectively as the Crime Prevention Division.)[35] The semi-autonomous status of the bureau had come to an end.

Davis's hostility toward policewomen was not unusual among police chiefs, especially during the Great Depression. Some of the hostility may have grown from a belief that policewomen were taking steady, good-paying jobs away from unemployed men. As Samuel Walker has noted, "The economic collapse of the 1930s had the curious effect of improving the relative economic status of police work. As the economy spiraled downward and unemployment figures steadily rose, jobs on police forces became highly prized."[36] Many Americans probably thought it wrong, if not shameful, that women police had such good jobs while men went without work. The feeling that women's place was in the home pervaded popular culture during the 1930s and influenced hiring practices. The Brotherhood of Railway and Steamship Clerks, for example, refused to employ married women whose husbands could financially support them.[37]

Davis's hostility toward policewomen also reflected his preference for strong-arm police tactics and his disdain for anyone who did not share his views. In 1927, when two LAPD detectives shot to death a suspected killer, Davis bragged that his men would continue to "hold court on gunmen in the Los Angeles streets." In an interview with the press about gangsters, he announced flatly, "I want them brought in dead not alive." He then added that he would "reprimand any officer who shows the least mercy to a criminal." Referring to the Cornero brothers, a notorious pair of local bootleggers, he claimed that "if the courts won't eliminate them, I will."[38] (Davis had a national reputation as a marksman.) Under his second administration in the mid-1930s, LAPD patrolmen were the only municipal police officers in the United States who wore their revolvers conspicuously on the outside of their uniforms. All other U.S. police departments instructed their patrolmen to wear revolvers under their coats.[39]

LAPD historian Joseph Gerald Woods has argued that Davis's aggressive personality contributed to the increase in the number of citizens' complaints of police brutality, or "cossackism" as it was known. Davis was cavalier and defensive in his response to these complaints, nearly always refusing to discipline the officers involved. According to Woods, Davis believed it was "only natural" that officers would physically attack citizens who offended or insulted them.[40] Davis's bellicose attitude represents the antithesis of pioneer policewomen's ideals of preventive justice.

Urban Politics and the Erosion of Female Activism

The silence of women activists over the relocation of the bureau in 1937 signifies another key change affecting policewomen's work: the increasingly beleaguered state of separate female institutions after the passage of the Nineteenth Amendment in 1920. The 1920s was a rocky decade for separate female institutions, in part because ideas stressing gender differences disappeared from white middle-class women's public discourse. During the Progressive Era, many middle-class women had asserted that women were needed in the public sphere because of the gender-specific contributions they could make, but beginning in the 1920s, they argued that in the workplace and other public arenas, both men and women should disregard gender identity and simply view women as workers and as citizens. Many separate female institutions withered and died under this formulation, and membership in women's clubs declined nationwide. In a parallel development, social activism decreased markedly during the 1920s among white middle-class women.[41] Diminished belief in women's gender-specific capabilities and the decline in female social activism inflicted serious wounds on the campaign for women police and other maternalist reform movements.

At first glance, the silence of organized women in Los Angeles over the relocation of the City Mother's Bureau in 1937 seems to typify the decline in female social activism and the weakened state of women's clubs. But some women in Los Angeles and elsewhere in the nation still spoke the language of maternalist reform in the 1930s, despite the hostility of conservative forces. And some women still wielded considerable political influence, particularly at the local and regional levels.[42] At times, however, opposing conservative forces overwhelmed organized women on a given issue, forcing them to put their limited resources elsewhere. Events in Los Angeles during 1930 exemplify women's forced retreat in the face of strong opposition. The power struggle there pitted the white female activist community against Mayor John C. Porter, an ambitious man who tried to reorganize the police department and make it answerable only to him; as part of his plan, he deliberately severed the ties between the City Mother's Bureau and local white women activists.

The events leading to Porter's actions began with his election in July 1929. During the mayoral campaign, Porter portrayed himself as a reform candidate, but like many so-called reform candidates in Los Angeles during the early twentieth century, he was a machine politician. Shortly after his election, Roy E. "Strong-

Arm Dick" Steckel became chief of police through Porter's political influence. Porter liked Steckel because he knew Steckel was an ambitious "yes-man."[43] To ensure that Steckel would do his bidding, he moved Steckel's office from the police department to City Hall and installed an electric buzzer so he could summon Steckel instantly to his side. Wags predicted that Steckel would soon develop callouses on his forehead from his continuous bowing and scraping.[44]

Porter ruled the police board and civil service commission almost as completely as he ruled Steckel. According to Woods, Porter's "regal disregard" for civil service rules led to the firing of many civil servants who thought their jobs were secure.[45] It probably also led to the civil service commission's controversial selection of Elizabeth Fiske as Aletha Gilbert's successor as City Mother.

In January 1930, six months after Gilbert's retirement, the civil service commission held examinations to select the new City Mother. Of the thirty-five women who took the examinations, Deanne Harris stood out as Gilbert's likely successor because she had fifteen years of experience as assistant City Mother, she enjoyed the backing of the entire City Mother's Advisory Board, and she was currently the acting City Mother. She and her supporters felt certain that she would win the appointment, but their confidence was misplaced. In late January, the civil service commission announced that only one of the applicants, Elizabeth Fiske, had passed both the written and the oral examinations. Harris supposedly had failed the oral examination. The commissioners accordingly submitted only Fiske's name to Chief Steckel.[46]

Harris and the City Mother's Advisory Board were outraged. Compared with Harris, Fiske had extremely limited experience. She had joined the LAPD only the year before as a "juvenile officer–female," and she had never worked in the City Mother's Bureau.[47] Soon after hearing the news, Harris sought the advice of an attorney, probably the bureau's legal advisor. Using the language and format of a legal petition, the attorney helped Harris to compose a formal letter of protest to all police and city officials. Harris made two accusations in her letter: that the civil service commissioners had failed to give proper credit to her for her years of service as assistant City Mother, and that they had failed to submit the names of the three highest-scoring candidates to the chief, as required by law. She then demanded that she be given the opportunity to take another set of examinations and that the second set be graded by an "impartial Board of Examiners" instead of the civil service commission.[48]

The letter breathed a lot of fire but got no results. The city council simply filed it away, smugly asserting that it had no authority over the civil service commission.[49] Meanwhile, Chief Steckel transferred Harris to a desk job in the Wilshire Division.[50] The transfer was akin to a demotion, and it probably frightened Harris into thinking that if she created more trouble, the chief might retaliate by firing her and taking away her pension rights—a fate that had befallen other LAPD officers who, for one reason or another, had displeased the Porter-Steckel administration. In one particularly notorious case, Steckel had fired a captain with nineteen years on the department. The captain would have been eligible to collect a pension after twenty years.[51]

The City Mother's Bureau Advisory Board had its own response to Fiske's appointment. In February, board members circulated a petition throughout Los Angeles requesting the city council to pass an ordinance to remove the City Mother's Bureau from the LAPD and to make it into an agency outside the purview of the civil service commission.[52] The petition failed, but its boldness so angered Porter that he summarily told the City Mother's advisors that they no longer could hold their meetings in City Hall.[53] A few weeks later, while the advisors were still reeling from this blow, Steckel fired the bureau's legal advisor, cut back the City Mother's secretarial support staff, limited the City Mother's use of a police car, then, in a final thrust, abolished the advisory board itself.[54]

Many in the police department probably cheered Steckel's actions. According to an interview with Alice Stebbins Wells in 1938, sentiment against the bureau had run high in some quarters of the LAPD during Gilbert's administration. Unidentified critics of the bureau charged that Gilbert undertook cases that did not properly belong to the bureau, that she had too many "outside" interests, and most telling of all, that she and her staff engaged in far too much political activity. This last criticism was a fine piece of hypocrisy because all high-ranking policemen in the LAPD owed their positions to a system of political patronage. Even the lowly patrolman on his beat knew he dared not offend politicians, lest he lose his job.[55] Furthermore, according to Wells, unnamed members of the LAPD charged that under Gilbert, the bureau "catered" to prominent people in Los Angeles, that it was "high-handed" with clients, and that it practiced class and racial discrimination. Unfortunately, Wells gave no details or evidence supporting these allegations.[56]

At first, the former members of the City Mother's Advisory Board tried to carry on their work by reorganizing as the City Mother's Emeritus Club under the direction of Aletha Gilbert. Their relationship with Fiske grew increasingly strained, however, when she refused to give back four thousand dollars they had raised for the bureau under Gilbert's administration. In September 1930, they sued her and lost.[57] Shortly thereafter, Gilbert, who had scrupulously remained above the fracas, died, and the Emeritus Club disbanded.

Urban politics, together with the weakened state of female social activism in the 1930s, ensured that Fiske never received the kind of support from women in Los Angeles that Gilbert had enjoyed. On one hand, the City Mother's Advisory Board cannot be blamed for resenting the fact that Fiske had received her appointment as a result of a corrupt mayor's machinations. However, no evidence exists to suggest that Fiske had any influence with Porter, Steckel, or the civil service commissioners prior to her appointment. In 1930, she was a relative new-comer to Los Angeles, having moved there from northern California less than five years before. The most likely explanation for the commissioners' selecting her over Harris is that they were responding to a directive from Porter to choose the applicant with the least experience and least clout in the department. Such appointees were usually grateful, loyal, and eager to please. On the other hand, the City Mother's Advisory Board should have recognized Fiske as a pawn. Had the advisors overcome their distaste for the process that elevated her to City Mother, they would have found that she had a heartfelt dedication to her work and a genius for getting things done under trying circumstances.

Fiske's appointment split LAPD women officers into two camps: Fiske supporters and Harris supporters. In autumn 1930, approximately seven months after Fiske took office, Captain Edward M. Slaughter of the Crime Prevention Division apparently bowed to the pressure of the Harris camp and told Fiske she was through as City Mother. She went to the chief and asked for an explanation. He told her that Slaughter had made a mistake. When asked by the press why Slaughter tried to fire her, Fiske bluntly replied that some women officers resented her and wanted her gone.[58] If other attempts were made to force her out, nothing came of them. Fiske remained City Mother for thirty-four years, until her retirement in 1964. No controversies would erupt over the selection of her successor; once she retired, the LAPD closed the City Mother's Bureau permanently.[59]

Sexual Regulation and Sex-Crime Panics

Politically, much had changed for the City Mother's Bureau by the time Fiske finished her first year as City Mother, but one trend remained steady: the continuing increase in the percentage of marital discord cases and the corresponding decrease in the percentage of "In Danger" cases. As noted in Chapter Three, this trend began in the mid-1920s; by 1939, approximately three-quarters of City Mother's Bureau cases involved marital discord, while less than 10 percent involved allegations of premarital sexual activity by unwed teenage girls and young women.[60]

Although Fiske and her assistants handled relatively few "In Danger" cases in the 1930s and early 1940s, policewomen in the LAPD Juvenile Bureau continued to arrest many girls and young women for sex delinquency. As in earlier years, a disproportionate percentage of those arrested were from the working class and racial and ethnic minority groups. From mid-1937 to mid-1938, for example, 40 percent of all arrests of girls under eighteen years old involved the charge of sex delinquency (396 of 997); 13 percent of those arrested on this charge were African Americans (51 of 396), while 21 percent were Latinas (84 of 396).[61] According to Ruth M. Alexander, working-class and minority female youth received a disproportionate share of police attention in the mid-twentieth century because police and other authorities knew that prostitution had not disappeared, and they thought that poor teenage girls easily drifted from premarital sexual experimentation to commercial sex work.[62] Racist stereotypes doubtlessly also influenced arrest rates. So although the "girl problem" had disappeared as a social crisis in the late 1920s, policewomen's work as agents of female sexual regulation continued into the 1930s and 1940s. At the same time, policewomen were losing their public image as crime prevention specialists and the "natural" protectors of girls and women in public. Nothing better illustrates the loss of this image than policewomen's negligible role in the sex-crime panic of the late 1930s.

The sex-crime panic of the late 1930s grew out of the alarm Americans felt about crime in general. According to sensationalized press coverage of crime, some of society's worst lawbreakers were psychologically twisted men who committed violent, sexual murders of women and children. These men, known as sexual psychopaths, supposedly harbored uncontrollable sexual urges. Almost overnight, stories about sexual psychopaths filled newspapers and magazines, making it seem that no woman or child was safe in public at any time. These stories were so numerous and horrifying that they played a major role in causing a sex-crime panic in the late 1930s, the first of several such panics stretching over a period of thirty years, from 1935 to 1965.[63]

At first glance, it seems surprising that the sex-crime panic of the late 1930s led to no new calls for women police; after all, women had originally entered police work largely on the basis of their claim that only women could protect women and girls from moral dangers, especially sexual dangers. Nor did policewomen's daily work change significantly as a result of the sex-crime panic. Los Angeles policewomen did not, for example, begin to patrol the neighborhoods around schools, looking for sexual psychopaths. Given the widely acknowledged need to protect women and children from sexual psychopaths, why did the movement for women police remain dormant in the late 1930s and why did policewomen remain on the sidelines?

Most of the answer to these questions lies in the nature of sex-crime panics themselves. As Estelle B. Freedman has argued, the central concern of sex-crime panics was men and masculinity, not violence against women and children. According to her analysis, masculinity became a significant social issue in the 1930s, when millions of unemployed men lost their traditional masculine status as breadwinners. At the same time, psychologists, psychiatrists, and others expanded their research into masculinity and the related topic of male sexual deviance. Their studies, together with extensive news accounts of sex murders committed by the so-called sexual psychopath, raised Americans' awareness of masculinity in general and male sexual deviance in particular.[64] But the issues of masculinity and male sexual deviance had never greatly interested women activists. During the 1930s and later, campaigns to pass laws regarding sexual psychopaths had little female and no feminist leadership.[65] Similarly, masculinity and male sexual deviance were issues that policewomen had never claimed as areas of expertise. Even during the Progressive Era, when the movement for women police was going strong, pioneer policewomen and their supporters evinced little interest in male sexual deviance. Their concern was the protection of women and girls from the dangers of premarital sex and male sexual license, or the "normal" male sex drive.[66]

Little documentation of policewomen's response to the sex-crime panic exists. Published interviews of policewomen became increasingly rare during the 1930s, and to make matters worse for the researcher, a major source of information about policewomen, the *Policewoman's International Bulletin*, distributed by the International Association of Policewomen, stopped publication in December 1930 because of a lack of funds. Unfortunately, therefore, policewomen's response to the sex-crime panic remains obscure. Yet even if the sex-crime panic had inspired some policewomen to try to stake out new occupational territory for themselves as regulatory agents of male sexual deviance, policewomen as a whole were in no position to undertake such bold action. As the 1930s advanced, policewomen in every city found themselves losing ground on many fronts.

Most of the defeats policewomen suffered in the 1930s were beyond their control, such as the loss of their public identity as crime prevention specialists, the prevalent sentiment against hiring women instead of men, and the erosion of middle-class women's social activism. But the pioneering generation of policewomen also suffered a setback that arose inside their ranks: the lack of interest among the second generation of women police in maintaining policewomen's dual occupational identity as preventive and protective social workers and police officers. To the dismay of the pioneering generation, second-generation policewomen rejected the social-work ideals of the pioneering generation and thereby helped to doom the crime prevention model of police work.

Second-Generation Policewomen

The second generation of women officers entered police departments from approximately 1930 to 1950. At the LAPD, the entry of the second generation coincided in the early 1930s with changes in personnel policies. Sometime in 1931 or 1932, the LAPD reversed its requirement that women officers be over thirty years old; now all women officers had to be under thirty at the time of their appointment. The LAPD also followed the lead of other U.S. police departments by dropping the ban against hiring unmarried women.[67] These policy changes accelerated the entry of women into the LAPD who had come of age in a social and political climate strikingly different from that of pioneer policewomen and who brought to police work a new set of attitudes about female gender identity and gender relations. Sex solidarity among women, for example, was highly prized by pioneer policewomen and their peers, but it was often seen as sex antagonism toward men during the 1920s.[68] To many younger women, sex solidarity seemed old-fashioned and pioneer policewomen themselves seemed to be antiques from a bygone age. This attitude carried over to pioneer policewomen's social case-work methods and attempts to be both social workers and police officers. According to Mary Galton Stevenson, a second-generation LAPD officer, the second generation strove for assimilation into the police department as police officers, not as social workers who carried a badge. For this reason, she and some of her peers wondered why the City Mother's Bureau continued to exist as a division of the police department. To them, the bureau resembled a social work agency much more than an arm of the law.[69]

Whether purposefully or not, the LAPD reinforced the second generation's rejection of the social-worker identity by routinely teaming rookie policewomen with veteran policemen, instead of veteran policewomen. Stevenson has recalled that because all her partners were men when she first joined the department, she never got to know personally any pioneer policewomen.[70] The practice of as-signing female rookies to male veterans had negative consequences for police-women's collective status in the department because it precluded the formation of close working relationships between pioneer and second-generation police-women. More important, male-female teams guaranteed that the second genera-tion learned the practice of police work from male officers, many of whom deeply resented having female partners; these male officers sometimes displayed their resentment by openly expressing doubts about women's proficiency in law en-forcement. Ultimately, teaming female rookies with male veterans helped to cre-ate a working environment for the second generation that was in its own way as hostile to women as the one the pioneering generation had endured.[71]

A study of the LAPD in the late 1930s by Margaret Saunders, a graduate stu-dent in social work at the University of Southern California, found that police-women were well aware that policemen of all ranks questioned women's ability to work under police discipline and organization. Saunders noted with obvious approval that policewomen's response to this criticism was to turn the other cheek.

> The policewomen . . . believe that, though police departments do not al-
> ways function according to women's ways of doing things, it is up to
> the women members to adapt themselves. They realize that effective
> service depends largely on the extent to which women police cooperate
> with men police.[72]

This passage points up a fundamental change in policewomen's attitudes since the 1910s. In the early days, policewomen had sought to infuse police work with values associated with women and social work. They knew all too well that policemen did not welcome them, but they forged ahead regardless, secure in their belief that as women, they had both a place and a mission in police departments. In the late 1920s, this attitude began to seem too strident, too combative, and even some leading pioneer policewomen adopted a more conciliatory tone. In an interview in 1928, Lieutenant Mina C. Van Winkle of the District of Columbia Police Department proclaimed that "the United States has no use for a sex war. . . . The hope of the woman movement and its logical progress lies in cooperation with men and not antagonism to them."[73] Although Van Winkle was referring to the woman's movement in general, her words held a special meaning for policewomen because of her position as president of the International Association of Policewomen.

Second-generation policewomen's rejection of the social-worker identity, together with their strong emphasis on cooperating with policemen, opened no new doors to them in police work. With few exceptions, LAPD women officers continued to serve as matrons in the Women's Jail and to handle cases involving women, girls, prepubescent boys, and domestic relations. Their work with female youths did not remain completely static, however. During the Great Depression, the number of female dependency cases rose steadily.

Broadly speaking, a dependency case involved a child who allegedly lacked a "proper" guardian. These cases usually came to the attention of the police through allegations of child neglect or child abuse by neighbors, schoolteachers, or relatives; through policewomen's investigation into truancy or other problems concerning a child; or through the arrest, death, desertion, or institutionalization of a child's parents.[74] In 1930–31, just over 21 percent of all female juveniles under arrest by the LAPD faced dependency charges. By 1940, this percentage had risen to nearly 53.[75] A report prepared in 1935 by the Children's Protective Association of Los Angeles indicates that the economic hardships arising from the Great Depression accounted for the increase. According to the report, the number of children placed in foster care in the city "increased a hundred-fold" during the early 1930s because many parents simply could no longer provide the necessities of life for their children.[76]

A few second-generation Los Angeles policewomen worked in undercover squads during the 1930s, but here, too, they had only two roles, both based solely on their sex/gender identity: to act as decoys and to handle any females or young boys involved in investigations. Policewoman Lula B. Lane worked in the Shoplifting Detail and the Pickpocket and Bunco Detail, Marie Dinuzzo worked in the Narcotics Detail, and Mary Ross worked in the Vice Detail.[77] When male detectives needed additional policewomen for an investigation, or when they needed a policewoman with certain physical traits to impersonate someone, they usually drafted policewomen from the Crime Prevention Division. According to

Fanchon Blake, a second-generation LAPD woman officer, detectives sometimes put policewomen into highly dangerous situations. Any policewoman who balked when asked to do something dangerous risked losing her career: "When policemen said jump, policewomen jumped."[78]

As Blake's comment suggests, the determination of second-generation policewomen to assimilate into the LAPD as police officers, not social workers, did not raise policewomen's overall standing in the department. They probably suffered more than their predecessors from their subordinate status because, unlike the pioneering generation, the second generation could not draw on a female network of support outside the department. The decline in female social activism left the second generation politically, socially, and psychologically stranded inside a hostile male institution. It also made women's presence in police work more puzzling to the public in general. Whereas during the 1910s pioneer policewomen were part of a large army of women demanding entry into male workplaces and institutions, by the early 1930s such demands had gone out of style. Recall, too, that during the Great Depression some Americans resented the presence of women on the police force because male unemployment was high. In sum, the public image of policewomen—never very good—did not improve in the 1930s. In Los Angeles newspapers increasingly began to refer to policewomen in playfully demeaning ways, a practice they continued into the 1940s and beyond. In place of the term "policewomen," reporters used "police beauties" and "sheminions of the law."[79] Los Angeles policemen were much more derogatory, openly referring to a policewoman, for example, as "Sgt. Tits." Second-generation policewomen generally bore all these names in silence.[80]

The negative public image of policewomen during the 1930s merits close examination because it shows how little some aspects of policewomen's lives had changed since the 1910s. At the root of policewomen's public image was the sentiment that they were "unfeminine." "Unfeminine" in this context had three shades of meaning that blended into each other. In its strongest formulation, "unfeminine" meant that policewomen were lesbians. A weaker and more frequently voiced definition held that policewomen lacked conventional feminine attributes, such as beauty, grace, and charm. As one journalist observed, most Americans believed a policewoman was "a tough, callous girl, about as alluring as the business end of a burp gun."[81] (Burp guns were automatic weapons, nicknamed "burp" because of the distinctive sound they made when fired.) Another slightly more subtle definition held that the masculine nature of police work robbed women of their "natural" feminine senses of modesty, delicacy, and refinement. It also suggested that any woman who was drawn to police work was somehow not quite respectable. Alice Ames Winter, an editor of the *Ladies' Home Journal*, dramatized this aspect of policewomen's public image in an article she wrote about Mina C. Van Winkle in 1927. "Policewoman?" she sneered. "Pound the pavements? Dip into dives and rub shoulders with filth and lawlessness? You can't get decent women to do that kind of work."[82]

The question of policewomen's lesbianism did not overtly arise in Los Angeles until the 1930s, when the LAPD dropped its ban against hiring unmarried women. The LAPD then tacitly acknowledged the lesbian stereotype by investigating the backgrounds of women applicants for signs of lesbian "tendencies" or evidence of "Boston marriages." If any rumors or signs of sexual "irregularities" surfaced, the LAPD automatically rejected the applicant. For example, the neighbors of one applicant told a LAPD investigator that they had surreptitiously observed the applicant and her female roommate exchange vows and rings in the backyard. This allegation killed the applicant's chances to become a policewoman in Los Angeles.[83] Because it involved a sexual taboo, the idea that policewomen were lesbians did not receive much public attention. However, the silence that surrounded the lesbian stereotype may have strengthened it.

The defeminizing stereotype—the notion that police work robbed women of their femininity—plagued both pioneer and second-generation policewomen. In the early 1910s, Aletha Gilbert cleverly discounted the stereotype in her answer to an interviewer's question about the "Nicotine Dance," a controversial dance show performed on the public stage in Los Angeles.

> *I found the dance very artistic, very beautiful, very chaste . . . but I did not rely entirely on my own judgment. I feared that what I have [been] accustomed to seeing and hearing as a policewoman might have blunted my sense of what was modest and decorous, so I took to the theatre several persons of known prudence of view, of some degree of unsophistication of judgment, and who by the worldly might be charged with a carefulness that could be called prudery and they sustained my opinion exactly.*[84]

Gilbert's remarks were disingenuous; she was far too self-confident to doubt her judgment in matters of taste and morality. Indeed, within a year or so of making this statement, she pushed for her appointment as City Mother, a position requiring the constant exercise of her judgment of "what was modest and decorous." She made the statement because she was acutely aware of the charge that police work robbed women of their "natural" feminine attributes, and she wanted to counter it openly. Decades later, an observation by New York City policewoman Dorothy Uhnak reveals the longevity of the defeminizing stereotype: "A policewoman, apparently, is supposed to look a certain way: big, heavy, hard, tough, obvious. She is generally expected to wear her experiences on her face, to have them glaring from her eyes or resounding in her voice"[85]

Policewomen's "unfeminine" public image received a boost in the 1930s when some police departments began to issue firearms to women officers for the

first time. Policewomen in New York City received guns and began pistol practice in 1934.[86] Five years later, the LAPD reversed its longstanding policy regarding the arming of women officers. Without much fanfare, Acting Chief David
I. Davidson notified women officers that they must attend a training course in
firearms, after which they would be issued .38-caliber pistols, popularly known
as "belly guns." The *Los Angeles Times* announced the change in policy with the
comment, "The female of the species, when it comes to cops, is truly as deadly, if
not more so, than the male."[87]

The arming of Los Angeles policewomen graphically illustrates the death of
the crime prevention model of police work and the distance LAPD women officers had traveled in the 1930s. At the beginning of the decade, policewomen still
wore civilian clothes and tucked their badges into handbags. They still thought
of themselves primarily as social workers, as the following remark made by policewoman Marguerite Curley in January 1930 reveals: "Every policewoman is
entitled to be called city mother, for every day, every one of us does the same kind
of work."[88] Nine years later, Los Angeles policewomen presented a very different image. They wore police uniforms with badges prominently displayed and
carried guns in their handbags (apparently the idea of a woman in uniform with
a gun visible on her hip was still too disturbing). In 1939, Los Angeles policewomen no longer resembled the motherly social worker and policewoman ideal
of the early 1910s.

Ironically, the arming of policewomen illustrates their loss of power. Because
policewomen no longer sought to infuse police work with the values associated
with women and social work, they no longer represented a threat to male hegemony. Even some policemen who initially opposed the employment of women social workers as police officers in the 1910s and 1920s now conceded that policewomen had their uses.[89] The uniform and the gun were therefore not marks of
policewomen's equal status with policemen. Instead, they were visible symbols of
policewomen's conformity with men's opinions about the nature of police work.
In a sense, policewomen had become domesticated within police departments.

Rise of the Crime Control Model

The death of the female-gendered crime prevention model during the 1930s occurred simultaneously with the rise of a new, male-gendered model of police work.
The new model, known as the crime control or militarized model, characterizes the
typical police officer as a crime fighter extraordinaire, a seasoned, well-armed, professional soldier in an unending and savage war on crime. The gender implications
of the crime control model were plain: women could not be combat soldiers.

Since the late 1960s, historians have examined the rise of the crime control
model and the militarization of U.S. police departments. Eric Monkkonen argues

that at the close of the nineteenth century, police departments began to jettison many tasks unrelated to crime, such as the provision of beds for homeless men. Gradually, as the functions of the police narrowed, the focus of police work shifted from class control to crime control.[90] Samuel Walker has offered a slightly different interpretation. He believes that in the early twentieth century the crime prevention model of policing competed with the crime control model, but during the 1930s long-term trends toward efficiency finally prevailed, resulting in the ascendancy of the crime control model.[91] Additionally, Walker asserts that FBI Director J. Edgar Hoover purposefully cultivated the crime-fighting image of the police during the 1930s. This image corresponded with Hoover's insistence that a tidal wave of crime threatened American civilization.[92]

Consideration of gender dynamics greatly augment these explanations. As we have seen, middle-class women led a national movement during the Progressive Era to make the police more responsive to the needs of women and children. Supporters of the movement for women police believed that if sufficient numbers of cities hired women social workers as police officers, society would benefit in two ways: police work would gradually become infused with values associated with women and social work, and police departments would become agencies for crime prevention. Proponents of women police possessed an extraordinarily strong belief in the power of female social workers to effect sweeping change. Yet because pioneer policewomen and their proponents cast their arguments in gender-specific terms, they unintentionally helped to pave the way for the eventual appearance of an antithetical, male-gendered model of police work. Specifically, by identifying some areas of police work as feminine and other areas as masculine, proponents of women police imposed gender divisions where none had existed before. Prior to women's mass entry into police departments, all police work was a "man's job." By dividing police work along gender lines, proponents of women police narrowed the functions of policemen and, in effect, prepared the ground for the crime control model through their insistence that policemen should specialize in crime detection and arrest. The crime control model adopted this definition of policemen's work in its entirety but rejected policewomen's crime prevention mission.

Considerations of gender dynamics also shed light on why the crime control model devalued women officers and excluded social work methods of crime prevention. Most of the architects of the crime control model were policemen or former policemen. In this respect they differed from earlier generations of police reformers. As a group, policemen disliked social workers, resented policewomen, and hated the crime prevention model of police work. They rightly associated social work with the crime prevention model, which valued policewomen's efforts to prevent crime more highly than it valued policemen's efforts to apprehend criminals. Moreover, policemen understood that the crime prevention model reversed gender hierarchy and directly challenged men's authority in a traditional male arena: the maintenance of law and order.

Even though the crime prevention model never achieved dominance in police work, its existence, together with the appointment of women social workers to police departments, posed a threat to male hegemony in police work during the 1910s and 1920s, an era of great turmoil, uncertainty, and change for municipal police departments. The Executive Board of the International Association of Chiefs of Police acknowledged the threat posed by policewomen and the crime prevention model in 1921, when board members warned policemen that if they did not improve their performance, they might lose their jobs to social workers. Given policemen's antipathy toward policewomen and social work, no wonder the architects of the crime control model conceived of the police role in masculine, crime-fighting terms.

By the end of World War II, the crime control model had eclipsed the crime prevention model and dominated U.S. municipal policing. Yet the crime control model was not responsible for robbing policewomen of their public identity as crime prevention experts. As we have seen, male-dominated groups of professionals and public administrators took over the cause of crime prevention in the early 1930s, prior to the ascendancy of the crime control model. Even some police chiefs in the 1930s took up the cause of crime prevention among youth; LAPD Chief James E. Davis, for example, organized the all-male "Predelinquent Detail" in 1935. Public discourse over crime in the 1930s changed so quickly, however, that by the time the Predelinquent Detail was a year old, its referrals of teenagers to scout troops and recreational programs were no longer completely in harmony with the national mood. In the late 1930s, a spirit of law and order had taken over the country, profoundly affecting law enforcement policies.[93]

"Law and order" became a byword among many Americans in the late 1930s because of their longing for stability. Mass unemployment triggered worries about the survival of traditional masculine roles, while soaring crime statistics and the presence of "drifters" in most cities and towns made Americans apprehensive about the possibility of social anarchy. FBI Director J. Edgar Hoover skillfully manipulated public uneasiness during this time by demonizing criminals, calling them "vermin of the worst type," "mad dogs," and "human vultures."[94] Against the backdrop of this kind of rhetoric and general anxiety, the idea of the police as tough, aggressive, authoritative he-men exerted great appeal. Similarly, the idea that the police should handle delinquent youths with "love, sympathy, encouragement, and personal interest," as Aletha Gilbert once summarized the crime prevention mission, appeared hopelessly naive.[95]

It is difficult to state precisely when the crime control model began to gain ascendancy nationwide. In Los Angeles, the mayoral election of 1938 helped to set the stage because it brought reformers into power for the first time since the early 1910s. Like their predecessors, the reformers of 1938 concentrated much of their attention on dissolving the ties between the police and organized vice operators. They succeeded remarkably well. Shortly after taking office, Mayor Fletcher Bowron expelled the entire board of police commissioners. Chief James E. Davis, realizing his cozy relations with vice lords had come to an end, took an early retirement. As soon as he left, the new police board discharged twenty-three high-ranking officers. Next, it asked Bruce Smith and A. J. Cavanaugh, nationally known police reformers and administrators, to come to Los Angeles to guide the process of choosing a new chief. Both men subscribed to the theory that police officers should be crime fighters, not social workers. Through a supposedly scientific selection process, they narrowed the field of candidates to Arthur C. Hohmann, an obscure lieutenant who had been with the LAPD since 1925. After some shilly-shallying (Mayor Bowron favored another candidate), the police board approved Hohmann's nomination.[96]

Chief Hohmann completely reorganized the department along military lines of command by dividing the city into four semi-autonomous zones and by establishing clearly separate line and staff functions.[97] A firm believer in the crime control model of police work, Hohmann explicitly rejected the image of police as social workers. In late 1939 he wrote that the officer in charge of juvenile cases "must maintain constant surveillance over the activities of his entire personnel to obviate any tendency toward retrogression into . . . the particular field of social welfare work."[98] Hohmann also scorned the idea that the police should be heavily involved in crime prevention. He abolished the Predelinquent Detail and changed the name of the Crime Prevention Division to the Juvenile Welfare Bureau. The new name lasted less than three years. In early 1942, Chief Clarence B. Horrall, Hohmann's successor, renamed the Juvenile Welfare Bureau the Juvenile Control Division, thereby making clear his view of police work among juveniles.[99]

By the end of World War II the crime control model prevailed at the LAPD. The wartime social conditions of the city, which placed a severe strain on the department, help to account for its fast rise. During the war, the population of Los Angeles increased sharply, as hundreds of thousands of people moved into the city and surrounding areas to work in war-related industries.[100] At the same time, thousands of soldiers and sailors on military leave jammed the streets nightly, looking for entertainment. Unfortunately for Chief Horrall, the upsurge in population increased the need for police services at the very time hundreds of policemen were leaving the LAPD to serve in the military or take better-paid jobs in war-related industries. (More lucrative local employment was not difficult for policemen to find, for their wages had not risen since 1926, despite recent rapid inflation.)[101]

The need to provide for civilian defense added another layer to the problems Horrall faced during the war. Within days of the U.S. entry into the war, rumors began to circulate that Japan had targeted Los Angeles for its next bombing raid. Horrall responded to the rumors by training 78,463 civilian volunteers in bomb reconnaissance and safety procedures. He also received permission from the civil service commission to create the rank of "emergency policeman" for the duration of the war. The requirements for this position were much less strict than those for regular policemen. Even with the addition of more than 250 emergency policemen, however, the LAPD still had over 500 vacancies during 1942 and 1943.[102] In desperation, Horrall argued that Los Angeles policemen merited deferment from the draft. As he explained, his men performed essential war work in their capacity as police officers because Los Angeles was a "combat zone" of the war.[103] His plea for draft deferments not only implied that policemen were soldiers but also revealed a siege mentality among LAPD officials bred by the combined influence of wartime social conditions and the crime control model of police work.[104]

Wartime social conditions in Los Angeles provided an ideal setting for the overtly masculine crime-fighting image of the police to thrive. During the war, LAPD officers exhibited so much aggression that citizens' complaints and lawsuits charging police brutality became commonplace. In one case, the court granted a twenty-thousand-dollar judgment against officers whose attack on the plaintiff resulted in the amputation of a leg. In another case, a policeman allegedly kicked a man so severely that the man died.[105]

Despite hundreds of vacancies at the LAPD, the number of policewomen increased by only nineteen during the war, rising from thirty-eight to fifty-seven.[106] This modest increase at a time when women were moving into many occupations previously held exclusively by men shows the strength of the bias against women in police work and the ascendancy of the male-gendered crime control model. Rosie the Riveter did not have her counterpart in Peggy the Patrol Officer. In late 1944, however, Los Angeles policewomen achieved a major victory when Chief Horrall reluctantly bowed to pressure from policewomen and created the rank of policewoman-sergeant. Horrall promoted two policewomen, Leola Vess and Laura Churchill, to the new positions and gave them a salary equal to that of male sergeants, $275 a month.[107] The Los Angeles Policewomen's Association and Women Peace Officers Association of California had campaigned for this victory for nearly twenty years; it would take nearly thirty years more before the next higher position, that of lieutenant, became open to policewomen.[108]

Postwar social conditions in Los Angeles seemed to justify the continuance of the crime control model of police work. Because of a rapid growth in population after 1945, Los Angeles had one of the lowest ratios of police officers to citizens in the nation throughout the 1940s, 1950s, and 1960s. These low ratios kept alive the siege mentality of the LAPD long after the end of the war.[109] In addition, postwar chiefs of police strengthened the military structure of the LAPD. After

Horrall retired in June 1949 in the wake of a major vice scandal, William A. Worton, a former Marine Corps general with no experience in police work, headed the department.[110] In August 1950, William H. Parker replaced Worton and soon gained a national reputation for his extremely authoritarian style. According to one account, Parker deliberately modeled the LAPD after the U.S. Marine Corps.[111]

In Los Angeles and other cities, the crime control model of police work marginalized policewomen by reinforcing the male working-class subculture of the police department. It did not, of course, rid police departments of every middle-class policewoman, but because it conceptualized police work as a constant war against crime, it reaffirmed the superiority of the "masculine" characteristics and values of aggression, dominance, physical strength, and toughness.[112] It also simplified police work. Under the crime control model, there was only one task—to fight crime—and one kind of crime-fighter—a man.

Although police departments continued to employ women officers in the postwar years, the ideals of preventive justice had disappeared. As we have seen, the rise of the crime control model did not, by itself, bring about the decline of the crime prevention model. During the 1930s, second-generation policewomen were both unable and unwilling to follow the lead of the pioneering generation: unable because male professionals and male public officials took over the cause of crime prevention, and unwilling because, like many other women who came of age in the postsuffrage era, policewomen sought assimilation into male institutions. The LAPD encouraged and participated in these trends. Two of its actions in this regard stand out: the establishment of an all-male Predelinquent Detail and the practice of assigning rookie policewomen to veteran policemen, rather than to veteran policewomen, for on-the-job training. On the national level, one clear sign of second-generation policewomen's lack of interest in maintaining a work identity separate from that of policemen was the dissolution in the 1930s of the International Association of Policewomen, the organization Alice Stebbins Wells had founded in 1915.

With few exceptions, second-generation policewomen in Los Angeles wore uniforms, carried guns, and distanced themselves from social work. Despite these changes, policemen did not consider policewomen "real" police officers. To policemen, only men could be "real" police officers because only men could be combat soldiers in the ceaseless war on crime. Unfortunately for policewomen, even as their sex/gender identity kept them from being accepted as policemen's equals, their occupational identity kept them from being accepted as truly "feminine" women by the public. According to popular stereotypes, policewomen were callous, graceless, and physically unattractive to men. The LAPD tacitly endorsed the "unfeminine" stereotype by investigating the sexual orientation of single women who wished to join the department.

The crime control model still dominates U.S. police work today. The fact that historians of the police have overlooked its overtly masculine character emphasizes the near-invisibility of gender in criminal justice history. It also underscores how comprehensively crime control triumphed over crime prevention as an organizing principle of police work: the triumph was so complete that it has seemed to scholars and to the police themselves to be the product of gender-neutral professionalization processes. But these processes were not gender neutral. Gender relations of power helped to shape the nature and direction of police work and police reform throughout the first half of the twentieth century.

Out for Justice:
The Legacy
of the
Crime Control Model

In April 1991, scarcely a month after the beating of Rodney King by four Los Angeles policemen, Warner Brothers released *Out for Justice,* a movie glorifying police violence. Its fictional hero, a police officer in New York City, assaults, maims, or kills dozens of people over the course of twenty-four hours, using whatever weapons come to hand, including a pool cue, a meat cleaver, a corkscrew, and a semi-automatic rifle. Newspaper advertisements for the movie show a full-length photograph of the policeman-hero cradling a rifle. The caption reads, "He's a cop. It's a dirty job . . . but somebody's got to take out the garbage."

Unfortunately, the idea that police work primarily entails the "dirty job" of "taking out the garbage" is more than an advertising slogan for a Hollywood movie; as the videotaped beating of Rodney King graphically illustrated to television audiences around the world, it is also an integral part of a flawed police subculture in the United States. Since the 1970s, sociologists and criminologists have probed deeply into the heart of this subculture. Their research has uncovered a world that, as one group of scholars concluded, operates "under a masculine value system in which the favored image is that of an armed man of action continuously involved in fighting crime and criminals."[1]

As this book reveals, the gender dimensions of modern police work and subculture first took shape in the early 1910s, when middle-class women mounted a nationwide campaign for the appointment of women social workers as municipal police officers. According to women active in the campaign, police departments needed women officers to handle female and juvenile cases, to represent the interests of women and children, and to transform police work into social work. Pioneer policewomen and their supporters believed that police departments should do more than detect crime and arrest criminals; they should prevent crime, eliminate bad social conditions, and protect women and girls from moral dangers, especially those associated with premarital sex. These aims reflected the maternalist ideals of women reformers in the Progressive Era who tried to refashion public policy to meet what they believed were the needs of women and children. Drawing on their understanding of the problems facing urban women, adolescent girls, and children, pioneer policewomen and their supporters constructed the crime prevention model of police work. Of course, the ways maternalist reformers defined women's and children's needs reveal a great deal about their own gender, class, race, and culture. Thus, the crime prevention model embodied maternalist reformers' vision of the state (and of themselves) as an empowering, protecting, and disciplining mother to women and children whom they saw as ignorant, misguided, or disadvantaged by circumstance.

Because normative standards of gender had always kept women out of police work, pioneer policewomen and their supporters built the crime prevention model by stretching female gender prescriptions to include specialized police work for women. By imposing gender divisions where none had existed before, the movement for women police profoundly changed the meaning and representation of police work in unintended ways. Hoping to transform police departments into social work agencies, pioneer policewomen and their proponents introduced a particular gendered conception of police work. Ultimately they lacked the power to transform police departments as they wished, but their gendered conception of police work survived in truncated form in the crime control model.

On the whole, policemen, including most police chiefs, vehemently opposed the movement for women police. In Los Angeles, conservative chiefs put constraints on policewomen's work, taking away their patrol duties and prohibiting them from arresting teenage boys and men. These policies lasted for decades. In 1954, a national magazine article on LAPD women officers reported that "lady cops are not permitted to arrest men except in extreme circumstances, [and they] must telephone for assistance." The subtitle of the article was "Policemen No Longer Try to Bar Women from Force."[2]

The author of the article was right; in the 1950s and early 1960s, most policemen no longer tried to bar women from police work because by that time the crime control model was solidly in place. This model equated police work with the masculine function of crime fighting. Some women continued to work in police departments as "lady cops," but their jobs were not viewed as "real" police work. Most policewomen handled juvenile and female cases, the kinds of cases that long had a low priority in police departments. Policemen, sociologist Egon Bittner notes, "shun assignments involving young people [because] . . . no points are gained by careful and considerate handling of a juvenile problem, and there is some risk that attention given to it will be judged excessive in relation to problems deemed more important."[3]

The second wave of feminism in the late 1960s and 1970s had a significant impact on the work and status of policewomen. In the late 1960s, a few women officers began to challenge the LAPD's sexist employment practices. In retaliation, top LAPD officials refused to hire any new women officers for four years; when eighteen policewomen vacancies occurred during this time, the department appointed male officers to fill them.[4] In 1971, Chief Ed Davis told women officers that they did not belong in patrol cars and that they could not be trusted with guns during "that time of the month."[5]

The LAPD and other major police departments did not begin to abandon sexist employment practices until forced to do so by the federal government. Of key importance in this regard was the passage in 1972 of Title VII of the Civil Rights Act, which prohibited employment discrimination on the basis of race, creed, color, sex, or national origin. This legislation enabled LAPD Sergeant Fanchon Blake, a twenty-four-year veteran with the department, to file a sex discrimination lawsuit against the LAPD in 1973. Prior to filing the lawsuit, Blake had petitioned the city council in vain for four years to permit her to take the promotional examination for lieutenant. (As a woman, she was barred from all ranks above that of policewoman-sergeant.) It took seven years for the courts to resolve the lawsuit in her favor. The LAPD then agreed to two consent decrees: to increase the number of women officers until women composed 20 percent of all sworn personnel and to increase minority representation until it equaled the minority representation in the Los Angeles work force.[6] Los Angeles policemen responded negatively to the consent decrees. Some of them argued that the department would have to add "one more pouch to officers' belts—to hold tissues for women's emotional outbursts."[7]

Recent studies reveal a continuing resentment by many policemen toward policewomen. The report of the Christopher Commission is particularly disturbing in this respect. Organized in 1991 to investigate the LAPD in the wake of the beating of Rodney King, the commission found ample evidence of pervasive sexism as well as racism at the LAPD. It discovered, for example, that many male training officers strongly believe that policewomen cannot perform police duties satisfactorily. (Training officers are assigned as partners to new officers during their first year; according to the Christopher Commission, training officers "play a major role in shaping the new officers' views of police work.") When asked their opinion of policewomen, many male training officers replied that policewomen were a liability to the LAPD because they were not as "capable, effective or trustworthy" as policemen.[8] A study undertaken in 1987 by the LAPD itself provides further evidence of male training officers' bias. In that study, researchers asked LAPD women officers if they had trouble being accepted into the working culture. Every policewoman interviewed stated that during her first year on the department, male training officers told her repeatedly that she would not be as good as a man in a "man's job."[9] Even LAPD Chief Daryl Gates admitted to the Christopher Commission that female officers had a "real tough time" achieving acceptance in the department; perhaps a tougher time, he conceded, than that faced by gay male officers.[10]

Policemen's generally low opinion of policewomen's capabilities flies in the face of numerous studies showing that policewomen perform as well as policemen in patrol and detective work.[11] Unfortunately, these studies have had no discernible impact on the perception of police work as a "man's job." The reason for the remarkable strength of this perception lies primarily in the macho subculture of police work, which equates peak job performance with masculinity and a ready willingness to use force. This subculture is a natural outgrowth of the crime control model. That is, once the crime control model defined police work as a constant war on crime and little else, a subculture evolved that encouraged the police to view the city as a combat zone where only aggressively masculine policemen-soldiers survive. Vivienne Gomez, a LAPD detective, commented on the macho subculture of the LAPD in an interview she gave in 1993. "With a male suspect and a male officer," she said, "it's like two dogs meeting on the street. They get their hair up on their backs."[12]

The Christopher Commission deplored the "hard-nose posturing" of Los Angeles policemen, declaring in its report that male officers' aggressive style "produces results at the risk of creating a siege mentality that alienates the officer from the community." The commission urged the LAPD to develop a new style of policing based on communication rather than confrontation. It also noted that policewomen are less likely than policemen to "abuse the public." Specifically, the commission pointed out that although women composed 13 percent of LAPD sworn personnel during the period 1986 to 1990, none of the LAPD's worst offenders in excessive use of force was a woman. In an analysis that linked the bias against policewomen with police brutality, the commission claimed that "the continued existence of discrimination against female officers can deprive the department of certain skills, and thereby contribute to the problem of excessive force."[13]

The commission's reference to female officers' "certain skills" would have pleased pioneer policewomen. They would have recognized in it a call to employ women police for the purpose of infusing police work with the characteristics and values commonly associated with women. Although nearly half a century has passed since the death of the movement for women police, the battles over the gendered representation of police work continue.

Notes

INTRODUCTION

1. "Women as Police Officers," quoted by Mrs. George B. Walker in "The Relationship of Policewomen and Social Service as Viewed from the Sidelines," *Minnesota State Conference of Social Work* 38 (1930): 164.

2. Alice Stebbins Wells, "Personal History of Los Angeles' First Policewoman," Los Angeles Police Associations, *Bulletin,* October 1940, p. 5.

3. Before 1971, the most reliable source of information on the number of police personnel in the United States, the *Uniform Crime Reports* published annually by the federal government, did not distinguish between male and female officers. Statistics on the number of policewomen between 1910 and 1970 therefore rely on scattered studies. For statistics from these studies, see Daniel J. Bell, "Policewomen: Myths and Realities," *Journal of Police Science and Administration* 10 (1982): 114; statistics for the post-1970 era can be found in *Uniform Crime Reports* (Washington, D.C.: U.S. Government Printing Office) for relevant years.

4. After decades of little scholarship on women police in the United States, the mid-1990s have witnessed a sudden spurt. An overview of the movement for women police and women's status in policing since World War II is in Dorothy Moses Schulz, *From Social Worker to Crimefighter: Women in United States Municipal Policing* (Westport, Conn.: Praeger, 1995). Kerry Segrave also offers an overview of women in policing, but her study encompasses England as well as the United States. Segrave, *Policewomen: A History* (Jefferson, N.C.: McFarland, 1995). Gloria E. Myers provides a detailed look at the experiences of a "protective officer" and pioneer policewoman in Progressive Era Portland, Oregon, in *A Municipal Mother: Portland's Lola Greene Baldwin, America's First Policewoman* (Corvallis: Oregon State University Press, 1995). Samuel Walker was the first to offer a serious historical discussion of policewomen. See Walker, *A Critical History of Police Reform: The Emergence of Professionalism* (Lexington, Mass.: Lexington Books, D. C. Heath, 1977).

5. Joan Wallach Scott, *Gender and the Politics of History* (New York: Columbia University Press, 1988), p. 179.

6. Thomas Gray, "Selecting for a Police Subculture," in *Police in America*, ed. Jerome Skolnick and Thomas Gray (Boston: Little, Brown, 1975), p. 48, quoted in Nanci Koser Wilson, "Women in the Criminal Justice Professions: An Analysis of Status Conflict," in *Judge, Lawyer, Victim, Thief: Women, Gender Roles, and Criminal Justice*, ed. Nicole Hahn Rafter and Elizabeth Anne Stanko (Boston: Northeastern University Press, 1982), p. 368.

7. Wilson, "Women in the Criminal Justice Professions," p. 360. Other sociological analyses of gender dynamics in policing include Susan Ehrlich Martin, *On the Move: The Status of Women in Policing* (Washington, D.C.: Police Foundation, 1990); idem., *Breaking and Entering: Policewomen on Patrol* (Berkeley: University of California Press, 1980); and Bruce L. Berg and Kimberly J. Budnick, "Defeminization of Women in Law Enforcement: Examining the Role of Women in Policing," in *Police and Law Enforcement*, vol. 5, ed. Daniel B. Kennedy and Robert J. Homant (New York: AMS Press, 1987).

8. Eric Monkkonen, *Police in Urban America, 1860–1920* (Cambridge: Cambridge University Press, 1981), analyzes the police practice of taking care of lost children and providing lodging to homeless men.

9. Walker, *Critical History*, analyzes the crime prevention model (which he calls the social-work/crime-prevention model), but he does not identify women as the model's chief proponents and architects, nor does he analyze its gender connotations; Monkkonen, *Police in Urban America*, pp. 158–59, argues that the crime prevention mission of the police formed part of their crime control focus. None of the recent works on women police cited in note 4 analyzes the crime prevention model.

10. In recent years, scholars have devoted considerable attention to the role of middle-class women in the creation of the welfare state. See, for example, Seth Koven and Sonya Michel, eds., *Mothers of a New World: Maternalist Politics and the Origins of Welfare States* (New York: Routledge, 1993); Theda Skocpol, *Protecting Soldiers and Mothers: The Political Origins of Social Policy in the United States* (Cambridge, Mass.: Harvard University Press, 1992); Linda Gordon, ed., *Women, the State, and Welfare* (Madison: University of Wisconsin Press, 1990); idem, "Putting Women and Children First: Women, Maternalism, and Welfare in the Early Twentieth Century," in *U.S. History as Women's History*, ed. Linda K. Kerber, Alice Kessler-Harris, and Kathryn Kish Sklar (Chapel Hill: University of North Carolina Press, 1995); idem, "Social Insurance and Public Assistance: The Influence of Gender in Welfare Thought in the United States, 1890–1935," *American Historical Review* 97 (February 1992): 19–54; idem, "Black and White Visions of Welfare: Women's Welfare Activism, 1890–1945," *Journal of American History* 78 (September 1991): 559–90; Robyn Muncy, *Creating a Female Dominion in American Reform, 1890–1935* (New York: Oxford University Press, 1990).

11. Lee Shippey, "The Lee Side of LA," *Los Angeles Times*, December 12, 1927; "City Mothers and Politics," *Los Angeles Chronicle*, [ca. 1930], Aletha Gilbert Papers, in private possession.

12. For an important and influential discussion of gender as a category of historical analysis, see Scott, *Gender and the Politics of History*, chap. 2; on the ways women and gender have shaped public policy in the United States, see Kerber et al., *U.S. History as Women's History*; and Mimi Abramovitz, *Regulating the Lives of Women: Social Welfare Policy from Colonial Times to the Present* (Boston: Southend Press, 1988).

CHAPTER ONE

1. Alice Stebbins Wells, "Personal History of Los Angeles' First Policewoman," Los Angeles Police Associations, *Bulletin*, October 1940, p. 5; undated handbill advertising lecture by Wells, and "People Worth Knowing About," unidentified magazine article, January 1911, Alice Stebbins Wells Papers, in private possession; Raymond Wells (grandson of Alice Stebbins Wells), interview by author, September 18, 1990, Long Beach, Calif.

Historians have found factual basis for the myth of the "Irish cop" in both nineteenth- and twentieth-century police departments. See Samuel Walker, *A Critical History of Police Reform: The Emergence of Professionalism* (Lexington, Mass.: Lexington Books, D. C. Heath, 1977), p. 11; James F. Richardson, *Urban Police in the United States* (Port Washington, N.Y.: National University Publications, Kennikat Press, 1974), p. 54.

2. Wells, "Personal History," p. 5.

3. Alice Stebbins Wells, "Reminiscences of a Policewoman," *Police Reporter*, September 1929, p. 23; "People Worth Knowing About."

4. Los Angeles City Council, Minutes, "Report of City Attorney," August 2, 1910, 82:33, Los Angeles City Archives.

5. "People Worth Knowing About"; Wells, "Reminiscences," p. 23; idem, "Personal History," p. 5. Although Wells has long been recognized as the first American to have the official title "policewoman," other women wielded police power prior to Wells's appointment to the LAPD. For example, in 1893, the Chicago Police Department granted Mary Owens, a widow of a Chicago policeman, both the title and the pay of a patrolman for her work in police investigations and the courts. She was a "patrolman" for thirty years. Chloe Owings, *Women Police: A Study of the Development and Status of the Women Police Movement*, Publications of the Bureau of Social Hygiene (New York: Frederick H. Hitchcock, 1925), p. 99. The city of Portland, Oregon, granted police power to Lola Baldwin in 1905. Gloria E. Myers, *A Municipal Mother: Portland's Lola Greene Baldwin, America's First Policewoman* (Corvallis: Oregon State University Press, 1995).

6. "Famous Policewoman Urges Prevention of Crime," *New York Times*, December 22, 1912, sec. 5, p. 13.

7. Wells, "Personal History," p. 10; on the number of policewomen in the United States, see Owings, *Women Police*, pp. 103–4, 121; Dorothy Moses Schulz, *From Social Worker to Crimefighter: Women in United States Municipal Policing* (Westport, Conn.: Praeger, 1995), p. 33. Other estimates of policewomen's numbers are in Women Peace Officers Association of California, *Yearbook 1928–29*, p. 9; Henrietta Additon, *Social Work Year Book* (1935) quoted in Josephine Nelson, "On the Policewoman's 'Beat,'" *Independent Woman*, May 1936, 138.

When Wells took her leave of absence in 1912, the LAPD hired two more women officers to handle her expanding workload. "Roster of the Los Angeles Police Department for the Fiscal Year Ending June 30, 1914," Los Angeles Police Department, *Annual Report, Police Department, City of Los Angeles, California, for the Fiscal Year Ending June 30, 1914*, p. 41. (Until 1939, all *Annual Reports* covered the fiscal year running from July 1 to June 30. Beginning in 1939 they covered the calendar year.)

8. Wells, "Personal History," p. 5.

9. For a collection of essays on maternalist reforms, see Seth Koven and Sonya Michel, eds., *Mothers of a New World: Maternalist Politics and the Origins of Welfare States* (New York: Routledge, 1993). Koven and Michel offer a deft analysis of the international scholarship in the field in "Womanly Duties: Maternalist Politics and the Origins of the Welfare States in France, Germany, Great Britain, and the United States, 1880–1920," *American Historical Review* 95 (October 1990): 1076–108. For other historical scholarship on maternalist reform, see also works cited in Introduction, note 10.

10. Peggy Pascoe, *Relations of Rescue: The Search for Female Moral Authority in the American West, 1874–1939* (New York: Oxford University Press, 1990), pp. xvi-xvii. The ideology of domesticity has received close and increasingly sophisticated attention from historians over the past quarter century, as Linda K. Kerber points out in "Separate Spheres, Female Worlds, Woman's Place: The Rhetoric of Women's History," *Journal of American History* 75 (June 1988): 9–39. See, for example, Jeanne Boydston, *Home and Work: Housework, Wages, and the Ideology of Labor in the Early Republic* (New York: Oxford University Press, 1990), Glenna Matthews, *"Just a Housewife": The Rise and Fall of Domesticity in America* (New York: Oxford University Press, 1987); Barbara Leslie Epstein, *The Politics of Domesticity: Women, Evangelism and Temperance in Nineteenth-Century America* (Middletown, Conn.: Wesleyan University Press, 1981); Mary P. Ryan, *Cradle of the Middle Class: The Family in Oneida County, New York, 1790–1865* (Cambridge: Cambridge University Press, 1981); Carl N. Degler, *At Odds: Women and the Family from the Revolution to the Present* (New York: Oxford University Press, 1980); Barbara Berg, *The Remembered Gate: Origins of American Feminism: The Woman*

and the City (New York: Oxford University Press, 1978); Nancy F. Cott, *The Bonds of Womanhood: "Woman's Sphere" in New England, 1780–1835* (New Haven: Yale University Press, 1977); Kathryn Kish Sklar, *Catharine Beecher: A Study in American Domesticity* (New Haven: Yale University Press, 1973); Barbara Welter, "The Cult of True Womanhood, 1820–1860," *American Quarterly* 18 (1966): 151–74.

11. On the gender roles of Latinas, Native American women, and Asian immigrant women during the nineteenth century, see Ramona Ford, "Native American Women: Changing Statuses, Changing Interpretations," in *Writing the Range: Race, Class, and Culture in the Women's West,* ed. Elizabeth Jameson and Susan Armitage (Norman: University of Oklahoma Press, 1997), pp. 42–68; in the same volume, see Darlis Miller, "The Women of Lincoln County, 1860–1900," pp. 147–71; Robert Griswold, "Anglo Women and Domestic Ideology in the American West in the Nineteenth and Early Twentieth Centuries," in *Western Women: Their Land, Their Lives,* ed. Lillian Schlissel, Vicki Ruiz, and Janice Monk (Albuquerque: University of New Mexico Press, 1988), pp. 15–29; Janet Lecompte, "The Independent Women of New Mexico, 1821–1846," in *New Mexican Women: Intercultural Perspectives* (Albuquerque: University of New Mexico Press, 1984), pp. 71–93; and Lucie Cheng Hirata, "Chinese Immigrant Women in Nineteenth-Century California," in *Women in America, History,* ed Carol Ruth Berkin and Mary Beth Norton (Boston: Houghton Mifflin, 1979), pp. 224–44.

12. Kathryn Kish Sklar, "The Historical Foundations of Women's Power in the Creation of the American Welfare State, 1830–1930," in Koven and Michel, *Mothers of a New World,* p. 52.

13. Many of the studies cited in note 10 analyze women's organized benevolent work in the nineteenth century. See also Lois A. Boyd and R. Douglas Brackinridge, *Presbyterian Women in America: Two Centuries of a Quest for Status* (Westport, Conn.: Greenwood Press, 1983); Mary Ryan, "The Power of Women's Networks: A Case Study of Female Moral Reform in Antebellum America," *Feminist Studies* 5 (spring 1979): 66–87; Carroll Smith-Rosenberg, "Beauty, the Beast, and the Militant Woman: A Case Study of Sex Roles and Social Stress in Jacksonian America," *American Quarterly* 23 (October 1971): 562–84.

14. Historical research on female solidarity has discovered the existence of many separate women's cultures. On black women's culture, see Carol Stack, *All Our Kin: Strategies for Survival in a Black Community* (New York: Harper & Row, 1974); on white working-class women, see Christine Stansell, *City of Women: Sex and Class in New York, 1789–1860* (New York: Alfred A. Knopf, 1986); on white middle-class women, see Carroll Smith-Rosenberg, "The Female World of Love and Ritual: Relations Between Women in Nineteenth-Century America," in *A Heritage of Her Own,* ed. Nancy F. Cott and Elizabeth H. Pleck (New York: Simon and Schuster, Touchstone, 1979), pp. 311–42.

15. Estelle B. Freedman, *Their Sisters Keepers: Women's Prison Reform in America, 1830–1930* (Ann Arbor: University of Michigan Press, 1981); on middle-class women's identification of "unfortunate" women, see Pascoe, *Relations of Rescue.*

16. Nancy A. Hewitt, *Women's Activism and Social Change: Rochester, New York, 1822–1872* (Ithaca, N.Y.: Cornell University Press, 1984).

17. Evelyn Brooks Higginbotham, "Beyond the Sound of Silence: Afro-American Women in History," *Gender and History* 1 (spring 1989) discusses how white women missionaries fostered the patriarchal ideal among southern blacks during the late nineteenth century. See also Jacqueline Jones, *Soldiers of Light and Love: Northern Teachers and Georgia Blacks, 1865–1873* (Chapel Hill: University of North Carolina Press, 1980). In her study of home missions during the late nineteenth century, Pascoe found that the women founders rejected the patriarchal ideal. Pascoe, *Relations of Rescue;* Lori D. Ginzberg points out that women who worked in state-related benevolent organizations after the Civil War "repudiated an ideology based on a peculiarly female identity as they sought to create an efficient [i.e., repressive] charitable elite with the men of their class" (p. 209). Ginzberg, *Women and the Work of Benevolence: Morality, Politics, and Class in the Nineteenth-Century United States* (New Haven: Yale University Press, 1990), pp. 25–35, 200–209; for a contrasting view, see John T. Cumbler, "The Politics of Charity: Gender and Class in Late Nineteenth-Century Charity Policy," *Journal of Social History* 14 (fall 1980): 99–111.

18. Mary P. Ryan, *Women in Public: Between Banners and Ballots* (Baltimore: Johns Hopkins University Press, 1990), p. 100.

19. Freedman, *Their Sisters' Keepers,* pp. 1, 15–16. See also David J. Pivar, *Purity Crusade: Sexual Morality and Social Control, 1868–1900,* Contributions in American History, no. 23 (Westport, Conn.: Greenwood Press, 1973), pp. 99–103, 152–54.

20. Ginzberg, *Women and the Work of Benevolence,* p. 210.

21. Kathryn Kish Sklar, "Two Political Cultures in the Progressive Era: The National Consumers' League and the American Association for Labor Legislation," in *U.S. History as Women's History: New Feminist Essays,* ed. Linda K. Kerber, Alice Kessler-Harris, and Kathryn Kish Sklar (Chapel Hill: University of North Carolina Press, 1995), pp. 36–62; see also idem, "Historical Foundations of Women's Power in the Creation of the American Welfare State, 1830–1930," in *Mothers of a New World.*

22. Class-based interpretations of the juvenile court include Anthony S. Platt, *The Child Savers: The Invention of Delinquency* (Chicago: University of Chicago Press, 1969); Robert M. Mennel, *Thorns and Thistles: Juvenile Delinquents in the United States, 1825–1940* (Hanover, N.H.: University Press of New England, 1973); Harold Finestone, *Victims of Change: Juvenile Delinquents in American Society* (Westport, Conn.: Greenwood Press, 1976); and Steven L. Schlossman, *Love*

and the American Delinquent: The Theory and Practice of "Progressive" Juvenile Justice (Chicago: University of Chicago Press, 1977). For an insightful discussion of the ways class and gender simultaneously shaped maternalist reform, see Linda Gordon, "Putting Children First: Women, Maternalism, and Welfare in the Early Twentieth Century," in *U.S. History as Women's History*, pp. 63–86.

23. Henriette Greenbaum Frank and Amalie Hofer Jerome, comps., *Annals of the Chicago Woman's Club, for the First Forty Years of Its Organization, 1876–1916* (Chicago: Chicago Woman's Club, 1916).

24. Ibid., p. 36.

25. Ibid., pp. 36–38. As Karen J. Blair has documented, Chicago clubwomen were not alone in their wish to broaden their club's activities. Blair asserts that many American clubwomen in the 1890s found public work more satisfying than cultural pursuits. *Clubwoman as Feminist: True Womanhood Redefined, 1868–1914* (New York: Holmes and Meier, 1980), p. 99. See also Anne Firor Scott, *Natural Allies: Women's Associations in American History* (Urbana: University of Illinois Press, 1991).

26. Frank and Jerome, *Annals of the Chicago Woman's Club*, p. 38.

27. On the police matron movement, see Dorothy Moses Schulz, *From Social Worker to Crimefighter: Women in United States Municipal Policing* (Westport, Conn.: Praeger, 1995), chap. 1; Freedman, *Their Sisters' Keepers*, p. 61; and Pivar, *Purity Crusade*, pp. 101–3.

28. Frank and Jerome, *Annals of the Chicago Woman's Club*, p. 42. The report for 1882–83 also notes members' decision to devote one afternoon to the presentation of reports relating to philanthropic and charitable work undertaken in Chicago.

29. Ibid.

30. Ibid.

31. Ibid., p. 75.

32. Ibid., p. 76; Walter Wyckoff, *The Workers: The West* (New York: Scribner, 1898), pp. 22–43, quoted in Eric Monkkonen, *Police in Urban America, 1860–1920* (Cambridge: Cambridge University Press, 1981), p. 91. Since their establishment in the mid-nineteenth century, U.S. police departments regularly provided bed and sometimes board for homeless people, the vast majority of whom were men. "Year after year these 'lodgers,' as the police referred to them, swarmed to the police stations in most large cities. . . . During very bad depression years or harsh winters, the number of overnight lodgings provided by a police department exceeded all annual arrests." Ibid., pp. 86–87.

33. Frank and Jerome, *Annals of the Chicago Woman's Club*, pp. 125–27, 135, 177.

34. Ibid., p. 127. On the sexual division of labor in probation departments, see Bernard Flexner and Roger N. Baldwin, *Juvenile Courts and Probation* (New

York: Century, 1914), pp. 46, 110–14; Emily Norma Heitman, "A Study of the Probation System for Juvenile Offenders in Los Angeles County" (M.A. thesis, University of Southern California, 1924), pp. 25–26; U.S., Department of Labor, Children's Bureau, *Juvenile Courts at Work: A Study of the Organization and Methods of Ten Courts*, by Katharine F. Lenroot and Emma O. Lundberg, Bureau Publication 141 (Washington, D.C.: Government Printing Office, 1925), p. 169; and Helen D. Pigeon, *Probation and Parole in Theory and Practice: A Study Manual* (New York: National Probation Association, 1942), p. 97.

35. Frank and Jerome, *Annals of the Chicago Woman's Club*, p. 127.

36. Ibid.

37. Ibid., p. 67.

38. Harriet Smith Farwell, *Lucy Louisa Flower, 1837–1920: Her Contribution to Education and Child Welfare in Chicago* (n.p., [1924]), p. 28.

39. Ellen Ryerson, *The Best-Laid Plans: America's Juvenile Court Experiment* (New York: Hill and Wang, 1978), p. 32.

40. In *Best-Laid Plans*, Ryerson ably examines some of these issues, as well as the history of the juvenile court movement.

41. Farwell, *Lucy Louisa Flower*, p. 30.

42. Louise DeKoven Bowen, "The Early Days of the Juvenile Court," in Jane Addams et al., *The Child, the Clinic, and the Court* (New York: New Republic, 1925), p. 301. Louise DeKoven Bowen published several pamphlets and books; the spelling of "DeKoven" varies among these publications. Two variants are "de Koven" and "De Koven." For the sake of consistency, all references to her herein use "DeKoven."

43. For a discussion of the transformation of child welfare into a mainstream political issue, see Muncy, *Creating a Female Dominion*.

44. In her biography of Flower, Farwell asserts that Illinois state legislators "deliberately attempted to cripple the bill" by depriving the court of public financial support. Farwell, *Lucy Louisa Flower*, p. 33.

45. Elisabeth Parker, "Personnel and Organization in the Probation Department of the Juvenile Court of Cook County (1899–1933)" (M.A. thesis, University of Chicago, 1934), pp. 7–8; Bowen, "The Early Days of the Juvenile Court," pp. 299–307; Farwell, *Lucy Louisa Flower*, pp. 32–34; Thomas D. Eliot, *The Juvenile Court and the Community* (New York: Macmillan, 1914), p. 107. Confusion has arisen over the years because of the existence of two Juvenile Court Committees in Chicago. One committee was composed entirely of the members of the Chicago Woman's Club; the other was composed of representatives from many women's organizations in Chicago, including the Chicago Woman's Club. To further complicate matters, both committees convened at the Chicago Woman's Club. Parker, "Personnel and Organization," pp. 15–16.

46. Zona Gale, "How Women's Clubs Can Co-operate with the City Offi-

cials," *American City*, June 1914, p. 537. Louise DeKoven Bowen, a member of the Juvenile Court Committee, also lamented "political interference" in the operations of the court. Bowen, "The Early Days of the Juvenile Court," pp. 308–9. On women's loss of power in federal child welfare policy, see Muncy, *Creating a Female Dominion*. Estelle B. Freedman argues that women's loss of political influence and reform energy in the 1920s has been somewhat exaggerated. See Freedman, "Separatism Revisited: Women's Institutions, Social Reform, and the Career of Miriam Van Waters," in *U.S. History as Women's History*, pp. 170–88, and idem, *Maternal Justice: Miriam Van Waters and the Female Reform Tradition* (Chicago: University of Chicago Press, 1996).

47. Sara Evans, *Born for Liberty: A History of Women in America* (London: Collier Macmillan, 1989), chap. 6, quoted in Koven and Michel, "Womanly Duties," p. 1094.

48. Sophonisba P. Breckinridge and Edith Abbott even went so far as to make the self-proclaimed "radical statement" that juvenile court judges should be female: "One [cannot] fail to realize that, even when the judge is a genius at understanding the child, or devotedly kind and genuinely sympathetic, there is often the need not merely of advice from a woman, but of deciding power exercised by a woman." Breckinridge and Abbott, *The Delinquent Child and the Home* (New York: Charities Publication Committee, Russell Sage Foundation, 1912), p. 175.

49. For a discussion of this aspect of maternalist reform, see Gordon, "Putting Children First."

50. In their dislike of separating children from parents, the court's founders followed in the footsteps of an earlier generation of women activists in the Children's Aid Society (CAS) of New York. Whereas the male members of CAS chose to solve the problem of numerous working-class children on the streets of New York City by sending the children away from their urban homes, the female members of CAS chose to keep children and parents together and take on the task of "educating" working-class mothers about child rearing. Christine Stansell, "Women, Children, and the Uses of the Streets: Class and Gender Conflict in New York City, 1850–1860," *Feminist Studies* 8 (summer 1982): 309–35.

51. "Women's Clubs in the Middle Western States," *The Annals of the American Academy of Political and Social Science* 28 (July–December 1906): 239; Hastings L. Hart, *Preventive Treatment of Neglected Children* (New York: Charities Publication Committee, Russell Sage Foundation, 1910), p. 211; Mary S. Gibson, comp., *A Record of Twenty-Five Years of the California Federation of Women's Clubs, 1900–1925* (n.p: California Federation of Women's Clubs, 1927), 1:35–39.

52. As Karen J. Blair remarks, "The new clubwoman of the 1890s was far more ready to tackle public problems than her mother and grandmother had been, due in large part to the success of the Woman Movement in creating jobs and schools for her." Blair, *Clubwoman as Feminist*, p. 119.

53. Linda Gordon points out that "the softening of methods of child-raising was part of a middle-class romanticization of domesticity, idealizing the home as a place of harmony and cooperation. Feminists were among the most ardent purveyors of this ideal." Gordon, *Heroes of Their Own Lives: The Politics and History of Family Violence, Boston 1880–1960* (New York: Viking Penguin, 1988), pp. 33–34.

54. For a discussion of the biological theory of crime, articulated most forcefully by Cesare Lombroso in the late nineteenth century, and women reformers' response to it, see Freedman, *Their Sisters' Keepers,* pp. 109–15.

55. Breckinridge and Abbott, *The Delinquent Child and the Home,* p. 74. According to Estelle B. Freedman, women social scientists were among the first criminologists to formulate an environmental theory of crime. She believes they may have rejected the hereditarian view because they had already personally rejected the separate female sphere and its biology-is-destiny connotations. Freedman, *Their Sisters' Keepers,* p. 125.

56. Thomas Stuart McKibbon, "The Origin and Development of the Los Angeles County Juvenile Court" (M.A. thesis, University of Southern California, 1932), pp. 17–18.

57. Ibid.

58. Gibson, *Record of Twenty-Five Years,* p. 36.

59. McKibbon, "Origin and Development," pp. 23–27.

60. Pigeon, *Probation and Parole,* p. 54.

61. Women's Society for the Prevention of Crime, Educational Committee, "Bulletin No. 1" (New York, 1910); idem., "Organization and Purposes" (1911). This association was not an auxiliary of the well-known Society for the Prevention of Crime founded in 1878 in New York City. For a discussion of private protective associations, see Ruth M. Alexander, *The "Girl Problem": Female Sexual Delinquency in New York, 1900–1930* (Ithaca, N.Y.: Cornell University Press, 1995), pp. 42–47; and Freedman, *Their Sisters' Keepers,* p. 127.

62. On police corruption, see Robert M. Fogelson, *Big-City Police* (Cambridge, Mass.: Harvard University Press, 1977), especially pp. 17–35.

63. Women activists in the Progressive Era were by no means the first reformers to undertake crime prevention work. See Paul Boyer, *Urban Masses and Moral Order in America, 1820–1920* (Cambridge, Mass.: Harvard University Press, 1978), pp. 162–66, and Kathleen Daly, "The Social Control of Sexuality: A Case Study of the Criminalization of Prostitution in the Progressive Era," *Research in Law, Deviance and Social Control* 9 (1988): 178–79.

64. Louise DeKoven Bowen, "The 'Block System' of the Juvenile Protective Association of Chicago," in *Speeches, Addresses, and Letters of Louise DeKoven Bowen: Reflecting Social Movements in Chicago,* ed. Mary Humphrey (Ann Arbor, Mich.: Edwards Brothers, 1937), pp. 419–23. In the same volume, see also "The

Road to Destruction Made Easy in Chicago," pp. 385–400; "President's Address, Juvenile Protective Association," pp. 507–18. On the Juvenile Protective Association of Los Angeles, see Dorothy Frances Allen, "The Changing Emphasis in Protective Services to Children with an Account of the Children's Protective Association of Los Angeles" (M.S.W. thesis, Graduate School of Social Work, University of California, 1943).

65. Boyer, *Urban Masses*, pp. 220–50; Roy Lubove, *The Progressives and the Slums: Tenement House Reform in New York City*, 1880–1917 (Pittsburgh: University of Pittsburgh Press, 1962).

66. Bessie D. Stoddart, "The Public Playgrounds of Los Angeles," *Pacific Municipalities* 26 (April 30, 1912): 175–81.

67. John D'Emilio and Estelle B. Freedman discuss these changes in *Intimate Matters: A History of Sexuality in America* (New York: Harper & Row, 1988), chap. 8; see also Kathy Peiss, *Cheap Amusements: Working Women and Leisure in Turn-of-the Century New York* (Philadelphia: Temple University Press, 1986); Joanne Meyerowitz, *Women Adrift: Independent Wage Earners in Chicago, 1880–1930* (Chicago: University of Chicago Press, 1988).

68. "Many Reasons for Women on Police Forces," *Ottawa Free Press*, January 17, 1913.

69. On the white slavery scare, see D'Emilio and Freedman, *Intimate Matters*, pp. 208–10; Barbara Meil Hobson, *Uneasy Virtue: The Politics of Prostitution and the American Reform Tradition* (New York: Basic Books, 1987), pp. 141–44; Meyerowitz, *Women Adrift*, p. 61; Mark Thomas Connelly, *The Response to Prostitution in the Progressive Era* (Chapel Hill: University of North Carolina Press, 1980). For a related perspective on female sexuality, see Ellen Carol DuBois and Linda Gordon, "Seeking Ecstasy on the Battlefield: Danger and Pleasure in Nineteenth-Century Feminist Sexual Thought," *Feminist Studies* 9 (spring 1983): 8–25.

70. Peiss, *Cheap Amusements*; Alexander, *The "Girl Problem."*

71. Daniel Scott Smith and Michael Hindus, "Premarital Pregnancy in America, 1640–1971: An Overview and Interpretation," *Journal of Interdisciplinary History* 5 (spring 1975): 537–70.

72. Peiss, *Cheap Amusements*, especially chap. 3; Alexander, *The "Girl Problem,"* chap. 1; D'Emilio and Freedman, *Intimate Matters*, chaps. 10, 11. It should be noted that middle-class female youth generally adopted tamer versions of working-class styles and behavior.

73. Alexander, *The "Girl Problem,"* pp. 39–40.

74. D'Emilio and Freedman, *Intimate Matters*, pp. 209–10; Alexander, *The "Girl Problem,"* pp. 40–41. The findings of vice commissions helped to expose the cozy relationship between the police, the machine, and owners of brothels and saloons. See Fogelson, *Big-City Police*, pp. 129–34.

75. On the social purity movement, see D'Emilio and Freedman, *Intimate*

Matters, pp. 150–56; Pivar, *Purity Crusade;* Ruth Rosen, *The Lost Sisterhood: Prostitution in America, 1900–1918* (Baltimore: Johns Hopkins University Press, 1982), pp. 9–13; Linda Gordon, *Woman's Body, Woman's Right: A Social History of Birth Control in America* (New York: Grossman, 1976), pp. 116–26.

76. Mary E. Odem, *Delinquent Daughters: Protecting and Policing Adolescent Female Sexuality in the United States, 1885–1920* (Chapel Hill: University of North Carolina Press, 1995), pp. 73–74.

77. Alexander, *The "Girl Problem,"* pp. 41–43.

78. Bowen, "Road to Destruction Made Easy" and "'Block System.'"

79. Freedman, *Their Sisters' Keepers,* p. 127; Bowen, "Road to Destruction Made Easy" and "'Block System.'"

80. Boyer, *Urban Masses,* p. 280. In Progressive Era Berkeley, California, Chief of Police August Vollmer instructed patrolmen to know by sight every person who lived or worked on their beats so they could immediately investigate any deviation from normal routine. On Vollmer's aggressive approach, see Julia Liss and Steven Schlossman, "The Contours of Crime Prevention in August Vollmer's Berkeley," *Research in Law, Deviance and Social Control* 6 (1984): 79–107.

81. D'Emilio and Freedman, *Intimate Matters,* pp. 150–56.

82. Allan M. Brandt, *No Magic Bullet: A Social History of Venereal Disease in the United States Since 1880* (New York: Oxford University Press, 1985), p. 83.

83. For a discussion of the shift in thinking about female sexuality during the Progressive Era, see Alexander, *The "Girl Problem,"* chap. 2.

84. Peggy Pascoe argues that home mission women sought female moral authority to strengthen women's power relative to men. Pascoe, *Relations of Rescue.*

85. Linda Gordon, "Black and White Visions of Welfare: Women's Welfare Activism, 1890–1945," *Journal of American History* 78 (September 1991): 579. Gordon points out that black female activists "were far in advance of white feminists in their campaigns against rape and their identification of that crime as part of a system of power relations, and they did not assume that only *white* men were sexual aggressors." (Emphasis in original.) See also Tullia Kay Brown Hamilton, "The National Association of Colored Women, 1896–1920" (Ph.D. diss., Emory University, 1978).

86. Female African American police and probation officers of the early twentieth century have received very little scholarly attention. Information on their work can be gleaned from widely scattered sources. See, for example, Alice Ward Smith, "Colored Policewomen of Washington," *Southern Workman* 51 (March 1922): 135–36; Florence Kelley, "A Burglar Four Years Old in the Memphis Juvenile Court," *Survey* 32 (June 20, 1914): 318–19; Lenroot and Lundberg, *Juvenile Courts at Work;* and Dorothy Willys Lawrence, "Some Problems Arising

in the Treatment of Adolescent Negro Girls Appearing Before the Los Angeles Juvenile Court" (M.S.W. thesis, Graduate School of Social Work, University of Southern California, 1941).

87. Seth Koven and Sonya Michel have argued that "in the name of friendship and in the interest of the health of the family and the nation . . . [women] reformers claimed the right to instruct and regulate the conduct of working-class women." Koven and Michel, "Womanly Duties," p. 1078.

88. Louise DeKoven Bowen, *Safeguards for City Youth at Work and at Play* (New York: Macmillan, 1914), p. 48.

89. Myers, *Municipal Mother*, pp. 8, 11–23; "Chief Jenkins's Portland, Ore., Police Force," *Police Journal*, February 1922, 10; Owings, *Women Police*, pp. 100–101.

90. Joseph Gerald Woods, "The Progressives and the Police: Urban Reform and the Professionalization of the Los Angeles Police" (Ph.D. diss., University of California, Los Angeles, 1973), pp. 32–38; Phil McArdle, "Oakland [Calif.] Police Department History, 1900–1919," pt. 2, typescript, n.d., p. 36; U.S. Department of Commerce, Bureau of the Census, *Thirteenth Census of the United States, 1910, Supplement for California, Statistics of Population*, p. 615.

91. Carey McWilliams, *Southern California Country: An Island on the Land* (New York: Duell, Sloan & Pearce, 1946), p. 157.

92. Willard Huntington Wright, "Los Angeles: The Chemically Pure," *The Smart Set Anthology*, ed. Burton Rascoe and Groff Conklin (New York: Reynal & Hitchcock, 1934), pp. 92–93, 95. For complementary analyses of the impact of Midwestern migrants to Los Angeles in the early twentieth century, see George J. Sánchez, *Becoming Mexican-American: Ethnicity, Culture, and Identity in Chicano Los Angeles, 1900–1945* (New York: Oxford University Press, 1993), pp. 88–93; Mike Davis, *City of Quartz: Excavating the Future of Los Angeles* (London: Verso, 1990); and Elaine Tyler May, *Great Expectations: Marriage and Divorce in Post-Victorian America* (Chicago: University of Chicago Press, 1980).

93. Burton Rascoe, "'Smart Set' History," *Smart Set Anthology*, p. xxii.

94. Woods, "Progressives and the Police," pp. 32–38; Raymond Wells, interview.

95. "Famous Policewoman Urges Prevention of Crime"; "The Need for Women in Police Work," *[Chicago] City Club Bulletin*, October 12, 1912, pp. 321–28; handbill advertising forthcoming speaking tour by Wells, [ca. 1912], Alice Stebbins Wells Papers, in private possession; Raymond Wells, interview.

96. Sidney Kirkpatrick, "Policewomen in the United States," Women's Police Officers Association of California, *Yearbook* 10 (1937): 3; Raymond Wells, interview.

97. "Famous Policewoman Urges Prevention of Crime."

CHAPTER TWO

1. "A Policewoman on Trial," *Survey*, April 15, 1922, pp. 69–70.

2. Ibid., p. 69.

3. Ibid.

4. Robert M. Fogelson, *Big-City Police* (Cambridge, Mass.: Harvard University Press, 1977), pp. 17–35.

5. Ibid., p. 56.

6. Ibid., p. 67.

7. On police corruption see, in addition to Fogelson, *Big-City Police,* Jerome Hopkins, *Our Lawless Police* (New York: Viking Press, 1931). For a very detailed account of reform and intercine battles for graft in the Los Angeles Police Department during the late nineteenth and early twentieth centuries, see Joseph Gerald Woods, "The Progressives and the Police: Urban Reform and the Professionalization of the Los Angeles Police" (Ph.D. diss., University of California, Los Angeles, 1973), chap. 1.

8. Woods, "Progressives and the Police," p. 31.

9. On police reform, see Fogelson, *Big-City Police;* Gene Carte and Elaine Carte, *Police Reform in the United States: The Era of August Vollmer* (Berkeley: University of California Press, 1975); James F. Richardson, *Urban Police in the United States* (Port Washington, N.Y.: National University Publications, Kennikat Press, 1974). Samuel Walker uses slightly different names for civic reformers and moral reformers. He calls them respectively efficiency/managerial reformers and social service/crime prevention reformers. Walker, *A Critical History of Police Reform: The Emergence of Professionalism* (Lexington, Mass.: Lexington Books, D. C. Heath, 1977).

10. On narrowing of police functions, see Fogelson, *Big-City Police*, especially p. 84; Walker, *Critical History*, pp. 31, 33. As Eric Monkkonen points out, the gradual narrowing of police functions in the early twentieth century stripped the police of their role as social welfare providers. He believes that this change created psychological and physical distance between the police and the citizenry, particularly between the police and the poor, because it "meant an end to police familiarity with the difficulties of the life of the poor." Monkkonen, *Police in Urban America*, p. 108.

Many female social welfare reformers wanted to end the practice of police lodging. As Monkkonen argues, "The fight against police lodging was part of a larger battle led by Josephine Lowell, among others, against the giving of outdoor relief, a form of aid that she felt merely perpetuated poverty." Ibid., p. 106. On Josephine Lowell and charity, see Lori D. Ginzberg, *Women and Benevolence: Morality, Politics, and Class in the Nineteenth-Century United States* (New Haven: Yale University Press, 1990).

11. The classic work on scientific management is Frederick Winslow Taylor, *Scientific Management* (New York: Harper & Brothers, 1911); for a Marxist in-

terpretation of scientific management, see Harry Braverman, *Labor and Monopoly Capital: The Degradation of Work in the Twentieth Century* (New York: Monthly Review Press, 1974).

12. Unidentified New York City alderman quoted in Fogelson, *Big-City Police*, p. 54.

13. Joan Wallach Scott, *Gender and the Politics of History* (New York: Columbia University Press, 1986), p. 48.

14. Duncan Mathews, "Law Enforcement and Causes of Crime," International Association of Chiefs of Police, *Proceedings, 31st Convention, 1924*, p. 122. (Hereafter, references to the proceedings of this body will be cited as follows: IACP, *Proceedings*, followed by year.)

15. Walter ("W. J.") Petersen, "The Chief of Police: THE GOAT for the Sins of Society," IACP, *Proceedings*, 1916, pp. 38–44.

16. Portraying reform and reformers as feminine was not a new practice in the Progressive Era. As Steven Stark notes, nineteenth-century American political culture depicted reformers as politically impotent. It also depicted men who were thinking of changing parties as "Miss-Nancys." "Gap Politics," *Atlantic Monthly*, July 1996, p. 74.

17. Walter J. Petersen to unidentified person, May 13, 1916, quoted in Phil McArdle, "Oakland [Calif.] Police Department History, 1900–1919," pt. 2, typescript, n.d., p. 41. Petersen's compliance with reformers' demands preceded California voters' approval of the Red Light Abatement Act. This act went into effect December 1914. Ibid., p. 40.

18. Ibid., p. 45.

19. Ibid., pp. 38–39.

20. Excerpt from unidentified article in the *San Francisco Chronicle*, [ca. March 1912], quoted in "Police Work," a pamphlet, Alice Stebbins Wells Papers, in private possession. The excerpt reads in part, "As a concrete result of the address given last night in Chabot Hall by Mrs. Alice Stebbins Wells . . . a committee of five will be named this week . . . to present plans for a second mass meeting of citizens for the appointment of policewomen in the Oakland Police Department."

21. See, for example, "Famous Policewoman Urges Prevention of Crime," *New York Times*, December 22, 1912, sec. 5, p. 13.

22. "L.A. Housewives Are Offered Lectures on Law," unidentified newspaper article, Aletha Gilbert Papers, in private possession (hereafter, AG Papers). On the need for a woman on police departments, see "Famous Policewoman," and "Many Reasons for Women on Police Forces," *Ottawa Free Press*, January 17, 1913.

23. "The 'Sesqui' Policewomen," *Woman Citizen* 11 (February 1927): 34. On appointment of women police in Seattle, Boston, and Portland, Oregon, see Gloria E. Myers, *Municipal Mother: Portland's Lola Greene Baldwin, America's First Policewoman* (Corvallis: Oregon State University Press, 1995), pp. 8–14, 146–48.

24. Sabina Marshall, "Development of the Policewoman's Movement in Cleveland, Ohio," *Journal of Social Hygiene* 11 (April 1925): 193–209; Tamar Hosansky and Pat Sparling, *Working Vice: The Gritty True Story of Lt. Lucie J. Duvall* (New York: HarperCollins, 1992), p. 23.

25. Chloe Owings, *Women Police: A Study of the Development and Status of the Women Police Movement*, Publications of the Bureau of Social Hygiene (New York: Frederick H. Hitchcock, 1925), pp. 104–5.

26. Owings, *Women Police*, p. 131.

27. Myers, *Municipal Mother*, pp. 14, 20–22, 162.

28. "Western Women as Police Officers," *Survey*, December 21, 1912, pp. 345–46. On the history and duties of railroad police, see H. S. Dewhurst, *The Railroad Police* (Springfield, Ill.: Charles C. Thomas, 1955).

29. Dorothy Moses Schulz, *From Social Worker to Crimefighter: Women in United States Municipal Policing* (Westport, Conn.: Praeger, 1996), p. 28; Los Angeles Police Department, *Annual Report, Police Department, City of Los Angeles, California, for the Fiscal Year Ending June 30, 1917; June 30, 1918; June 30, 1919*.

30. Owings, *Women Police*, p. 122; "Here and There with the Policewomen," *Policewoman's International Bulletin* 5 (May 1929): 7; Schulz, *From Social Worker to Crimefighter*, p. 91.

31. Schulz, *From Social Worker to Crimefighter*, pp. 71, 92.

32. On the federal anti-vice program during World War I, see Allan M. Brandt, *No Magic Bullet: A Social History of Venereal Disease in the United States Since 1880* (New York: Oxford University Press, 1985), and David Kennedy, *Over Here: The First World War and American Society* (New York: Oxford University Press, 1980). For an insightful discussion of the impact of the anti-vice campaign during World War I on gay men in New York City, see George Chauncey, *Gay New York: Gender, Urban Culture, and the Making of the Gay Male World, 1890–1940* (New York: Basic Books, 1994).

33. Winthrop D. Lane, "Girls and Khaki: Some Practical Measures of Protection of Young Women in Time of War," *Survey* 39 (December 1, 1917): 236–40. On the work of the CPWG, see Owings, *Women Police*, pp. 110–11. An exhaustive account of the Commission on Training Camp Activities is in Brandt, *No Magic Bullet*, chap. 2.

34. Owings, *Women Police*, pp. 113–14; Mary E. Odem, *Delinquent Daughters: Protecting and Policing Adolescent Female Sexuality in the United States, 1885–1920* (Chapel Hill: University of North Carolina Press), pp. 121–27.

35. Schulz, *From Social Worker to Crimefighter*, p. 33.

36. John G. Buchanan, "War Legislation Against Alcoholic Liquor and Prostitution," *Journal of the American Institute of Criminal Law and Criminology* 9 (February 1919): 525, quoted in Brandt, *No Magic Bullet*, p. 76.

37. Miner to Fosdick, August 6, 1917, National Archives, Record Group 165,

Box 585, quoted in Mary Ellen Odem, "Delinquent Daughters: The Sexual Regulation of Female Minors in the United States, 1880–1920" (Ph.D. diss., University of California, Berkeley, 1989), p. 198.

38. Maude Miner to Ethel S. Dummer, April 17, 1918, Dummer Papers, quoted in Brandt, *No Magic Bullet*, p. 86.

39. Odem, *Delinquent Daughters*, pp. 125–27.

40. The difference between Miner and Rippen on this issue illustrates the split in opinion among social workers regarding sexually active teenage girls. As Estelle B. Freedman points out, some social workers in the 1910s and 1920s worried more about the girls' role in spreading venereal disease than they did about the welfare of the individual girl; other social workers worried more about the individual girl. Estelle B. Freedman, *Maternal Justice: Miriam Van Waters and the Female Reform Tradition* (Chicago: University of Chicago Press, 1996), p. 86.

41. Within the middle class, notions of gender differences were sharper in the late nineteenth and early twentieth centuries than they had been earlier. See John D'Emilio and Estelle B. Freedman, *Intimate Matters: A History of Sexuality in America* (New York: Harper & Row, 1988), pp. 173–80.

42. Josephine Nelson, "On the Policewoman's 'Beat,'" *Independent Woman*, May 1936, 138. Emphasis in original.

43. "The Need for Police Women in City Work," *[Chicago] City Club Bulletin*, October 31, 1912, 325.

44. "Many Reasons for Women on Police Forces."

45. "Famous Policewoman Urges Prevention of Crime."

46. Alice Stebbins Wells, untitled speech, IACP, *Proceedings*, 1914, p. 129.

47. Louise DeKoven Bowen, *Safeguards for City Youth at Work and at Play* (New York: Macmillan, 1914), pp. 154–55. The idea that the criminal justice system discriminated against women was not new. It surfaced in the nineteenth century as part of the movement for separate prisons for women. See Estelle B. Freedman, *Their Sisters' Keepers: Women's Prison Reform in America, 1830–1930* (Ann Arbor: University of Michigan Press, 1981), pp. 58–59.

48. New Haven, Connecticut, newspaper editorial quoted in "Progress in New Haven," *Policewoman's International Bulletin* 4 (September 1928): 6.

49. Irene Vandyck, "No Man's Land in Police Work," *Police Journal*, May 1922, p. 17.

50. "Functions and Work of the Woman's Bureau of a Police Department and Tests for Selection of Policewoman," *Public Personnel Studies* 5 (December 1927): 247.

51. Alice Stebbins Wells, "Women on the Police Force," *American City*, April 1913, p. 401.

52. Mary E. Hamilton, *The Policewoman: Her Service and Ideals* (New York: Frederick A. Stokes, 1924), p. 70.

53. Henrietta T. Additon, an advocate of women police, remarked in 1924, "I remember talking with a group of very respectable, wealthy club women who were quite cold to the idea of *policewomen,* but when I spoke of *public chaperons,* their attitude completely changed." (Emphasis in original.) "The Policewoman," *Community Treatment of Delinquency,* Annual Report and Proceedings of the Eighth Annual Conference of the National Probation Association (New York: National Probation Association, 1924), pp. 238–39.

54. Miner to Fosdick, August 6, 1917, National Archives, Record Group 165, Records of the War Department General and Special Staff, Box 585, quoted in Odem, "Delinquent Daughters," p. 198. Even during the 1920s, when the revolution in sexual culture had spread from the working class to the middle class, and the existence of the female sexual drive was widely acknowledged, most Americans still believed that men were naturally more lustful than women; therefore, the idea that men "led girls astray" retained much of its persuasive power. On the persistence of some nineteenth-century gender stereotypes regarding sexuality, see Freedman and D'Emilio, *Intimate Matters,* pp. 256–74.

55. Myers, *Municipal Mother,* pp. 35–36.

56. "Warfare Waged on Love Pirates of Jitney Bus," *Los Angeles Examiner,* January 9, 1915, AG Papers.

57. Aletha Gilbert et al. to Los Angeles City Council, April 4, 1927, City Council File 2680, Los Angeles City Archives.

58. Walker, *Critical History,* pp. 38, 81.

59. Michael J. Regan, untitled speech, IACP, *Proceedings,* 1911, p. 149.

60. Joseph M. Quigley, "Prevention of Crime," IACP, *Proceedings,* 1912, p. 105.

61. Both speeches are in the IACP *Proceedings* of 1915. James L. Beavers, "The Efficiency of the Police Department," p. 78; Walter "W. J." Petersen, "The Constructive Police," p. 70.

62. Julia Liss and Steven Schlossman, "The Contours of Crime Prevention in August Vollmer's Berkeley," *Research in Law, Deviance and Social Control* 6 (1984): 84–85, 89–93.

63. August Vollmer, "The Policeman as a Social Worker," IACP, *Proceedings,* 1919, pp. 32–38.

64. Ibid., p. 36.

65. Elisabeth Lossing, "The Crime Prevention Work of the Berkeley Police Department," in *Preventing Crime: A Symposium,* ed. Sheldon Glueck and Eleanor Glueck (New York: McGraw-Hill, 1936), p. 244.

66. The major exception to police chiefs' silence about policewomen was the resolution passed in 1922 at the convention of the International Chiefs of Police stating that policewomen were "a necessity." William P. Rutledge, "Report of Section on 'Police Organization and Administration,'" IACP, *Proceedings,* 1922, p.

38. This resolution was the work of a special committee whose membership and deliberations are not recorded in the published proceedings. The 1922 convention was unique in other ways as well. It featured numerous speakers from outside law enforcement, including academic criminologists and clinical psychologists. Vollmer was doubtlessly instrumental in lining up academic speakers at the conference because he served as president of the IACP in 1922, the conference that year was held in San Francisco (near his home turf), and he was known for his championship of college-trained policemen. It seems ironic that he presided over the convention in which policewomen were declared a "necessity," yet the Berkeley Police Department, which he headed, did not employ a policewoman for three more years.

67. "Western Women as Police Officers," *Survey*, December 21, 1912, p. 346.

68. Quoted in "Policewomen in Chicago," *Literary Digest*, August 23, 1913, p. 271.

69. Wells, "Women on the Police Force," p. 401; Dorothy Thomas, "Crime Prevention Is Our Job," *Independent Woman*, January 1935, p. 32; Martha Strayer, "Daily News Representative Discovers Human Side of Policewomen at Regional Conference," *Policewoman's International Bulletin* 3 (August–September 1927): 5; Louis Brownlow, "The Policewoman's Sphere," *National Municipal Review* 17 (March 1928): 136; Mary E. Hamilton, "The Policewoman's Point of View," *Police Journal*, January 1924, p. 30.

70. August Vollmer, "The Policewoman and Pre-Delinquency," *Woman Citizen*, March 1926, p. 30.

71. Vandyck, "No Man's Land," pp. 16–17.

72. Vollmer, "The Policewoman and Pre-Delinquency," p. 30. Vollmer made this statement shortly after the Berkeley Police Department hired its first woman officer. Vollmer was a latecomer to the movement for women police, but after 1925 he took up the cause with more enthusiasm than most chiefs of police.

73. A crime study undertaken in 1917 by the New York City Police Department concluded that juvenile delinquency was "due mainly to lack of parental control arising from such conditions as poverty, ignorance as to how to bring up children, gross neglect, drunken parents, and the loss of one or both parents." "Report, 1914–1917," Police Department, City of New York, pp. 76–77, quoted in Clarence B. Smith, "The True Sphere of Policewomen," *Police Journal*, April 1922, p. 19.

74. Rhoda J. Miliken, "We Don't Carry Nightsticks!" *Prison World* 6 (March–April 1944): 5. Emphasis in original. Miliken served as Van Winkle's assistant in the Women's Bureau of the District of Columbia Police Department during the 1920s. Susan Bordo discusses the origins of a masculine cognitive style (stressing emotional detachment and concern for abstract principles) in "The Cartesian Masculinization of Thought," *Signs* 3 (spring 1986): 439–56.

75. Louis Brownlow, "The City and the Citizen," *Policewomen's International Bulletin* 3 (October 1927): 2.

76. New Haven, Connecticut, newspaper editorial quoted in "Progress in New Haven," p. 6. Some policemen were well aware of their unsavory public image. See, for example, California Peace Officers Association, *Proceedings*, 1931, pp. 86–95, quoted in Walker, *Critical History*, p. 134.

77. Roche, a graduate of Vassar College, did not last long in her job as a policewoman; she left the Denver Police Department in August 1913. "Denver's Policewoman Quits," *New York Times*, August 6, 1913, p. 7.

78. For this analysis I mined approximately 150 articles published between 1912 and 1940 that discussed the work of women police; several books written by or about pioneer policewomen; the annual proceedings of the conventions of the International Association of Chiefs of Police, 1913–30; the *Policewoman's International Bulletin*, 1925–29; and the *Annual Reports* of the City Mother's Bureau and the Crime Prevention Bureau of the Los Angeles Police Department, 1914–40.

79. For a succinct discussion of how contests over meanings involve the introduction of new pairs of opposition, see Scott, *Gender and the Politics of History*, pp. 6–7.

80. Wells, untitled speech, IACP, *Proceedings*, 1914, p. 129.

81. "Functions and Work of the Woman's Bureau," p. 247.

82. "Editorial," *Policewoman's International Bulletin* 3 (August–September 1927): 4.

83. Fred N. Valz, "Policewomen Fill Long Felt Need in Jacksonville, Fla.," *Police Journal*, August 1927, p. 32.

84. Mrs. George B. Walker, "The Relationship of Policewomen and Social Service as Viewed from the Sidelines," Minnesota State Conference and Institute of Social Work, *Proceedings* 38 (1930): 166.

85. Helen D. Pigeon, "The Relationship of the Juvenile Court to the Police," *The Courts and the Prevention of Delinquency*, Annual Reports and Proceedings of the Twentieth Annual Conference of the National Probation Association, Cleveland, Ohio, May 23–27, 1926 (New York: National Probation Association, 1926), p. 197.

86. Mina C. Van Winkle, "Preface," in Owings, *Women Police*, p. xi.

87. Ibid., p. x.

88. Estelle B. Freedman discusses female institution building in "Separatism as Strategy: Female Institution Building and American Feminism, 1870–1930," *Feminist Studies* 5 (fall 1979): 512–29.

89. Owings, *Women Police*, p. 164, quoting New York Police Commissioner Richard E. Enright.

90. "Her Ears Hear Women's Woes," *Los Angeles Times*, October 4, 1914, pt. 2, p. 10.

91. "The City Mothers Bureau of Los Angeles, California," *Journal of Social Hygiene* 1 (June 1915): 495.

92. Vandyck, "No Man's Land," p. 51.

93. Photograph captioned "City Mothers' Row Over Ousting Up to City Attorney," unidentified newspaper article, AG Papers.

94. Hamilton, *Policewoman*, p. 59.

95. Letter from Mina C. Van Winkle to the Superintendent of Police of Washington, D.C., quoted in part in "Here and There," *Policewoman's International Bulletin* 3 (August–September 1927): 8.

96. U.S., Congress, House Committee on the District of Columbia, Subcommittee on Police and Firemen, Hearings on H.R. 7848, 69th Congress, 1st sess., 1926, p. 13. It is difficult to state how many woman's bureaus ever existed because no one kept reliable records. The editors of the *Policewoman's International Bulletin* asserted in March 1928 that they received reports every year regarding woman's bureaus that were abolished (p. 4). They also occasionally reported the establishment of new bureaus.

97. Dr. Mary B. Harris, "The Socialized Policewoman," *Woman Citizen*, June 27, 1925, p. 15.

98. Owings, *Women Police*, p. 257.

99. Van Winkle, "Address," IACP, *Proceedings*, 1926, pp. 243–45.

100. Van Winkle, "Purpose and Scope of a Woman's Bureau," IACP, *Proceedings*, 1922, p. 9.

101. Van Winkle was a feminist who came to police work after eight years of serving as head of the Woman's Political Union of New Jersey, a suffrage organization. An informative discussion of her police career is in Ann Sadler, "The Ideal Policewoman: An Interview with Mrs. Mina Van Winkle, President of the International Association of Policewomen," *Welfare Bulletin* 19 (May 1928): 638–44.

102. Aletha Gilbert, "The Duties of a 'City Mother,'" *American City*, March 1922, p. 239.

103. Vandyck, "No Man's Land," p. 17.

104. Barbara Wells, "The Feminine Arm of the Law," *Independent Woman*, February 1948, p. 36.

105. Valeria H. Parker, "A Policewoman's Life," *Woman Citizen* June 28, 1924, p. 16.

106. Virginia M. Murray, "Policewomen in Detroit," *American City*, September 1921, p. 209.

107. Mrs. John P. (Irene) Buwalda, "The Policewoman's Function in the Community," IACP, *Proceedings*, 1922, p. 19.

108. Walker, "The Relationship of Policewomen and Social Service," p. 166. Emphasis in original.

109. Clarence B. Smith, Jr., "The True Sphere of Policewomen," *Police Jour-*

nal, April 1922, p. 61. Owings discusses cartoonists' portrayal of Wells in *Women Police*, p. 103; see also T. Earl Sullenger, *Social Determinants in Juvenile Delinquency* (New York: John Wiley, 1936), p. 210.

110. Helen D. Pigeon, "Policewomen in the United States," *Journal of the American Institute of Criminal Law and Criminology* 18 (November 1927): 376.

111. Hamilton, *Policewoman*, p. 69.

112. "Uniform a Vexing Problem to Policewomen," *Police Journal*, July 1922, p. 23. By the 1910s, some reform-minded police chiefs also believed that arrests of women and children should be made as discreetly as possible. See, for example, Richard Sylvester, "The Treatment of the Woman Delinquent from the Police Standpoint," IACP, *Proceedings*, 1911, p. 153.

113. Mary Jane Spurlin, "Women's Contribution to Crime Prevention," *Oregon Law Review* 14 (April 1935): 419.

114. "Uniform a Vexing Problem to Policewomen," p. 23.

115. When the police department of Chicago hired the first black policemen in the United States in the late nineteenth century, it did not permit them to wear uniforms. Walker, *Critical History*, p. 10.

116. "Here and There with the Policewomen," *International Association of Policewomen* 3 (November–December 1927): 10–11.

117. Eric Monkkonen observes that when American police departments first required uniforms in the mid- to late nineteenth century, policemen strongly resisted wearing them on the grounds that uniforms were both undemocratic and "servantlike." Monkkonen, *Police in Urban America*, pp. 44–45.

118. "Women on the LAPD: It Ain't a New Phenomenon," Los Angeles Police Relief Association, *Guardian*, first quarter 1990, p. 4.

119. Nelson, "On the Policewoman's 'Beat,' " p. 138.

120. IACP, *Proceedings*, 1921, p. 45.

121. Sadler, "Ideal Policewoman," pp. 638–44.

122. A federally sponsored survey of police departments in the United States during the late 1920s revealed that 60 percent of policemen had no high-school education at all. Richardson, *Urban Police*, p. 135.

123. Walker, *Critical History*, p. 91. The working-class identity of the police has deep historical roots. As Egon Bittner notes, medieval watchman were "recruited from among the ranks of the destitute." Centuries later, the first modern municipal police force in the world, the Metropolitan Police of London established by Parliament in 1829, hired very poor working-class men as patrolmen. Neither British policemen nor their counterparts in the United States during the late nineteenth and early twentieth centuries needed much formal education or specialized skills to enter police work. A strong back, a strong arm, and a willingness to carry out orders (including at times the orders of corrupt city and police officials) were the primary requirements. As late as the mid-1920s, leading U.S. police chiefs still

seriously debated whether the minimum entry requirements for policemen should be the ability to read and write. In contrast, requirements for policewomen throughout the 1910s, 1920s, and 1930s demanded at least a high school diploma, and preferably a college degree. On the working-class nature of police and how it has affected their reputation and work, see Egon Bittner, *Aspects of Police Work* (Boston: Northeastern University Press, 1990), pp. 89–232.

124. Sadler, "Ideal Policewoman," p. 638.

125. IACP, *Proceedings, 1920*, p. 121.

126. "Need for Police Women in City Work," pp. 322–23.

127. It should be noted that class differences between pioneer policewomen and policemen probably correlated to some degree with ethnic and nativity differences, but little evidence exists to prove it categorically.

128. Quoted in Hosansky and Sparling, *Working Vice*, p. 23 (no citation given for source of original quotation).

129. New Haven, Connecticut, newspaper editorial quoted in "Progress in New Haven," p. 6.

130. Van Winkle, Preface to Owings, *Women Police*, p. ix.

131. Edith Abbott, "Training for the Policewoman's Job," *Woman Citizen*, April 30, 1926, p. 30.

132. "The Policewoman's Sphere," p. 138. The study whose conclusions Brownlow discusses is cited in note 50 herein.

133. Joseph A. Gerk, "Policewomen," IACP, *Proceedings, 1930*, p. 161.

134. "City Policewomen to Wear Uniforms," *New York Times*, January 14, 1935, p. 17, quoted in Kerry Segrave, *Policewomen: A History* (Jefferson, N.C.: McFarland, 1995), p. 88.

135. Mina C. Van Winkle, "Women Police and General Social Welfare," IACP, *Proceedings, 1920*, p. 53. The phrases quoted from her speech to the chiefs in 1926 is found on p. 245 of the IACP *Proceedings* for that year.

136. Sadler, "Ideal Policewoman," p. 642.

137. Untitled speech by Sarah V. Dunn, IACP, *Proceedings, 1928*, p. 93.

CHAPTER THREE

1. "Report of Cases of the City Mother's Bureau Since the First of the Fiscal Year," July 1927, Aletha Gilbert Papers, in private possession (hereafter, AG Papers); Margaret Saunders, "A Study of the Work of the City Mother's Bureau of the Los Angeles Police Department" (M.S.W. thesis, Graduate School of Social Work, University of Southern California, 1939), p. 90.

Mary Lockyer and Nancy Lockyer are fictitious names. The true names of all clients of the City Mother's Bureau whose cases I discuss have been changed to insure the confidentiality of these records. The fictitious names have the same eth-

nic content as the true names. I have devised a numbering system to refer to specific cases I discuss. The Lockyer case is no. 32. Anyone who has permission to
look at the Aletha Gilbert Papers may write to me through Temple University
Press for the key to my coding system.

2. U.S., Department of Commerce, Bureau of the Census, *Thirteenth Census
of the United States, 1910: Supplement for California, Statistics of the Population*, p. 569.

3. Arthur W. Sjoquist, "From Posses to Professionals: A History of the Los
Angeles Police Department" (M.S. thesis, California State University, Los Angeles, 1972), p. 118.

4. "Assistant Matron," unidentified newspaper article, [ca. March 1902],
AG Papers.

5. Family genealogy chart, AG Papers; John Stevens McGroarty, *Los Angeles from the Mountains to the Sea* (Chicago: American Historical Society, 1921),
2:402–3.

6. Ibid.; undated handwritten note by Gilbert showing date (March 17,
1902) she quit the sales job with the wholesale grocery company; *Aletha Gilbert v.
Thomas M. Gilbert*, Los Angeles Superior Court Index, 1897. Court documents relating to Gilbert's divorce have either disappeared or been misfiled, so the specific legal grounds for the divorce remain unknown. Mutual incompatibility was
not valid grounds for divorce in California in 1897, even though California had
among the most liberal divorce laws of any state in the nation in the late nineteenth century. On divorce in Los Angeles, see Elaine Tyler May, *Great Expectations: Marriage and Divorce in Post-Victorian America* (Chicago: University of
Chicago Press, 1980), pp. 5–6.

7. "Busiest Officer on the Force," *Los Angeles Times*, January 25, 1901;
"Woman Who Feared Not," *Los Angeles Times*, March 1, 1904. Both AG Papers.

8. Ibid.; Estelle Lawton Lindsey, "Low Wages Cause of Girls' Downfall, So
Says Mrs. Gilbert, Jail Matron," *Los Angeles Record*, July 27, 1911, AG Papers; Estelle B. Freedman, *Their Sisters' Keepers: Women's Prison Reform in America, 1830–
1930* (Ann Arbor: University of Michigan Press, 1981), pp. 123–24.

9. "Matron of Police to War on Mashers," *Los Angeles Examiner*, April 22,
1911, AG Papers. Sebastian's support for women police is evidenced not only by
his willingness to employ them but also by his strong endorsement of them in a
speech he gave to the International Association of Chiefs of Police (IACP) entitled
"Women as Police Officers." He was the first person to speak on their behalf at an
IACP convention. IACP, *Proceedings*, 1913, pp. 140–44. Alice Stebbins Wells did
not address the IACP convention until 1914.

10. Los Angeles Police Department, *Annual Report, Police Department, City
of Los Angeles, California, for the Fiscal Year Ending June 30, 1914*, pp. 26, 40–49; photograph of LAPD Juvenile Bureau (ca. 1914) showing all members, AG Papers.
For discussion of the early years of Juvenile Bureau, see Chapter Four.

11. Joseph Gerald Woods, "The Progressives and the Police: Urban Reform and the Professionalization of the Los Angeles Police" (Ph.D. diss., University of California, Los Angeles, 1973), p. 27.

12. Ibid., pp. 9–13, 27–47.

13. Ibid., pp. 32–39, 46.

14. Ruth Rosen, *The Lost Sisterhood: Prostitution in America, 1900–1918* (Baltimore: Johns Hopkins University Press, 1982), p. 172.

15. "Los Angeles Worse Than Ever, Says Jail Matron," *San Diego Union,* October 13, 1912, p. 10, AG Papers. (The *San Diego Union* probably referred to Gilbert as a jail matron because its staff was not yet accustomed to the idea of women police officers.) Gilbert's remarks about the closing of the segregated district could be interpreted to mean that she favored re-opening it. However, in the absence of other evidence to indicate her support of a restricted district, the opinions she voiced in San Diego should be interpreted as criticism of male sexual license rather than as criticism of the closing of the segregated district.

16. "Two Probation Officials Are on Carpet," *Los Angeles Express,* October 19, 1912, p. 22; "Digging for Bottom Facts," *Los Angeles Examiner,* October 20, 1912, AG Papers. The *Los Angeles Express* was not wrong in calling Gilbert and Marden probation officers because in the early 1910s, the terms "probation officers," "police probation officers," and "juvenile officers" were used interchangeably to refer to officers assigned to the LAPD Juvenile Bureau.

17. "Her Ears Hear Women's Woes," *Los Angeles Times,* October 4, 1914, pt. 2, p. 10.

18. Steven Schlossman and Stephanie Wallach, "The Crime of Precocious Sexuality: Female Juvenile Delinquency in the Progressive Era," *Harvard Educational Review* 48 (February 1978): 65–95. See also Ruth M. Alexander, *The "Girl Problem": Female Sexual Delinquency in New York, 1900–1930* (Ithaca, N.Y.: Cornell University Press, 1995).

19. Mary Ellen Odem, *Delinquent Daughters: Protecting and Policing Adolescent Female Sexuality in the United States, 1885–1920* (Chapel Hill: University of North Carolina Press, 1995), pp. 135–36. See also idem, "Delinquent Daughters: The Sexual Regulation of Female Minors in the United States, 1880–1920" (Ph.D. diss., University of California, Berkeley, 1989), pp. 235, 302. Odem notes that by "families" she also means guardians.

20. "Her Ears Hear Women's Woes."

21. Gertrude M. Price, "City Mothers' Bureau," *Los Angeles Sun,* June 29, 1915; "Police Badges Given Women Who Will Advise Girls, Boys and Parents," unidentified newspaper article, AG Papers. Leo Jones, who reported on the bureau for the *National Municipal Review,* summarizes the argument for a separate location by describing police stations in harsh terms: "The prison atmosphere, the morbid crowd . . . the reporters of the sensational press eager to give publicity to the shame of some

girl or boy—such an environment, far from encouraging the reformation of youthful wrong-doers, tends to . . . break down their self-respect." "The City Mother's Bureau of Los Angeles," *National Municipal Review* 9 (August 1920): 485.

22. After Gilbert died, Alice Stebbins Wells was among those who criticized her. See Saunders, "Study of the Work of the City Mother's Bureau," pp. 53–55.

23. Los Angeles City Council, Minutes 97 (September 21, 1914): 533, Los Angeles City Archives; "Policewomen Take Up Cudgel to Protect Girls from Loose Men," *Los Angeles Record,* May 2, 1913; "Need 30 More Policewomen; Will Aid Crusade on Vice," *Los Angeles Examiner,* May 3, 1913; "Beware! Girls Dropping into Pitfalls," unidentified newspaper article, [ca 1912]; "'City Mother' Plan Receives New Impetus," *Los Angeles Record,* September 9, 1914; "'City Mother' May Be Domiciled at Normal," unidentified Los Angeles newspaper article. All AG Papers.

24. Gertrude M. Price, "City Mothers' Bureau," *Los Angeles Sun,* June 29, 1915.

25. Unidentified newspaper article, *Los Angeles Tribune,* November 29, 1914; "City Mothers," *Riverside (Calif.) Press,* December 15, 1914. Both AG Papers.

26. "Her Ears Hear Women's Woes."

27. Aletha Gilbert, "What Is Wrong with Modern Children," undated speech, typescript, AG Papers.

28. Aletha Gilbert, untitled, undated speech on "The normal, modern girl," typescript, AG Papers.

29. Aletha Gilbert, untitled, undated speech on "The place of the policewoman in the police department," typescript, AG Papers.

30. Gilbert, "The normal, modern girl."

31. Allan M. Brandt, *No Magic Bullet: A Social History of Venereal Disease in the United States Since 1880* (New York: Oxford University Press, 1985), pp. 13–22.

32. Odem, "Delinquent Daughters," p. 237.

33. "Need 30 More Policewomen, Will Aid Crusade on Vice," *Los Angeles Examiner,* May 3, 1913, p. 10.

34. Ibid.

35. Woods, "Progressives and the Police," pp. 42–43, 46; for information on the fate of Sebastian's proposal for five policewomen and twenty-five special appointees, I thank Jay Jones, city archivist of Los Angeles. Telephone interview by author, July 29, 1996.

36. "Police Badges Given Women Who Will Advise Girls, Boys and Parents," *Los Angeles Tribune,* November 29, 1914; "Women Flock to Help Sisters," *Los Angeles Times,* October 13, 1914; "New City Mothers to Take Office," unidentified newspaper article. All AG Papers.

37. Los Angeles Settlement Association, *Annual Report, 1904/05,* p. 10; "Urge Trial by Woman Judge of All Girl Cases," *Los Angeles Herald,* October 2,

1914, AG Papers. (Women judges of the juvenile court were long known as "referees," not as judges.) Claire Hosler Coombs, "The Women's Court," *Out West*, March 1916, pp. 115–17; "Police Chief Will Talk to Clubwomen," *Los Angeles Examiner*, January 16, 1916; "Woman Judge Opens Court, Justice, Not Cold Law, to Rule," *Los Angeles Tribune*, January 11, 1916, AG Papers.

On the female activist community of Los Angeles, see Dana W. Bartlett, *The Better City: A Sociological Study of a Modern City* (Los Angeles: Neuner Company Press, 1907), and Gloria Ricci Lothrop, "Strength Made Stronger: The Role of Women in Southern California Philanthropy," *Southern California Quarterly* 71, 2/3 (1989): 143–94.

38. Willard Huntington Wright, "Los Angeles: The Chemically Pure," *The Smart Set Anthology*, ed. Burton Rascoe and Grof Conklin (New York: Reynal & Hitchcock, 1934), p. 95.

39. "'City Mothers' Not to Be Merged with Police," unidentified newspaper article, October 28, 1919.

40. "Arguing City Mother's Job," *Los Angeles Evening Express,* n.d.; "Thorpe Opposes Davis in Mother Bureau Dispute," *Los Angeles Illustrated Daily News*, December 4, 1929. Both AG Papers. Linda K. Kerber has noted that in the 1980s historians of women began to analyze closely the relationship between gender relations of power and the control of physical spaces. As she points out, an important essay that discusses this topic is Estelle B. Freedman, "Separatism as Strategy: Female Institution Building and American Feminism, 1870–1930," *Feminist Studies* 5 (fall 1979): 512–29. Linda K. Kerber, "Separate Spheres, Female Worlds, Woman's Place: The Rhetoric of Women's History," *Journal of American History* 75 (June 1988): 30–33.

41. "New City Mothers' Bureau Will Open Today," *Los Angeles Examiner,* November 28, 1914, AG Papers.

42. "City Mother Plan Proves Big Success," unidentified newspaper article, October 28, 1914, AG Papers.

43. Ibid.

44. See, for example, remarks made by Timothy D. Hurley, the chief probation officer of the Cook County Juvenile Court in "State Conference of Charities," *Juvenile Record* [Chicago] 2 (NS), no. 2, p. 6.

45. Grace Abbott, "History of the Juvenile Court Movement Throughout the World," in Jane Addams et al., *The Child, the Clinic, and the Court* (New York: New Republic, 1925), p. 267.

46. LAPD, *Annual Report,* fiscal year 1916–17, p. 46; City Council File 1300 (1930), Los Angeles City Archives.

47. "New City Mothers' Bureau Will Open Today."

48. "City Mothers Tell What They Hope Bureau Will Accomplish," *Los Angeles Examiner*, November 28, 1914, AG Papers.

49. "City Mother Observes 30th Year in LA Work," *Los Angeles Evening Herald,* April 14, 1922, AG Papers. The reference to "30th Year" probably included in its tabulation Gilbert's work as an unpaid assistant to her mother when her mother was the jail matron.

50. Eric Monkkonen, *Police in Urban America, 1860–1920* (Cambridge: Cambridge University Press, 1981), pp. 108–9, 158. See Chapter Four herein for discussion of specific incidents in which parents sought the help of the Los Angeles police in controlling their children. For a discussion of the interactive relationship between the poor and social work agencies, see Linda Gordon, *Heroes of Their Own Lives: The Politics and History of Family Violence, Boston 1880–1960* (New York: Viking Penguin, 1988).

51. LAPD, *Annual Report,* fiscal year 1916–17, pp. 26–27, 29–30.

52. For a discussion of the class control functions of the police, see Robert M. Fogelson, *Big-City Police* (Cambridge, Mass.: Harvard University Press, 1977), and Monkkonen, *Police in Urban America.*

53. On the number of people from ethnic and racial minorities in twentieth-century Los Angeles, see George J. Sánchez, *Becoming Mexican American: Ethnicity, Culture, and Identity in Chicano Los Angeles, 1900–1945* (New York: Oxford University Press, 1993); Kevin Starr, *Material Dreams: California Through the 1920s* (New York: Oxford University Press, 1990), p. 120; Lawrence B. de Graaf, "Negro Migration to Los Angeles, 1930–1950" (Ph.D. diss., University of California, Los Angeles, 1962). See also U.S., Department of Commerce, Bureau of the Census, *Fifteenth Census of the United States, 1930: Population,* 3:1, "Report of Statistics," p. 248.

In an interview with a graduate student at the University of Southern California in 1939, eight years after Gilbert's death, policewoman Alice Stebbins Wells asserted that the City Mother's Bureau under Gilbert practiced racial and class discrimination. Wells did not elaborate on this statement. Unfortunately, little evidence survives to investigate this issue. Saunders, "City Mother's Bureau," p. 54.

54. Elsdon C. Smith, *New Dictionary of American Names* (New York: Harper & Row, 1956).

55. "Report of Cases," case no. 42.

56. Ibid., case no. 32.

57. Gilbert discussed her use of parental probation in an untitled speech she gave to the California Conference of Social Agencies in May 1923 in Yosemite, California. Typescript of speech in AG Papers.

Ruth M. Alexander notes that "twentieth-century educators, social workers, and mental hygienists argued that young women and adolescent girls were most likely to heed parental wishes when they were certain of their elders' understanding and respect." Alexander, *The "Girl Problem,"* pp. 110–11. Gilbert's use of parental probation reflects the same point of view.

58. "Report of Cases," case no. 45.

59. Ibid., case no. 12. On police probation, see LAPD, *Annual Reports*, fiscal years 1916–17, p. 22, and 1929–30, p. 37.

60. "Report of Cases," case nos. 14 and 33.

61. Ibid., case no. 4.

62. Gordon, *Heroes of Their Own Lives*.

63. Aletha Gilbert, "Is the Old-Fashioned Girl Extinct? Modesty Gone?" *Los Angeles Examiner*, [ca. 1915–17], AG Papers. Gilbert's disapproval of early marriages is interesting because she married when she was sixteen, as had her mother, who eloped. McGroarty, *Los Angeles*, pp. 402–3.

Pioneer policewomen in Portland, Oregon, battled with their local juvenile court over the issue of early marriages. Like Gilbert, they disapproved of court officials' policy of encouraging early marriage. They even disliked the policy in cases involving premarital pregnancy. See Allen East, "The Genesis and Early Development of a Juvenile Court: A Study of Community Responsibility In Multnomah County, Oregon, for the Period 1841–1920" (M.A. thesis, University of Oregon, 1939), p. 55, n. 50.

64. "Warfare Waged on Love Pirates of Jitney Bus," *Los Angeles Examiner*, January 9, 1915, AG Papers.

65. Ibid.; McGroarty, *Los Angeles*, p. 403.

66. Committee of City Mothers and School Women, letter; Aletha Gilbert, "What the City Mothers' Bureau of Los Angeles Hopes to Do," *Los Angeles Times*, January 12, 1915; untitled newspaper article from *Whittier (Calif.) News*, February 19, 1915. All AG Papers.

67. Gilbert, "What Is Wrong with Modern Children."

68. Gilbert, "The normal, modern girl."

69. Gilbert, "Afraid to Tell; Hides Her Shame," *Los Angeles Examiner*, August 25, 1915, AG Papers.

70. Gilbert, "Batter Down Door; Save Girl," *Los Angeles Record*, November 29, 1915, AG Papers.

71. Woods, "Progressives and the Police." On Sebastian's trial, see Adela Rogers St. Johns, *Final Verdict* (New York: Doubleday, 1962), pp. 487–90.

72. Woods, "Progressives and the Police," pp. 44–47.

73. "Mrs. Gilbert Quits," *Los Angeles Record*, November 30, 1915, AG Papers.

74. Peggy Pascoe has argued in her study of women who founded home rescue missions that they made similar compromises. Pascoe, *Relations of Rescue: The Search for Female Moral Authority in the American West, 1874–1939* (New York: Oxford University Press, 1990).

75. Gilbert, "City Mothers Make Dancing Refined," unidentified Los Angeles newspaper article, AG Papers.

76. John D'Emilio and Estelle B. Freedman, *Intimate Matters: A History of Sexuality in America* (New York: Harper & Row, 1988), pp. 194–201.

77. Aletha Gilbert, "City Mothers Make Dancing Refined"; "Modern Dances Defended by 'City Mother'"; Mrs. Frank Stoddard, "First Municipal Dance is Success Says City Mother," *Los Angeles Herald,* February 20, 1915. All AG Papers. Stoddard was a member of the City Mother's Advisory Bureau.

78. Gilbert, "City Mothers Make Dancing Refined."

79. "City Mothers Will Make Phone Girls Happy with Dance," *Los Angeles Express,* April 2, 1915; "Shop Girls Take Up Tango and Fox Trot," ibid., April 19, 1915, AG Papers.

80. Gilbert, "City Mothers Make Dancing Refined."

81. "City Mothers to Give Municipal Dance," unidentified Los Angeles newspaper article; "To Make Dancing Safe," unidentified Los Angeles newspaper article; "City Mother to Give Municipal Dance," unidentified Los Angeles newspaper article. All circa February 1915, AG Papers.

82. "Oh Joy! Next City Dance is on Saturday," *Los Angeles Record,* May 26, 1915, AG Papers.

83. "City Mother Opens Drive on Cheek Dancing," unidentified Los Angeles newspaper article; "City Dances Here Win Fame North," *Los Angeles Tribune,* October 1, 1915. Both AG Papers. D'Emilio and Freedman discuss popular dance styles of the 1910s and 1920s in *Intimate Matters,* pp. 195–96. See also Russell B. Nye, "Saturday Night at the Paradise Ballroom; or, Dance Halls in the Twenties," *Journal of Popular Culture* 7 (summer 1973): 14–22.

84. As Kathy Peiss has noted, "The essence of the tough dance was its suggestion of sexual intercourse." Peiss, *Cheap Amusements: Working Women and Leisure in Turn-of-the-Century New York* (Philadelphia: Temple University Press, 1986), p. 102.

85. "Traffic Officers Direct Dancers," *Los Angeles Times* April 9, 1915, AG Papers.

86. "Censored Dance Is to Be Program for City Mother's Ball," unidentified Los Angeles newspaper article, n.d.; "L.A. City Dance Season Opens Tomorrow," unidentified Los Angeles newspaper article, n.d. Both AG Papers.

87. Even Gilbert felt the lure of Hollywood; in the early 1920s she submitted a story to Cecil B. DeMille loosely based on the experiences of a young couple she had advised in her capacity as City Mother. DeMille thanked her but turned down the story. AG Papers.

88. Nye, "Saturday Night," pp. 19–20.

89. LAPD, *Annual Reports,* fiscal years 1917–18, p. 41; 1925–26, p. 20; 1926–27, p. 32.

90. LAPD, *Annual Reports,* fiscal years 1916–17, p. 23 (149 of 1,158 cases); 1917–18, p. 41 (114 of 928 cases); 1918–19, p. 37 (119 of 1,104 cases); 1919–20, p. 32 (137 of 1,054 cases); 1920–21, p. 25 (105 of 995 cases); 1925–26, p. 20. These statistics do not reflect all the marital discord cases handled in a given year because

Gilbert and her assistants sometimes arbitrarily classified a marital discord case under the heading "Dependent" rather than "Domestic Relations." For example, in July 1927, Evelyn Dixon went to the bureau to seek advice on how to obtain child support from her husband, who had deserted her and their four-year-old daughter. Gilbert referred Dixon to the Failure-to-Provide Department of the City Prosecutor's Office, then closed the case, labeling it a "Dependent" case and listing it under the name of Dixon's daughter. That same month, Helen Smith went to the bureau with the same request: her husband had deserted her and their children, and she wanted to know how to obtain child support. Gilbert also referred Smith to the Failure-to-Provide Department, then closed the case. But she called the Smith case a "Domestic Relations" case and listed it under Helen Smith's name, not the children's names. The percentage of marital discord cases was therefore probably much higher than LAPD statistics indicate. "Report of Cases," case nos. 17 and 50.

91. Woods, "Progressives and the Police," pp. 113–15, 229–38, 252–56, 262–63.

92. "Real Home Life Lacking, Says Mrs. Gilbert," *Los Angeles Examiner*, June 4, 8; Flavia Gaines Leitch, "City Mother Gilbert Cures Heart Aches and Puts Wayward Feet on Right Path," *Los Angeles Examiner*, n.d.; "Report of Cases." All AG Papers.

93. An early discussion of the "revolution in morals and manners" is in Frederick Lewis Allen, *Only Yesterday* (New York: Harper & Brothers, 1931; reprint ed., New York: Bantam Books, 1959), pp. 75–77.

94. May, *Great Expectations*, p. 96.

95. Ernest W. Burgess and Paul Wallin, *Engagement and Marriage* (Philadelphia: J. B. Lippincott, 1953), pp. 324, 332–33 discussed in D'Emilio and Freedman, *Intimate Matters*, pp. 257–58.

96. On Vollmer's year at the LAPD, see Woods, "Progressives and the Police," chap. 5.

97. Sample list of crimes drawn from LAPD *Annual Report*, fiscal year 1925–26, pp. 21–23.

98. *Information Please Almanac and Yearbook, 1993*, 46th ed. (Boston: Houghton Mifflin, 1993), p. 831.

99. D'Emilio and Freedman, *Intimate Matters*, pp. 265–70.

100. George Staininger, grandson of Aletha Gilbert, interview by author, December 11, 1990, Glendale, California.

101. "Here and There with the Policewomen," *Policewoman's International Bulletin*, February 1928, p. 7.

102. "Here and There with the Policewomen," *Policewoman's International Bulletin*, October 1927, p. 9.

103. Gilbert first lamented the lack of a public day nursery when she was

chief jail matron, and she urged the city to build one. "Jail Matron Favors Nursery for Poor," unidentified newspaper article, n.d.; "City Becomes Official 'Ma'; Nursery Open," unidentified newspaper article, March 2, 1919; "City Care for Little Folks," unidentified newspaper article, March 2, 1919; "Mothering a Whole City," *Ogden City, Utah Standard-Examiner*, January 17, 1928. All AG Papers.

CHAPTER FOUR

1. Mary Sullivan, *My Double Life: The Story of a New York Policewoman* (New York: Farrar and Rinehart, 1938), p. 302.

2. Joseph Gerald Woods, "The Progressives and the Police: Urban Reform and the Professionalization of the Los Angeles Police" (Ph.D. diss., University of California, Los Angeles, 1973), p. 32.

3. Ibid., pp. 32–38.

4. On juvenile delinquency, vice, and commercial places of amusement, see, Louise DeKoven Bowen, "The Road to Destruction Made Easy in Chicago" and "Fighting to Make Chicago Safe for Children," in *Speeches, Addresses, and Letters of Louise DeKoven Bowen: Reflecting Social Movements in Chicago* (Ann Arbor, Mich.: Edwards Brothers, 1937), pp. 385–400; 560–73; "Split Skirt Is First Dual Life Step," *Los Angeles Evening Herald*, July 31, 1913, Aletha Gilbert Papers, in private possession (hereafter, AG Papers); John D'Emilio and Estelle B. Freedman, *Intimate Matters: A History of Sexuality in America* (New York: Harper & Row, 1988), p. 199.

5. The Juvenile Protective Association of Los Angeles grew out of the Juvenile Court Committee, which was first formed in 1903–4. Dorothy Frances Allen, "The Changing Emphasis in Protective Services to Children, with an Account of the Children's Protective Association of Los Angeles" (M.S.W. thesis, Graduate School of Social Work, University of Southern California, 1943); Marlou Belyea, "The Joy Ride and the Silver Screen: Commercial Leisure, Delinquency, and Play Reform in Los Angeles, 1900–1980" (Ph.D. diss., Boston University, 1983), p. 23; Woods, "Progressives and the Police," pp. 37–41.

6. Leo W. Marden to Chief Charles E. Sebastian, September 29, 1911, AG Papers; Alice Stebbins Wells, "Personal History of Los Angeles' First Policewoman," Los Angeles Police Associations, *Bulletin* 1 (October 1940): 5, 8.

7. Los Angeles Police Department, *Annual Report, Police Department, City of Los Angeles, California, for the Fiscal Year Ending June 30, 1914*, pp. 26, 41; and fiscal year 1914–15, p. 57.

8. LAPD, *Annual Report*, fiscal year 1913–14, p. 26. State law defined female juveniles as girls younger than twenty-one years.

9. "Policewomen Able as 'Arms of Law,'" *Los Angeles Examiner*, [ca. 1914], AG Papers.

10. Mary Ellen Odem, "Delinquent Daughters: The Sexual Regulation of Female Minors in the United States, 1880–1920" (Ph.D. diss., University of California, Berkeley, 1989), p. 237.

11. "Policewomen Able as 'Arms of Law.'"

12. "Policewomen Take Up Cudgel to Protect Girls from Loose Men," *Los Angeles Record*, May 2, 1913, AG Papers.

13. On the coercive aspects of pioneer policewomen's work, see Mary E. Odem and Steven Schlossman, "Guardians of Virtue: The Juvenile Court and Female Delinquency in Early Twentieth-Century Los Angeles," *Journal of Social History* 25 (April 1991): 186–203.

14. "Policewomen Able as 'Arms of Law.'"

15. Anna Hamm, "Pitfalls Facing L.A. Girls, Policewoman Warns Mothers," *Los Angeles Examiner*, July 20, 1914, p. 2.

16. Estelle Lawton Lindsey, "Low Wages Cause of Girls' Downfall, So Says Mrs. Gilbert, Jail Matron," *Los Angeles Record*, July 27, 1911; Aletha Gilbert, "Parents Cause Delinquency, Policewoman Explains How," *Los Angeles Examiner*, [ca. 1912]. In the mid-1910s, Gilbert pushed hard for the establishment of a public, residential industrial training school for girls. "LA City Mothers Plan Girls' Colony: A Useful Arts School Is Proposed," *Los Angeles Evening Herald*, July 1, 1916, p. 1. All AG Papers.

17. Robert A. Woods and Albert J. Kennedy, ed., *Young Working Girls: A Summary of Evidence from Two Thousand Social Workers* (Boston: Houghton Mifflin, 1913), pp. 2–3, quoted in Ruth M. Alexander, *The "Girl Problem": Female Sexual Delinquency in New York, 1900–1930* (Ithaca, N.Y.: Cornell University Press, 1995), p. 39. Alexander provides an insightful discussion of the views of reformers and women social activists regarding working-class female youth in chap. 2.

18. On the reinvention of female adolescence, see Alexander, *The "Girl Problem"*; Kathy Peiss, *Cheap Amusements: Working Women and Leisure in Turn-of-the-Century New York* (Philadelphia: Temple University Press, 1986); Elizabeth Ewen, *Immigrant Women in the Land of Dollars: Life and Culture on the Lower East Side, 1890–1925* (New York: Monthly Review Press, 1985); and Paula S. Fass, *The Damned and the Beautiful: American Youth in the 1920's* (New York: Oxford University Press, 1977).

19. Alexander, *The "Girl Problem,"* pp. 20–24.

20. On class dynamics and the police, see Egon Bittner, *Aspects of Police Work* (Boston: Northeastern University Press, 1990), especially chap. 7.

21. The sociologist Egon Bittner believes that even today, working-class people call on the police to perform services that the middle class typically pay professionals to provide. As he explains, "The lives of the poor, although rich in their own self-help mechanisms, are virtually devoid of such formal remedial resources as lawyers, psychiatrists and marriage counselors, many of whom serve

only those who can afford their services." Ibid., p. 284. Moreover, as Ruth M. Alexander observes, by the 1920s, the middle-class ideal of female purity had waned, and middle-class parents began to accept "a more permissive ideology of female adolescence." Alexander, *The "Girl Problem,"* pp. 150–51.

22. "Policewomen Able as 'Arms of Law.'"

23. "The Need for Police Women in City Work," *[Chicago] City Club Bulletin,* October 12, 1912, p. 327. See also, "Many Reasons for Women on Police Forces," *Ottawa Free Press,* January 17, 1913; and "Famous Policewoman Urges Prevention of Crime," *New York Times,* December 22, 1912, sec. 5, p. 13.

24. Hamm, "Pitfalls."

25. "Policewomen Take Up Cudgel."

26. Although Gilbert's choice of words exaggerated the youth of working-class females, many female workers were only fourteen to sixteen years old. For example, 32 percent of the fourteen- and fifteen-year-old girls appearing before the Los Angeles County Juvenile Court in 1920 had jobs. Odem, "Delinquent Daughters," p. 232. Additionally, it should be noted that nineteenth-century tales of seduction nearly always depicted the seducer as a member of the upper or middle classes, his "victim" as a member of the working class. Gilbert's remark that the "kids" had fathers who were themselves on the prowl implied that both the "mature" man and the "kid" came from the same social class.

27. John B. Rae, *The American Automobile* (Chicago: University of Chicago Press, 1965), pp. 61, 200. According to Rae, the average retail price of passenger cars declined from $1,719 in 1909 to $1,157 in 1919. Used car prices from survey of classified advertisement section "Things on Wheels" from *Los Angeles Times,* May–July 1913. On the cost and class implications of car ownership during the Progressive Era, see Virginia Scharff, *Taking the Wheel: Women and the Coming of the Motor Age* (New York: The Free Press, Macmillan, 1991), pp. 17–20, 46, 56. Wage statistics from Jonathan Hughes, *American Economic History,* 2d ed. (Glenview, Ill.: Scott, Foresman, 1987), p. 420.

28. In her speeches across the United States and Canada during the early 1910s, Alice Stebbins Wells professed a strong belief in middle- and upper-class women's power to shame men into abandoning the double standard of morality. For example, according to the *Indianapolis Star,* November 3, 1912, Wells claimed that "if society women cut their invitation lists with equal regard to the morals of men as they do of women, the double standard would soon vanish."

29. IACP, *Proceedings,* 1913, pp. 140–44.

30. No mention of policewomen's patrol duties appears in LAPD *Annual Reports* after 1915.

31. LAPD, *Annual Reports,* fiscal years 1913–14 through 1930–31. The 1913–14 and 1914–15 statistics for "Contributing" do not distinguish between men and women; typically, men were arrested for this crime in much greater numbers than

women. The crime of "seduction" was exclusively a male crime. According to policewoman Eleonore Hutzel, "Seduction is ordinarily defined as the sexual violation of a previously chaste female on the promise of marriage. The element of force is not material; on the contrary, consent is implied." Hutzel, *The Policewoman's Handbook* (New York: Columbia University Press, 1933), p. 116. LAPD *Annual Reports* arrest tables do not distinguish between the crimes of rape and statutory rape.

Sidney Reeve, a judge of the Los Angeles County Juvenile Court, referred to policemen's reluctance to arrest men for the crime of "contributing" and other [hetero]sexual offenses in 1920. While hearing a case involving a sailor accused of statutory rape, Reeve said, "Now the great difficulty is that it seems the double standard is very prominently fixed in the eyes of the Police Department and they want the girl filed on and put away and they want to let the boys be turned loose. I don't believe in it and never have believed in it." Reeve was particularly upset about the case then under his review because the sailor involved was an adult at the time of the alleged crime, and therefore Reeve thought that the case should have been tried in an adult court. Reeve lamented the relatively light sentence the sailor would receive in juvenile court: "The worst I could do with him would be two years in Ione [a state reformatory], whereas if this girl is under the age of 18 he might get 50 years in the penitentiary." Los Angeles County Superior Court, Juvenile Department, Case 15969. Hereafter, all citations of Los Angeles County Juvenile Court cases will have only the case number.

In her study of female juvenile delinquency, Mary E. Odem asserts that "in numerous cases, they [male police officers in Los Angeles] detained the young women but released the men found with them in hotel rooms or other trysting spots." *Delinquent Daughters: Protecting and Policing Adolescent Female Sexuality in the United States, 1885–1920* (Chapel Hill: University of North Carolina Press, 1995), p. 155.

32. "Famous Policewoman."

33. The names of the various departments and subdepartments in the LAPD changed frequently over the years. In the mid-1920s, the Juvenile Bureau, the City Mother's Bureau, the Men's Probation Bureau, and the Women's Probation Bureau were consolidated into the Crime Prevention Division. I discuss some of the name changes of the Juvenile Bureau in Chapter Five. To avoid confusion, I use the term "Juvenile Bureau" throughout this chapter.

34. LAPD, *Annual Report*, fiscal year 1930–31, p. 38.

35. According to Robert Freeman, former Director of Los Angeles City Archives, the only extant internal records of the LAPD from the early and mid-twentieth century are the chiefs' files. To see these files, a researcher must obtain authorization from the LAPD. Freeman states that over the years the LAPD has reluctantly given such authorization to only a handful of people. Interview by author, September 5, 1990, Los Angeles, California.

36. August Vollmer, one of the foremost advocates of scientific police work, became chief of the LAPD in August 1923. While chief, he fully indulged his passion for collecting statistics. It is therefore not surprising that the LAPD began to publish detailed juvenile arrest statistics in the mid-1920s. For an account of Vollmer's short career with the LAPD, see Woods, "Progressives and the Police," chap. 5.

37. LAPD, *Annual Report*, fiscal year 1917–18, p. 40.

38. "Los Angeles Women Cops Become Real Peace Officers," *Los Angeles Express*, December 12, 1928, AG Papers.

39. Marguerite Curley to Editor, *Los Angeles Examiner*, March 12, 1930 (typescript), AG Papers.

40. LAPD, *Annual Report*, fiscal year 1926–27, pp. 32–37.

41. In 1925, Katharine F. Lenroot and Emma O. Lundberg of the U.S. Children's Bureau noted in their study, *Juvenile Courts at Work*, that Los Angeles police did not file petitions in juvenile court on many of the youths they arrested. Lenroot and Lundberg made particular mention of the work of LAPD women officers: "Investigations in girls' cases were made by women officers. Many cases were adjusted without court action, and children were often released on promise of good behavior." U.S., Department of Labor, Children's Bureau, *Juvenile Courts at Work: A Study of the Organization and Methods of Ten Courts*, by Katharine F. Lenroot and Emma O. Lundberg, Bureau Publication no. 141 (Washington, D.C.: Government Printing Office, 1925), pp. 42–43.

42. LAPD, *Annual Report*, fiscal year 1926–27, pp. 32–37.

43. Statistical information published by the LAPD about juvenile arrests varied somewhat from year to year in the 1920s and 1930s. In 1925–26, for example, the LAPD published the total number of girls' cases (1,907) and the number of girls arrested or investigated (838 or 43.9 percent), but it did not publish information about the disposition of the arrests. LAPD, *Annual Report*, fiscal year 1925–26, pp. 20–21. At first glance, the report for 1927–28 appears to give the same kind of statistical information as 1926–27, but its statistics do not distinguish between cases handled by the City Mother's Bureau and cases handled by the Juvenile Bureau. LAPD, *Annual Report*, fiscal year 1927–28, p. 32. In its report for 1928–29 and in all reports thereafter until the early 1940s, the LAPD dropped statistics on the number of girls investigated but not "booked" as arrests.

44. LAPD, *Annual Report*, fiscal year 1934–35, p. 31.

45. Police scholars have amply documented that police officers exercise a greater degree of discretionary freedom in proceeding against a citizen than any other public official. Moreover, as Egon Bittner has pointed out: "An officer's decision not to make an arrest is not a matter of record, contrary to the decision of the prosecutor not to prosecute, and the decision of the judge to dismiss or acquit. The condition creates something of a legal paradox because, according to the dis-

covered facts, the policeman who is in terms of the official hierarchy of power, competence, and dignity, on the lowest rung of the administration of justice, actually determines . . . what the business of his betters will be." *Aspects of Police Work,* p. 192.

46. "Calls Daughter Liar, Is Fined $10," *Los Angeles Examiner,* August 28, 1912, AG Papers; George Staininger, grandson of Aletha Gilbert, interview by author, December 11, 1990, Glendale, Calif.

47. Sullivan, *My Double Life,* p. 267. Sullivan linked this familial tension to the conflict between "Old World notions of foreign-born parents and the Americanized point of view of their children." On generational tensions, see Leslie Tentler, *Wage-Earning Women: Industrial Work and Family Life in the United States, 1900–1930* (New York: Oxford University Press, 1979), chap. 4; Peiss, *Cheap Amusements,* pp. 67–72; Odem, *Delinquent Daughters,* chap. 6.

48. Odem, *Delinquent Daughters,* p. 158. Ruth M. Alexander has also documented parents' willingness during the early twentieth century to use the criminal justice system to try to enforce their authority over their daughters. In her analysis of New York State's reformatories for women, Alexander found that nearly a quarter of the inmates she studied were sentenced to reformatories at the request of family members (22 of 100). Alexander, *The "Girl Problem,"* p. 49.

49. Odem, "Delinquent Daughters," p. 302.

50. On the hearing of juvenile cases in Los Angeles, see, Lenroot and Lundberg, *Juvenile Courts at Work,* pp. 127, 129; Deloss H. Bowers, "The Juvenile Court of Los Angeles County" (M.A. thesis, University of Southern California, 1931), pp. 77–78; Francis H. Hiller, *The Juvenile Court of Los Angeles County: Report of A Survey* (New York: National Probation Association, 1928), pp. 19–20.

51. Recent studies of relations between middle-class social workers and the working class include Odem, *Delinquent Daughters,* and Linda Gordon, *Heroes of Their Own Lives: The Politics and History of Family Violence, Boston 1880–1960* (New York: Penguin Books, 1988).

52. Odem, *Delinquent Daughters,* p. 167.

53. On the female physician employed by the Los Angeles Juvenile Court, see Lenroot and Lundberg, *Juvenile Courts at Work,* p. 95.

54. Case no. 10568. Eleanor Chapman is a fictitious name. To protect the confidentiality of juvenile court records, I have substituted fictitious names for the true names of all persons (except police and court personnel) mentioned in the cases I discuss. The fictitious names have the same ethnic content as the true names.

55. Ibid.

56. Ibid. Pregnancy brought many unmarried teenage girls and young women into court. According to studies of the Los Angeles County Juvenile Court, 25 percent of all female youths appearing before the court in the 1920s

were pregnant. Estelle B. Freedman, *Maternal Justice: Miriam Van Waters and the Female Reform Tradition* (Chicago: University of Chicago Press, 1996), p. 87.

57. Case no. 10648.

58. Kathy Peiss asserts that "women's wage labor and the demands of the working-class household offered daughters few resources for entertainment. At the same time, new commercial amusements offered a tempting world of pleasure and companionship beyond parental control." Peiss, "'Charity Girls' and City Pleasures: Historical Notes on Working-Class Sexuality, 1880–1920," in *Powers of Desire: The Politics of Sexuality*, ed. Ann Snitow, Christine Stansell, and Sharon Thompson (New York: Monthly Review Press, 1983), p. 84. See also, Joanne Meyerowitz, *Women Adrift: Independent Wage Earners in Chicago, 1880–1930* (Chicago: University of Chicago Press, 1988). Estelle B. Freedman notes that by the 1920s, treating had lost much of its economic basis, even among working-class young women. Freedman, *Maternal Justice*, p. 86.

59. According to the 1930 federal census, blacks composed 3.1 percent of the population of Los Angeles in 1930. U.S., Department of Commerce, Bureau of the Census, *Fifteenth Census of the United States, 1930: Population*, vol. 3, "Report of Statistics," p. 248.

60. Kevin Starr states that a census taken in 1926 in Los Angeles showed a population of 1.3 million, with "45,000 Hispanics, 33,000 blacks, and 30,000 Asians." Starr does not indicate the census to which he refers. According to the figures he gives, Latinos composed just under 3.5 percent of the city's population in 1926. *Material Dreams: Southern California through the 1920s* (New York: Oxford University Press, 1990), p. 120. According to George J. Sánchez, the Mexican population of the city of Los Angeles in 1930 was at least 97,000. This figure indicates that Mexicans and Mexican Americans composed 8 percent of the total population. As Sánchez notes, census figures for ethnic groups usually underestimate the number of people from ethnic minorities. Sánchez, *Becoming Mexican American: Ethnicity, Culture, and Identity in Chicano Los Angeles, 1900–1945* (New York: Oxford University Press, 1993), pp. 90, 293.

61. D'Emilio and Freedman, *Intimate Matters*, pp. 35–36, 88–90; racist stereotypes about black women at the turn of the century are analyzed by Beverly Guy-Sheftall, "'Daughters of Sorrow': Attitudes Toward Black Women, 1880–1920 (Ph.D. diss., Emory University, 1984), especially pp. 62–86; Darlene Clark Hine, "Lifting the Veil, Shattering the Silence: Black Women's History in Slavery and Freedom," in *The State of Afro-American History: Past, Present, and Future*, ed. Darlene Clark Hine (Baton Rouge: Louisiana State University Press, 1986), pp. 223–49; and Paula Giddings, *When and Where I Enter: The Impact of Black Women on Race and Sex in America* (New York: William Morrow, 1984), pp. 82–86.

62. Margaret Saunders, "A Study of the Work of the City Mother's Bureau

of the Los Angeles Police Department" (M.S.W. thesis, University of Southern California, 1939), pp. 65, 97.

63. Odem, *Delinquent Daughters*, p. 159. Odem specifically refers to "Latin American immigrants," a group that excludes Latinos born in the United States.

64. The figure of 80 percent comes from Odem, *Delinquent Daughters*, p. 134.

65. Joan Moore et al., *Homeboys, Gangs, Drugs, and Prison in the Barrios of Los Angeles* (Philadelphia: Temple University Press, 1978), p. 59.

66. Saunders, "City Mother's Bureau," pp. 65, 97; Odem, *Delinquent Daughters*, p. 159.

67. On black women's social activism, see Stephanie J. Shaw, *What a Woman Ought to Be and to Do: Black Professional Women Workers During the Jim Crow Era* (Chicago: University of Chicago Press, 1996); Jacqueline Jones, *Labor of Love, Labor of Sorrow: Black Women, Work and the Family from Slavery to the Present* (New York: Vintage Books, 1985); Beverly W. Jones, "Mary Church Terrell and the National Association of Colored Women," *Journal of Negro History* 67 (spring 1982): 20–33.

Studies of the history of Mexican American women's activism include Cynthia E. Orozco "Alice Dickerson Montemayor: Feminism and Mexican American Politics in the 1930s," in *Writing the Range: Race, Class, and Culture in the Women's West*, ed. Elizabeth Jameson and Susan Armitage (Norman: Oklahoma University Press, 1997), pp. 435–456; idem, "Beyond Machismo, La Familia, and Ladies Auxiliaries: A Historiography of Mexican-Origin Women in Voluntary Associations and Politics in the United States, 1870–1990," *Renato Rosaldo Lecture Series*, monograph no. 10, 1992–93 (Tucson: Mexican American Studies and Research Center, 1995), pp. 37–78; and Margaret Rose, "Gender and Civil Activism in Mexican American Barrios in California: The CSO from 1948 to 1962," in *Not June Cleaver*, ed. Joanne Meyerowitz (Philadelphia: Temple University Press, 1994).

On Mexican Americans in Los Angeles, see Sánchez, *Becoming Mexican American*. Scholarship on Mexican American family life includes Norma Williams, *The Mexican American Family: Traditions and Change* (Boston: G. K. Hall, 1990); Rosalinda M. González, "Chicanas and Mexican Immigrant Families, 1920–1940: Women's Subordination and Family Exploitation," in *Decades of Discontent: The Women's Movement, 1920–1940*, ed. Lois Scharf and Joan Jensen (Westport, Conn.: Greenwood Press, 1983); Alfredo Mirandé, "The Chicano Family: A Reanalysis of Conflicting Views," *Journal of Marriage and the Family* 39 (1977), pp. 750–51; David Alvirez and Frank D. Bean, "The Mexican American Family," in *Ethnic Families in America*, ed. Charles H. Mindel and Robert W. Haberstein (New York: Elsevier, 1976); Miguel Montiel, "The Social Science Myth of the Mexican American Family," *El Grito: A Journal of Contemporary Mexican American Thought* 3 (1970): 56–63.

68. There may have been other minority women officers in the Juvenile Bureau, but unfortunately, the LAPD stopped listing the names of officers in its *An-*

nual Reports in the mid-1920s, and so their names and length of employment remain unknown. Information on identity of minority policewomen from Homer F. Broome, Jr., *LAPD's Black History, 1886–1976* (Norwalk, Calif.: Stockton Trade Press, 1977), pp. 213–15; "Women on the LAPD," p. 4; list of police personnel of LAPD Crime Prevention Division, [ca. mid-1920s], AG Papers; Woods, "Progressives and the Police," pp. 193–97. Woods notes the existence of unproven rumors that the LAPD did not hire American Jews in the early twentieth century.

69. "'City Mothers' Bureau for All Negro Cases," *Los Angeles Express,* October 5, 1915; "To Help the Race," *Los Angeles Times,* October 5, 1915. Both AG Papers.

70. Tullia Kay Brown Hamilton, "The National Association of Colored Women, 1896–1920" (Ph.D. diss., Emory University, 1978), pp. 22–25; Darlene Clark Hine, "Rape and the Inner Lives of Black Women in the Middle West: Preliminary Thoughts on the Culture of Dissemblance," in *Unequal Sisters: A Multicultural Reader in U.S. Women's History,* ed. Ellen Carol DuBois and Vicki L. Ruiz (New York: Routledge, 1990), p. 295. For comparative analyses of black and white women activists' reforms, see Eileen Boris, "The Power of Motherhood: Black and White Activist Women Redefine the 'Political,'" in *Mothers of a New World: Maternalist Politics and the Origins of Welfare States,* ed. Seth Koven and Sonya Michel (New York: Routledge, 1993), pp. 213–45; and Linda Gordon, "Black and White Visions of Welfare: Women's Welfare Activism, 1890–1945," *Journal of American History* 8 (1991): 559–90.

71. "Sojourner Truth Industrial Club, Inc., a Brief History," undated document courtesy of Ruth Gordon, president, Sojourner Truth Industrial Club, Inc. (The club celebrated its ninetieth birthday in 1994.)

72. "'City Mothers' Bureau for All Negro Cases."

73. "First Negro Policewoman Joined L.A. Force in 1916," *Ebony,* September 1954, p. 32; Gail F. Johnson, "In Memory of Georgia Ann Robinson, LAPD's First Black Policewoman, 1916–1928," *The Link,* summer 1993, p. 6. On the history of African American police, see W. Marvin Dulaney, *Black Police in America* (Bloomington: Indiana University Press, 1996).

74. Case no. 15868.

75. Ibid.; "Sojourner Truth Industrial Club, Inc., A Brief History."

76. Case no. 15868.

77. Hamilton, "National Association of Colored Women," lists members of the Sojourner Truth Industrial Club in Los Angeles in "Appendix: Biographical Data," pp. 139–55.

78. On the average age of female youths before the Los Angeles County Juvenile Court, see Odem, "Delinquent Daughters," p. 231.

79. Case no. 44608.

80. Ibid.

81. Ibid.

82. Odem, *Delinquent Daughters*, p. 163.

83. Case no. 44594; Sánchez, *Becoming Mexican American*, p. 259. Linda Gordon has pointed out in her study of family violence that many middle-class white professionals in the twentieth century have accused people from racial and ethnic minorities of subnormal intelligence. Gordon, *Heroes of Their Own Lives*, p. 14.

84. Ibid., p. 14; case no. 44594.

85. Odem, *Delinquent Daughters*, p. 135.

86. Case no. 16265.

87. Case no. 110979.

88. Case no. 10644.

89. Ibid.; LAPD, *Annual Report*, fiscal year 1917–18, p. 19.

90. As LAPD Officer Gail Johnson has pointed out, Georgia Robinson was a tireless advocate of desegregation in Los Angeles. After her retirement, she worked closely with the Los Angeles branch of the National Association for the Advancement of Colored People on civic projects such as the desegregation of local beaches and the desegregation of hiring practices in Los Angeles City Schools. Johnson, "In Memory"; Nancy McCard Rene, granddaughter of Robinson, telephone interview by author, April 17, 1993.

91. "Field Notes," Women Peace Officers Association of California, *Yearbook, 1928–1929*, p. 12; ibid., "Big Sister League," *Yearbook, 1931–1932*, p. 11; LAPD, Public Affairs Division, "Women in Law Enforcement, Los Angeles Police Department" (typescript), February 1974; Myra Nye, "Asks for Return of Whipping Post," unidentified, undated newspaper article, AG Papers.

92. One typical letter to Gilbert from a former inmate of the Women's Jail reads in part, "Mrs. Gilbert you do not know how glad I am to be home, and how thankful I am to you for what you did for me. Surely you know how much I appreciate it and I just can't forget you." Another former inmate wrote in a similar vein: "At last I am home and in a position to be able to write you and *try* to tell you how much I appreciated your attitude towards me while I was under your care. The last week has been a nightmare for me and the happiest spot in it was when I was with you." Another correspondent mentioned Gilbert's gift of sufficient money for a ticket home to Davenport, Iowa: "Thanks you very much for helping me get back as it would of been some time before he [the writer's husband] could of save the money. . . . I wrote him the day I left and told him I was coming home but he didn't no how I got the money." AG Papers.

93. Linda Gordon makes the same point about social workers' intervention in the private lives of their clients: "The social work/social control establishment did not arise out of the independent agenda of the ruling class, or even of the middle class. Rather it developed out of conflicts that had gender and generational as well as class 'sides.'" Gordon, *Heroes of Their Own Lives*, p. 296.

CHAPTER FIVE

1. Ursula Vils, "Lady Cops and Robbers," *Los Angeles Times,* March 21, 1965; Los Angeles Police Department, *Annual Report, Police Department, City of Los Angeles, California, for the Fiscal Year Ending June 30, 1929,* p. 12; "Origin," Women Peace Officers Association of California, *Yearbook 1928–1929,* p. 16. Policemen assigned to work with juveniles were sometimes informally called "juvenile officers," but their official designation remained "policeman."

2. Samuel R. Blake, "The Acknowledgment of Community Responsibility for the Reduction of Delinquency," *Proceedings of the Sixty-Fourth Annual Congress of the American Prison Association* (Baltimore: American Prison Association, 1934), p. 28.

3. Samuel Walker, *A Critical History of Police Reform: The Emergence of Professionalism* (Lexington, Mass.: Lexington Books, D.C. Heath, 1977), pp. 153–54.

4. Raymond B. Fosdick and Albert L. Scott, *Toward Liquor Control* (New York: Harper & Brothers, 1933), pp. 13–19, quoted in George Chauncy, *Gay New York: Gender, Urban Culture, and the Making of the Gay Male, World, 1890–1950* (New York: Basic Books, HarperCollins, 1994), p. 335.

5. Frederick Lewis Allen, *Since Yesterday: The Nineteen Thirties in America, September 3, 1939—September 3, 1939* (New York: Harper & Brothers, 1939; reprint ed., New York: Bantam Books, 1961), p. 145; Walker, *Critical History,* pp. 153–54.

6. Estelle B. Freedman, "'Uncontrolled Desires': The Response to the Sexual Psychopath, 1920–1960," *Journal of American History* 74 (June 1987): 83–106.

7. Psychiatrists started moving into the field of crime prevention at the turn of the century. In 1909, philanthropist Ethel Sturges Dummer of the Juvenile Protective Association of Chicago offered to pay for a five-year study of the psychological causes of juvenile delinquency. The Juvenile Protective Association hired the English psychiatrist William Healy to conduct the study. His work in Chicago at the Juvenile Psychopathic Institute, and after 1917 at the Judge Baker Foundation in Boston, inspired the establishment of similar clinics in other major American cities during the 1910s. But it was not until the early 1930s that crime prevention became a top priority among psychiatrists, other professionals, and government administrators in general. For a discussion of Healy and other early twentieth-century theorists of juvenile crime and crime prevention, see Robert Mennel, *Thorns and Thistles: Juvenile Delinquents in the United States, 1825–1940* (Hanover, N.H.: University Press of New England, 1973), chap. 6.

8. Margo Horn, "'Gee, Officer Krupke, What Are We to Do?': The Politics of Professions and the Prevention of Delinquency, 1909–1940," *Research in Law, Deviance and Social Control* 8 (1986): 57–58.

9. Sheldon Glueck and Eleanor Glueck, "Introduction," *Preventing Crime: A Symposium,* ed. Sheldon Glueck and Eleanor Glueck (New York: McGraw-Hill, 1936), p. 6.

10. Ibid.

11. Horn, "Officer Krupke," p. 58. Psychiatric theories of crime and delinquency were a vital part of the emerging "mental hygiene" field of the late 1910s and 1920s. A number of scholars have addressed various issues regarding the intersection of crime prevention and the mental hygiene movement, including Julia Liss and Steven Schlossman, "The Contours of Crime Prevention in August Vollmer's Berkeley," *Research in Law, Deviance and Social Control* 6 (1984): 79–107; David Rothman, *Conscience and Convenience* (Boston: Little, Brown, 1980); and Mennel, *Thorns and Thistles*, chap. 6.

12. Horn, "Officer Krupke," p. 59.

13. John H. Ehrenreich, *The Altruistic Imagination: A History of Social Work and Social Policy in the United States* (Ithaca, N.Y.: Cornell University Press, 1985), p. 76.

14. Freedman, "Uncontrolled Desires," pp. 88, 90–91.

15. John Ehrenreich has traced the retreat from environmentalism and social reform among social workers to their eagerness to be recognized as full-fledged professionals by the upper class. Ehrenreich, *Altruistic Imagination*, p. 75. To a lesser extent, the same explanation may hold true for criminologists. On women social scientists, see Ellen Fitzpatrick, *Endless Crusade: Women Social Scientists and Progressive Reform* (New York: Oxford University Press, 1990).

16. In this respect, the programs illustrate one aspect of women's paradoxical role in the evolution of the welfare state. On the one hand, middle-class women activists spearheaded countless campaigns in the late nineteenth and early twentieth centuries to expand the role of the state in maternal and child welfare. On the other hand, once women carved out a place for themselves in public welfare bureaucracies, they steadily lost much of their influence to male politicians, physicians, and bureaucrats. Seth Koven and Sonya Michel, "Womanly Duties: Maternalist Politics and the Origins of the Welfare States in France, Germany, Great Britain, and the United States, 1880–1920," *American Historical Review* 95 (October 1990); Robyn Muncy, *Creating a Female Dominion in American Reform, 1890–1935* (New York: Oxford University Press, 1990). See also Penina Migdal Glazer and Miriam Slater, *Unequal Colleagues: The Entrance of Women into the Professions, 1890–1940* (New Brunswick, N.J.: Rutgers University Press, 1987).

17. Christopher G. Ruess, "The Prevention of Juvenile Delinquency in Los Angeles County Through Coordinating Councils," California Association for Social Welfare, *Bulletin* 16 (November 1932): 28; Norman Fenton, "Child Guidance in California Communities," *Journal of Juvenile Research* 21 (January 1937): 22–23.

18. Kenyon J. Scudder, "A Community Organizes to Prevent Delinquency," *Probation: The Official Bulletin of the National Probation Association* 12 (December 1933): 10.

19. Karl Holton, "Coordinating Community Forces," in American Prison

Association, *Proceedings of the Seventieth Annual Conference, 1940* (New York: American Prison Association, 1940), pp. 74–75.

20. C. W. Lester, "Modern Police Methods and Problem Children," *Transactions of the Commonwealth Club of California*, pt. 2, 29 (July 1934): 120.

21. Martin H. Neumeyer, "The Los Angeles County Plan of Co-Ordinating Councils," *Sociology and Social Research* 19 (May–June 1935): 460–71; Norman Fenton, "Purposes and Accomplishments of the Coordinating Councils," *Journal of Juvenile Research* 19 (April 1935): 98–103; Lawrence Riggs, "An Opportunity for the School in Community Cooperation: The Coordinating Council," *School and Society* 51 (May 11, 1940): 602. See also Erle Fiske Young, "The Coordinating Council Plan in Los Angeles County," *Journal of the American Institute of Criminal Law and Criminology* 26 (1935–36): 34–40; Fenton, "The Coordinating Council in Child Welfare," *Journal of Juvenile Research* 21 (January 1937): 39; Leonard W. Mayo, "Town and Village Councils," *Yearbook of the National Probation Association, 1936* (New York: National Probation Association, 1936), pp. 78–88; Sanford Bates, "Where Prisoners Come From," *Journal of Juvenile Research* 20 (July 1936): 130–37.

22. Neumeyer, "Los Angeles County Plan"; Kenneth S. Beam, "A National Movement for the Prevention of Delinquency Through Community Coordination," *Journal of Juvenile Research* 20 (October 1936): 181.

23. Riggs, "An Opportunity for the School," p. 602. See articles listed in note 21 for comparisons of coordinating councils to New England town meetings.

24. LAPD, *Annual Report*, fiscal year 1934–35, p. 69. Earlier reports do not list coordinating councils in the juvenile arrest tables. John Henry Good noted the reluctance of LAPD officers during the early 1940s "to work cooperatively with coordinating councils." Good, "A History of the Delinquency Control Institute: Its Program to Combat Juvenile Delinquency" (M.S. thesis, University of Southern California, 1967), p. 60. The Delinquency Control Institute was a police training program established in Los Angeles in the 1940s.

25. At first glance, the reluctance of police officers to refer cases to the councils seems at odds with the glowing descriptions of the councils in the LAPD *Annual Reports* of the early 1930s. But these accounts were written, not by the rank and file, but by high-ranking officials who may have had political reasons to praise the councils.

26. The sociologist Egon Bittner has observed that juvenile cases are more likely than adult cases to have "untoward consequences" that will reflect badly on the police officer handling the case. For that reason, most police officers avoid dealing with juveniles whenever possible. Bittner, *Aspects of Police Work* (Boston: Northeastern University Press, 1990), p. 334.

27. LAPD, *Annual Report*, fiscal year 1935–36, p. 35; Women Peace Officers Association of California, *Yearbook, 1935*, p. 17.

28. LAPD, *Annual Report*, fiscal year 1935–36, p. 35.

29. Ibid.

30. Ibid., fiscal year 1936–37, p. 29.

31. "Women on the LAPD: It Ain't a New Phenomenon," Los Angeles Police Relief Association, *Guardian* 9 (first quarter 1990): 4; "Uniforms for Women Police? Davis Says 'No,'" unidentified Los Angeles newspaper article, [ca. 1929], Aletha Gilbert Papers, in private possession (hereafter, AG papers).

32. Stephen Leinen, *Black Police, White Society* (New York: New York University Press, 1984), pp. 146–49.

33. Margaret Saunders, "A Study of the Work of the City Mother's Bureau," (M.S.W. thesis, University of Southern California, 1939), p. 59. The City Mother's Bureau, originally domiciled in the Normal Hill Center, was moved to the Hub Building on Main Street in 1923 because the city planned to demolish the Normal Hill Center. According to Saunders, the LAPD moved the Juvenile Bureau into the same building; other sources differ on this point. In 1928, the bureau was moved once again, this time to the City Hall. The record is not clear, but the Juvenile Bureau may have also been located in or near the City Hall in the late 1920s and early 1930s, rather than in the central police station. When Davis relocated the bureau to the Georgia Street Division in 1937, he also moved other units of the Crime Prevention Division there.

34. Ibid., p. 121.

35. LAPD, *Annual Report*, fiscal year 1926–27.

36. Walker, *Critical History*, p. 139. Clarice Feinman has noted that in 1938, more than five thousand women applied to take the civil service examination to fill twenty-nine policewomen position vacancies with the New York Police Department; the twenty-nine position vacancies were not filled until 1942. Feinman, *Women in the Criminal Justice System* (New York: Praeger, 1986), p. 87.

37. Gary B. Nash et al., *The American People: Creating a Nation and Society* (New York: Harper & Row, 1986), 2:805. Mary P. Ryan, *Womanhood in America: From Colonial Times to the Present*, 3d ed. (New York: Franklin Watts, 1983), pp. 250–51, points out that discrimination against women workers was "littered" throughout New Deal agencies.

38. Joseph Gerald Woods, "The Progressives and the Police: Urban Reform and the Professionalization of the Los Angeles Police" (Ph.D. diss., University of California, Los Angeles, 1973), p. 246. Kevin Starr also mentions the Cornero brothers in *Material Dreams: California Through the 1920s* (New York: Oxford University Press, 1990), p. 169.

39. Fred Gilbert Blakeslee, *Police Uniforms of the World* (Norwood, Mass.: Plimpton Press, 1934), p. 16.

40. Woods, "Progressives and the Police," pp. 244–46. Perhaps the most notorious episode of Davis's police career occurred in 1936, when he organized the Border Patrol Detail to stop people from out of state from crossing the border into

California. Also known as the "bum blockade," the Border Patrol Detail had instructions to single out dispossessed families from the Dust Bowl region. These families poured into California at the rate of one hundred thousand persons a year in the mid- and late 1930s. The 136 policemen assigned to this detail received special permission from law enforcement agencies in border counties to station themselves along major highways and turn back people who could not prove they were California residents. Davis claimed that by turning back the "refuse of other states," he reduced crime in Los Angeles by 20 percent. Lawsuits questioning the constitutionality of the Border Patrol Detail brought it to a swift end. Ibid., pp. 342–45; Walton Bean and James J. Rawls, *California: An Interpretive History*, 4th ed. (New York: McGraw-Hill, 1983), pp. 400–401.

41. Historians who have discussed the fate of the woman's movement in the 1920s include Nancy F. Cott, *The Grounding of Modern Feminism* (New Haven: Yale University Press, 1987); Rayna Rapp and Ellen Ross, "The Twenties' Backlash: Compulsory Heterosexuality, the Consumer Family, and the Waning of Feminism," in *Class, Race and Sex: The Dynamics of Control*, ed. Amy Swerdlow and Hanna Messinger (Boston: G. K. Hall, 1983), 93–107; Estelle B. Freedman, "Separatism as Strategy: Female Institution Building and American Feminism, 1870–1930," *Feminist Studies* 5 (fall 1979): 512–29. Gloria Ricci Lothrop notes that women's clubs in Los Angeles lost interest in reform in the 1930s in "Strength Made Stronger: The Role of Women in Southern California Philanthropy," *Southern California Quarterly* 71, 2/3 (1989): 168–69.

42. Estelle B. Freedman discusses the persistence of women's political activism at the local level in "Separatism Revisited: Women's Institutions, Social Reform, and the Career of Miriam Van Waters," in *U.S. History as Women's History: New Feminist Essays*, ed. Linda K. Kerber, Alice Kessler-Harris, and Kathryn Kish Sklar (Chapel Hill: University of North Carolina Press, 1995), pp. 170–88. See also idem, *Maternal Justice: Miriam Van Waters and the Female Reform Tradition* (Chicago: University of Chicago Press, 1996).

43. Woods, "Progressives and the Police," pp. 270–71. According to Woods, David I. Davidson originally scored higher than Steckel on the chief's examination in 1930, but "someone later lowered his grade." Ibid., p. 371.

44. Ibid., p. 279.

45. Ibid., pp. 270, 282–84.

46. "Mrs. Harris Out of City Bureau Job," unidentified newspaper article, AG Papers; "Only One Passes in Test," *Los Angeles Times*, February 6, 1930, sec. 2, p. 1.

47. Ibid.

48. Deanne Harris to Mayor John C. Porter et al., February 10, 1930, Los Angeles City Council File 1300, Los Angeles City Archives.

49. Los Angeles City Clerk Robert Dominguez to Deanne Harris, February 20, 1930, Los Angeles City Council File 1300, Los Angeles City Archives.

50. Gertrude M. Price, "City Mother Bureau Shake-Up Stirs Ire of Strong Supporters," *Los Angeles Record*, March 20, 1930, AG Papers; "Mrs. Harris Out of City Bureau Job."

51. Woods, "Progressives and the Police," pp. 281–84.

52. Price, "City Mother Bureau Shake-Up."

53. "City Mothers in 'Ouster' Protest," unidentified Los Angeles newspaper article, AG Papers.

54. Saunders, "City Mother's Bureau," pp. 54–55.

55. According to Joseph Gerald Woods, the term "political activity" in Los Angeles during the early 1930s meant opposition to Porter. Specifically, Woods discusses the firing of Captain John A. McCaleb, a twenty-two-year veteran of the LAPD in 1933. McCaleb lost his job through charges of "neglect of duty, pernicious political activity and unbecoming conduct." According to Woods, "'political activity' was the key phrase. McCaleb refused to support Mayor Porter's reelection and worked to elect Frank L. Shaw. Following Shaw's victory, the police commission reinstated McCaleb." Woods, "Progressives and the Police," p. 284.

56. Saunders, "City Mother's Bureau," pp. 53–54.

57. "City Mothers' Suit Pending," unidentified newspaper article dated September 3, 1930, AG Papers.

58. "City Mother's Desk Center of Political Move," unidentified Los Angeles newspaper article, September 4, 1930, AG Papers.

59. "City Mother to Be Honored on Retirement," *Los Angeles Times*, June 19, 1964; "Honor Mrs. Fiske, Last City Mother," *Los Angeles Herald-Examiner*, June 18, 1964. Elizabeth Fiske Papers, in private possession.

60. Saunders, "City Mother's Bureau," pp. 65, 92–96. Saunders analyzed one hundred "representative" cases handled by the City Mother's Bureau in 1938.

61. LAPD, *Annual Report*, fiscal year 1937–38, pp. 81–83.

62. Ruth M. Alexander, *The "Girl Problem": Female Sexual Delinquency in New York, 1900–1930* (Ithaca, N.Y.: Cornell University Press, 1995), p. 151.

63. Freedman, "'Uncontrolled Desires.'"

64. Ibid.

65. Ibid., pp. 87–91, 96.

66. According to Freedman, the sex-crime panic of the late 1930s represents "a significant departure from the nineteenth-century emphasis on maintaining female purity . . . toward a modern concern about controlling male violence." Ibid., p. 85.

67. Mary Galton Stevenson, retired second-generation LAPD officer, interview by author, September 15, 1990, Laguna Hills, Calif.

68. Nancy Cott, *Grounding of Modern Feminism*, p. 279. Victoria Bissell Brown explores young women's rejection of "sex-consciousness" in "Golden

Girls: Female Socialization in Los Angeles, 1880 to 1910" (Ph.D. diss., University of California, San Diego, 1985).

69. Interview with Stevenson; Patti Smith, second-generation retired LAPD officer, interview by author, September 15, 1990, Laguna Hills, Calif.; Saunders, "City Mother's Bureau," p. 55.

70. Interview with Stevenson.

71. Policemen's resentment of female partners arose in part from their feeling that having a female partner trivialized their work. Marital tension was another source of policemen's resentment. According to Mary Galton Stevenson, policewomen often unwittingly created domestic difficulties for married policemen because some women became jealous of the time their husbands spent with female partners. Interviews with Stevenson, Smith; Fanchon Blake, retired second-generation LAPD officer, telephone interview by author, August 10, 1990.

72. Saunders, "City Mothers Bureau," p. 21.

73. Ann Sadler, "The Ideal Policewoman: An Interview with Mrs. Mina Van Winkle, President of the International Association of Policewomen," *Welfare Bulletin* 19 (May 1928): 642.

74. Eleonore Hutzel, *The Policewoman's Handbook* (New York: Columbia University Press, 1933), p. 63.

75. LAPD, *Annual Reports,* fiscal years 1930–31 through 1938–1939. Beginning in 1939, arrest statistics published by the LAPD listed arrests made during the calendar year, rather than the fiscal year of July 1 to June 30. The number of male youths arrested for dependency increased nearly 600 percent in the 1930s, from 4 percent of all arrests in 1930–31 to just under 24 percent in 1939. This huge increase probably reflected to some degree the large number of boys who left their homes during the Depression and hitchhiked, walked, and rode the rails throughout the country. For an account of how Los Angeles handled the influx of "drifting boys," see Kenyon J. Scudder, "How California Anchors Drifting Boys," *Survey,* March 1933, pp. 101–2.

76. Children's Protective Association, *Ten Years of Promoting the Welfare of Children, 1925–1935* (Los Angeles: Children's Protective Association, 1935), p. 12.

77. "Metropolitan Policewomen," Women Peace Officers Association of California, *Yearbook, 1931–1932,* p. 9; Joseph F. Taylor, untitled article, Women Peace Officers Association of California, *Yearbook, 1933,* p. 47.

78. Blake, telephone interview; see also, "Lady Cops," *Ebony,* September 1954, p. 28.

79. "City's Female Police Armed First Time," *Los Angeles Times,* March 30, 1939; "Police Beauties Get Escort for Skidrow Tours of Duty," *Los Angeles Daily News,* June 30, 1948. Courtesy of the Los Angeles Public Library, Special Collections. An exception to the demeaning references to Los Angeles policewomen in

the 1930s is "Unsung Policewomen Aid Crime Prevention," *Los Angeles Times,* November 12, 1934, sec. 2, p. 5.

80. Patt Morrison, "Despite Bias, Women Cops Excel, L.A. Panel Finds," *Sacramento Bee,* July 12, 1991, sec. A, pp. 1, 22; Fanchon Blake states that police-men were using "Sgt. Tits" and other such terms to refer to policewomen when she first joined the LAPD during the late 1940s. Telephone interview.

81. "Lady Cops," p. 26.

82. Alice Ames Winter, "The Policewoman of Policewomen," *Ladies' Home Journal* (1927); reprint, *Policewoman's International Bulletin,* October 1927, 12.

83. Interview by author with retired, second-generation LAPD police-woman who prefers to remain unidentified.

84. Otheman Stevens, "Girl Defends 'Nicotine Dance,' Policewoman Finds It Chaste," *Los Angeles Examiner,* [ca. 1913], AG Papers.

85. Dorothy Uhnak, *Policewoman: A Young Woman's Initiation into the Reali-ties of Justice.* (New York: Simon and Schuster, 1963), p. 9. Bruce L. Berg and Kim-berly J. Budnick discuss other aspects of the alleged defeminization of police-women in "Defeminization of Women in Law Enforcement: Examining the Role of Women in Policing," in *Police and Law Enforcement,* ed. Daniel B. Kennedy and Robert J. Homant (New York: AMS Press, 1987), pp. 159–71.

86. Dorothy Moses Schulz, *From Social Worker to Crimefighter: Women in United States Municipal Policing* (Westport, Conn.: Praeger, 1995), p. 90.

87. "City's Female Police Armed for First Time," *Los Angeles Times,* March 30, 1939. In a statement astonishing in its inaccuracy, the *Times* also asserted that the newly-armed women officers were "the vanguard of a flying petticoat squadron which will number in the hundreds." Thirty years later, the number of LAPD women officers still did not number in the hundreds.

Although the LAPD did not issue guns to women officers until 1939, or al-low them to carry them while on duty, in 1925 it began to allow policewomen to practice target shooting at the Elysian Park range. Whether this privilege was later rescinded remains unknown. Los Angeles Police Department, *Commemora-tive Book, 1869–1984* (Los Angeles: Los Angeles Police Revolver and Athletic Club, 1984), p. 149.

88. "Policewoman, City Mother; One of 26, Favors Mrs. Fiske," *Los Angeles Record* [ca. January 1930], AG Papers.

89. See, for example, Captain Duncan Mathews, "Women Protective Offi-cers," Women Peace Officers Association of California *Yearbook, 1933,* p. 17. In the 1920s, Mathews, an officer with the San Francisco Police Department, vehemently opposed the idea that the police should be social workers. For a sample of his views, see "Law Enforcement and the Causes of Crime," International Associa-tion of Chiefs of Police, *Proceedings, 31st Convention,* 1924, p. 122.

90. Eric Monkkonen argues that police functions narrowed to a focus on

crime control in the early twentieth century as part of "the general spatial reinte-
gration and centralization of increasingly specialized city services and administration." Monkkonen makes no mention of the movement for women police, and
he portrays the crime prevention activities of the police as part of their crime control mission. In Monkkonen's opinion, the new emphasis on crime control was
"doomed to failure, for it was the one thing at which the police had never been
especially successful." Monkkonen, *Police in Urban America, 1860–1920* (Cambridge: Cambridge University Press, 1981), pp. 4, 152–53.

91. Walker, *Critical History*, p. 169.

92. Ibid.

93. Ibid., chap. 6. By 1938, the LAPD Predelinquent Detail had only one police officer assigned to it; this officer supervised a staff of Works Progress Administration (WPA) workers. The WPA workers made "home investigations of
children who have reported by the school, a juvenile officer, or a citizen, to be in
danger of falling into delinquent behavior habits." The availability of WPA workers made it easy for the LAPD to continue a juvenile delinquency prevention program while reducing drastically the number of officers assigned to it. It is interesting to note that the WPA workers often made referrals to coordinating
councils. Iva Hood, "Crime Prevention Methods of the Los Angeles Police Department with Reference to Girls under Eighteen during 1938" (M.S. thesis, University of Southern California, 1939), p. 50.

94. Descriptions of criminals and crime problem are from the U.S. Attorney
General's Conference on Crime, December 10–13, 1934, *Proceedings* (Washington,
D.C.: Government Printing Office, 1934), quoted in Walker, *Critical History*, p. 153.

95. Aletha Gilbert, "The Duties of a 'City Mother,'" *American City* 26 (1922):
239.

96. Woods, "Progressives and the Police," pp. 350–72.

97. Ibid., pp. 373–74.

98. LAPD, *Annual Report*, 1939, p. 7.

99. LAPD, *Annual Report*, 1942.

100. Between 1940 and mid-1944, an estimated 305,723 people moved to the
city of Los Angeles; nearly 200,000 more settled in the remainder of Los Angeles
County. Statistics from LAPD, *Annual Report*, 1943, p. 4.

101. Woods, "Progressives and the Police," pp. 389–90, 393.

102. Peace Officers Association of the State of California, *Proceedings of the
1942 War Conference*, p. 47 (hereafter referred to as Peace Officers Association, *Proceedings, 1942;*) Board of Police Commissioners, City of Los Angeles, "Minutes,"
Regular Meetings, September 22, 1942, and September 29, 1942, Los Angeles City
Archives; Woods, "Progressives and the Police," p. 390; LAPD, *Annual Report*,
1943, p. 4.

103. Peace Officers Association, *Proceedings, 1942*, p. 47.

104. For a discussion of how the siege mentality shaped the LAPD's response to the Zoot-Suit Riots of 1943, see Janis Appier, "Juvenile Crime Control: Los Angeles Law Enforcement and the Zoot-Suit Riots," *Criminal Justice History* 11 (1990): 149–70.

105. Woods, "Progressives and the Police," p. 390.

106. LAPD, *Annual Report*, 1943, p. 8.

107. During the war, the Women Peace Officers Association of California stepped up its efforts to secure the rank of policewoman-sergeant at the LAPD. See, for example, Board of Police Commissioners, City of Los Angeles, "Minutes," Regular Meetings, September 22, 1942 and November 10, 1942, Los Angeles City Archives. "Women on the LAPD" identifies Vess and Churchill as the first policewomen-sergeants, but misstates the date of their promotion as May 1945 (p. 4). According to the LAPD, *Annual Report*, 1944, p. 8, two policewomen-sergeants were on duty as of December 31, 1944.

108. "Women on the LAPD," pp. 5–6.

109. In 1950, Los Angeles had 2.1 sworn officers per 1,000 residents; in 1960, it had 1.8 sworn officers per 1,000 residents. In 1950, both the International Association of Chiefs of Police and the International City Managers Association agreed that 3 sworn officers per 1,000 residents was the safe ratio in urban areas. Woods, "Progressives and the Police," p. 430. According to a survey taken in 1986 of the six largest cities in the United States (New York, Los Angeles, Chicago, Philadelphia, Detroit, and Houston), Los Angeles had the lowest ratio of sworn police officers per resident (2:1000). Police Foundation, *The Big Six: Policing America's Largest Cities*, quoted in *Report of the Independent Commission on the Los Angeles Police Department* (Los Angeles: The Commission, 1991), p. 22.

110. Arthur W. Sjoquist, "From Posses to Professionals: A History of the Los Angeles Police Department" (M.S. thesis, California State University, Los Angeles, 1972), p. 264.

111. Woods, "Progressives and the Police," p. 417; John Gregory Dunne, "Law and Disorder in LA: Part Two," review of *Report of the Independent Commission on the Los Angeles Police Department*, by the Independent Commission on the Los Angeles, and of "Daryl Gates: A Portrait of Frustration," *Los Angeles Times*, August 15 and 16, 1982, by Bella Stumbo, in *New York Review of Books*, October 24, 1991, p. 62.

112. For a discussion of the link between commonly attributed gender differences and occupational subculture in criminal justice professions, see Nanci Koser Wilson, "Women in the Criminal Justice Professions: An Analysis of Status Conflict," in *Judge, Lawyer, Victim, Thief: Women, Gender Roles, and Criminal Justice*, ed. Nicole Hahn Rafter and Elizabeth Anne Stanko (Boston, Mass.: Northeastern University Press, 1982), pp. 359–74.

EPILOGUE

1. Catherine Higgs Milton et al., *Women in Policing: A Manual* (Washington, D.C.: Police Foundation, 1974), p. 32.

2. "Lady Cops," *Ebony*, September 1954, p. 28.

3. Egon Bittner, *Aspects of Police Work* (Boston: Northeastern University Press, 1990), p. 334.

4. "Women on the LAPD: It Ain't a New Phenomenon," Los Angeles Police Department, *Guardian* 9 (first quarter 1990): 5.

5. Sonia Nazario, "Force to Be Reckoned With," *Los Angeles Times*, June 5, 1993, sec. A, p. 12.

6. Beth Ann Krier, "Crusading Cop," *Los Angeles Times*, October 1, 1990, sec. E, p. 1. Blake retired in 1974 because of the harsh treatment meted out to her by supervisors and co-workers after she filed the lawsuit.

7. Nazario, "Force to Be Reckoned With."

8. Independent Commission, *Report of the Independent Commission,* p. 86. This commission was known as the Christopher Commission because its chair was Warren Christopher.

9. Ibid., p. 85.

10. Ibid.

11. Daniel Bell, "Policewomen: Myths and Realities," *Journal of Police Science and Administration* 10 (1982): 112–20, discusses studies evaluating policewomen's job performance. In the 1970s, the Police Foundation carried out an extensive study of policewomen's performance. For its conclusions, see Peter Block, Deborah Anderson, and Pamela Gervais, *Policewomen on Patrol: Final Report* (Washington D.C.: Police Foundation, 1974).

12. Nazario, "Force to Be Reckoned With."

13. Patt Morrison, "Despite Bias, Women Cops Excel, L.A. Panel Finds," *Sacramento Bee*, July 12, 1991, sec. A, pp. 1, 22; Independent Commission, *Report of the Independent Commission*, pp. 85–88. A survey taken in 1993 revealed that 83 percent of LAPD women officers agree that female officers have a different style of policing than male officers. Nazario, "Force to Be Reckoned With."

Index